MARCHING WITH A
BILLION

MARCHING WITH A
BILLION

ANALYSING NARENDRA MODI'S GOVERNMENT

UDAY MAHURKAR

EBURY
PRESS

An imprint of Penguin Random House

EBURY PRESS

USA | Canada | UK | Ireland | Australia
New Zealand | India | South Africa | China | Singapore

Ebury Press is part of the Penguin Random House group of companies
whose addresses can be found at global.penguinrandomhouse.com

Published by Penguin Random House India Pvt. Ltd
4th Floor, Capital Tower 1, MG Road,
Gurugram 122 002, Haryana, India

First published in Viking by Penguin Random House India 2017
Published in Ebury Press by Penguin Random House India 2019

ISBN 9780143449454

Typeset in Bembo Std by Manipal Digital Systems, Manipal

Printed at Repro India Limited

www.penguin.co.in

This is a legitimate digitally printed version of the book and therefore might not
have certain extra finishing on the cover.

Shri Khandoba Prasanna
Shri Renukadevi Prasanna

At the feet of
Brahmaleen Swami Pranavanandaji
of the Bharat Seva Ashram Sangh,
and two of the greatest saints of the Datta Sampradaya,
Brahmaleen Swami Vasudevanand Saraswati and
Brahmaleen Pujyashri Rang Avadhoot,
and my living guru,
His Holiness Pujyashri Rajarshi Muni of Jakhan, Limdi

Contents

Foreword

I have been an observer, partner and friend of India for over three decades and have always been a believer in the immense potential of the country. It has been thirty-five years since my first visit to India and I have never felt more optimistic about the country's future than now. Under the leadership of Prime Minister Narendra Modi, India will have a great influence in shaping our global future as the country pursues a more inclusive path going forward—'together with all, development for all'.

I first met Prime Minister Modi in 2003 at the India Economic Summit in New Delhi, and again at our first Annual Meeting of the New Champions, in Dalian, People's Republic of China, in 2007. The then chief minister of Gujarat clearly struck me as a passionate leader who saw the power of innovation as a resounding driver of economic growth and social progress.

Over the last forty-five years, I have had the great privilege of meeting almost every world leader. Thus, I am often asked, 'What makes a good leader?' Time and again, I have observed four defining qualities: brains, soul, heart and good nerves. There are only a handful of leaders in the world who, in my view, possess all four qualities, and Prime Minister Modi is one of them.

First, a leader must have the necessary contextual intelligence—the 'brains'—to connect the dots. Prime Minister

Modi has been an innovative force in embracing technology to improve India's economic prosperity, civic participation and digital governance. It comes as no surprise that the prime minister is one of the most followed global leaders on Twitter, with over 28 million followers, engaging them by providing policy updates, inviting ideas and feedback, and sharing the progress being made by the government.

Second, in a rapidly changing world, leaders need values and vision to serve as their radar and compass in navigating the future. The 'soul' helps provide this vision and direction. Without a compass, a leader cannot exercise leadership responsibly, and without a radar system, leaders cannot be responsive. Much has been said and written about the key initiatives of the prime minister, from Make in India to Digital India to Skill India, to name but a few. The 'red thread' throughout all these initiatives is his ability to create strong narratives and mobilize resources to help implement the vision.

Third, a leader needs 'heart'—namely passion and empathy. Knowing the prime minister's philosophy, it doesn't surprise me that he is developing an inclusive growth agenda focused on empowering the poor and providing them with an enabling environment by expanding direct benefit transfer through bank accounts to electrifying remote villages, among others.

Fourth, a leader must be able to combine a strong vision with the ability to translate that vision into action, and to effectively address the many simultaneous and complex challenges that we are facing. This requires what I call 'good nerves'. Here, what stands out is Prime Minister Modi's ability to take critical, and sometimes unpopular, decisions for the long-term benefit of the country and its citizens. The recent demonetization initiative is a good example of this.

Prime Minister Modi's consistent focus on responsible and responsive citizenship highlights the power of brains, soul, heart and good nerves in action. Initiatives such as Swachh Bharat

Abhiyan and Namami Gange focus on the power of citizen engagement in helping restore and regenerate India's natural environment and ecosystems. There is purity of purpose in this. *Marching with a Billion* provides a uniquely detailed account of the prime minister's many initiatives. And while it may be too early to assess their success, it is clear they are consistently driven by the red thread of vision and passion.

As the forum continues to deepen its engagement with India, I personally believe in a promising future for the country for many reasons, among which are a vibrant democracy and pluralistic society, the quality of Indian entrepreneurs, the country's demographic dividend, an energetic leadership and the significant multiplier effect of the reform and innovation policies that are being enacted.

In my conversations with business leaders, politicians, academics and young people from around the world, Indians everywhere feel deeply engaged, energized and empowered to participate in Prime Minister Modi's new vision for India. With such a decisive and strong leader, there is a great opportunity for Indians to participate in not only reforming, but also transforming India—responsively and responsibly.

April 2017   Klaus Schwab
                                   Founder and executive chairman,
                                        World Economic Forum

Author's Note

This book is not just about numbers or facts. It looks at the whole narrative of a transformational government, where each move is linked to another in some way or the other—as in an intricate, carefully tuned machine. It covers the key aspects of the government's style of functioning under a leader who leads from the front and aims to tap the latent energy of the people by awakening a sense of national pride. Presenting both a macro as well as micro view, it brings out the best of the government even while critically evaluating its performance in key areas like infrastructure, fiscal management, foreign affairs, digital technology and social sectors. To get the whole picture, I had to understand the motivations of the people, particularly officers, who actually drive this government, inspired by the vision of their leader.

As I dug deeper, I started to comprehend the nature of its governance. Broadly, it is defined by three terms: transparency, innovation and a marked commitment to good governance. The impression I got was that Narendra Modi was turning out a better narrative in Delhi than he did in Gujarat. The chapters on fiscal management and foreign affairs turned out to be unusually interesting for me as I got new insights into both. Writing about the manifold increase in India's global standing, thanks to the prime minister's more than fifty skilfully planned and executed foreign visits, and the admirable management of key fiscal parameters necessary for the nation's good financial health, gave me a lot of satisfaction.

All the facts, figures and data in this book are culled from the official records of the ministries concerned and archives of MyGov, the Modi government's innovative digital platform for furthering the public's participation in governance.

Introduction

On the sociopolitical turf of India, deeply divided by personal interests and the exigencies of vote-bank politics, it is difficult to arrive at an objective estimate of a government without being influenced by perceived notions. It is only a dispassionate approach that enables one to come to accurate conclusions. And that is what I have tried to do in writing this book, which takes stock of the Narendra Modi government at a little over the halfway point and devotes a full chapter to the analysis of the prime minister's momentous demonetization exercise on 8 November 2016—a step that changed the complexion of the Indian economy, and proved the doomsayers wrong on the economic as well as the political fronts. Demonetization, however, shouldn't dissuade us from looking at other multidimensional aspects of the government, chief among which is the passing of the Goods and Services Tax (GST) in Parliament, a giant step towards the economic integration of India. This introduction focuses on precisely those features.

When the Modi government completed two years, there was a slew of articles in the media, some extolling the government's policies and steps, and others criticizing and lamenting the weakened health of the economy under Modi's rule. Some were also critical of the slow pace of economic reforms, disinvestment and low exports in the first two years. In any case, at around 7.5 per cent growth before demonetization in November 2016, and 7.2 per cent in 2017 and 7.7 per cent for 2019 (as predicted by the World Bank for India in April 2017), with both the fiscal deficit and inflation under control and the Indian rupee gaining in strength, the economy could not have been in a better position against the backdrop of a global slowdown and the two consecutive years of drought that the nation had faced before the onset of a favourable monsoon in 2016. In terms of growth, India is ahead of China. It is also on the top of the BRICS table, which also includes Russia, South Africa and Brazil. The inflow of foreign direct investment (FDI) in India has, in fact, broken all past records, surpassing China's.

The pace of reforms saw a sudden rise, coinciding with the government's completion of two and a half years in office. It touched diverse sectors, including aviation. But the job scenario is still not encouraging, with the slowdown in manufacturing continuing despite a significant recovery in early 2017. The confidence of both consumers and investors is picking up further after a slowdown and there are clear signs of a gradual recovery in the real estate sector. But I think there are more precise ways of measuring the government's performance.

The best way to assess the Modi government's accomplishment is to take note of the changes it has introduced in core governance. Some of these changes have happened for the first time in India's recent history and greatly benefited the common man. The middlemen culture, marked by fixers, and the significant role played by powerful corporate houses not just in policymaking but also in ministry formation, has been nearly abolished in Delhi for the first time in more than three decades. There was a time when corporate bigwigs and their liaison men played a role even in the creation of ministries. This was suggested by the revelations of the Radia tapes, which were leaked when the United Progressive

Alliance (UPA) government was in office. From a time when middlemen held sway over ministers to a new phase in which such power brokers find it difficult to enter the premises of key ministries, a lot has changed in the corridors of Delhi.

The high-profile ministries dealing with infrastructure, such as coal, power, railways, petroleum, and transport and roads, were dominated by influential corporate houses and middlemen, who tried to affect policies or win crucial contracts through bribery. All that corruption has been largely eliminated. In the process, a level playing field has been created for the corporate houses dealing with government sectors. Even less lucrative Union ministries, such as the Ministry of Human Resource Development (HRD), had at one time small fixers operating as middlemen. But they are nowhere to be seen now. Clearly, crony capitalism has been dealt a big blow. It is noteworthy that the government has not faced any major allegation of corruption in its tenure of nearly three years. Even the government under Atal Bihari Vajpayee had not been able to reach such a level of transparency in spite of its apparent honesty of purpose. On another plane, the dramatic turnaround of the infrastructure ministries, as evident in their impressive, even unprecedented, performance, is seen as a new benchmark in governance.

Even the nation's civil aviation industry is witnessing a great turnaround under the Modi government. It is set to cross the 100 million passenger mark in 2017, outpacing Japan to become the third-largest domestic market after the US and China. In 2016, the domestic market saw a significant growth rate of 23 per cent, towards addition of new airports, and also a reduction of over 25 per cent in airfares. The rise has also been a bonanza for the common man. A one-hour flight will now cost just ₹2500 on 50 per cent of the total seats in a set of airlines dedicated to these shorter routes—the government has ensured this by giving tax concessions to those airlines operating on these short routes. However, the government's bid to develop the aviation sector has not come without a fight as the Federation of Indian Airlines has challenged its decision to impose around ₹7500 on every flight to create a fund for the development of regional airports.

As the country debates the performance of the government in sectors like skill development, what is unmistakable is the administration's concern for the common man and the poor. This matters in a country where poverty elimination remains a major challenge. The path that the Modi government has taken to achieve this is important. The government has pitched for an enabling model to help the poor, rejecting the marked tendency of previous governments to waive loans and distribute freebies with an eye on votes rather than on empowerment. The loan waiver promised by the prime minister's party to small farmers of Uttar Pradesh on the eve of the 2017 state elections is, of course, an unfortunate exception. One example of this is the change brought about in the structure of issuing subsidies for LPG connections by making a successful appeal to the middle class to give up the subsidy it gets on LPG cylinders so that the savings could be extended to people in the Below Poverty Line (BPL) category.

That more than 1 crore LPG connection holders surrendered their subsidy at Narendra Modi's behest shows what national pride can achieve where government actions fail. The steps to usher in transparency in the area of LPG distribution are equally laudable. By linking the LPG subsidy to the Aadhaar card and ensuring the direct payment of the subsidy amount in the beneficiary's bank account, the middlemen operating in the system have been wiped out at one stroke. The subsidy worth ₹21,000 crore being saved annually following the implementation of these two measures is now being used to cover 5 crore BPL families, or 25 crore persons, under the government's Pradhan Mantri Ujjwala Yojana—a good example of an enabling model to help the poor with subsidy. It also shows how the government has used technology to target corruption and bring transparency.

In the national capital, which was also the capital of all sorts of fixers and middlemen, transparency is visible across the board in the dealings of the government. Public-sector banks are some of the cleaner institutions among the lot (after the NDA took over), although they are yet to act on the problem of the bad loans of the past that are affecting their non-performing assets (NPAs), which would continue to increase unless bad loans are addressed. The reason: there is no pressure on the banks any more to appoint inappropriate people as directors, who could use their position to bestow questionable loans on a select few, an 'under-table premium', of course. With the dawning of this new culture of transparency in the banking sector, the nation can feel relieved—there will hopefully be no Vijay Mallyas in the future. Mallya's arrest in the UK on 18 April 2017 and the starting of the extradition proceedings against the wilful defaulter following pressure built on the UK by Modi and Finance Minister Arun Jaitley is a shining example of both the government's commitment to bring the high and mighty to book as required by the law and the cleaning up of the banking system. It gave sanctity to Modi's statement in a public function only a few weeks earlier: 'My government is not going to spare a single defaulter howsoever big he might be. The money they have swindled belongs to the poor people of India.' The government's approach towards the banking sector will go a long way in ensuring that new NPAs are prevented—a positive sign for the economy.

Democracy is not just about electing governments but also about making the common man a part of the development process. In a poor country like India, with its diverse population and varied problems, it is all the more necessary to involve the people, creating a sense of pride and oneness. Modi's government is probably the first since Independence that has made a real attempt to involve the people in the process and, that too, quite successfully. There are examples that show the government's commitment to the ideal. National public schemes are no longer being launched just from Delhi's Vigyan Bhavan, the favourite place of previous leaders to inaugurate nationwide programmes. These are now being flagged off from areas where they make a difference to the target group and give people a sense of involvement in the process.

In 2016, the LPG scheme for poor families was launched by Modi from Ballia in Uttar Pradesh, while the landmark Gram Uday Se Bharat Uday Abhiyan was launched from Mhow in Madhya Pradesh. When, in 2015, Modi launched the revolutionary Jan Suraksha insurance schemes from Kolkata in West Bengal, a state ruled by an opposition party—the Trinamool Congress—he showed both his government's commitment to federalism and its focus on developing the backward eastern parts of India. This step, along with the Centre's special focus on the development of India's east and the north-east, was in tune with the promise made several times by the prime minister during his campaign for the 2014 Lok Sabha polls: 'No person can be called fit if one of his arms is undernourished. India can't be called developed if its eastern parts remain underdeveloped. If the west has developed well, we have to develop the east too.'

The government's involve-people-in-development resolve is further demonstrated by its exceptional measure of seeking and implementing the suggestions of the public in governance through its digital platform called MyGov, launched in 2014. Using the website as a pathway, ministries invite inputs from people on particular areas of administration and apply some of the innovative suggestions. It is certainly one of the most unique experiments of independent India—a democracy that has been, for many, a device to attain power rather than a tool for changing the lives of ordinary people by taking them along in the process of growth.

Some of the most crucial measures implemented by the Modi government have come in the form of people's suggestions on this interactive platform. Probably for the first time, ordinary people are playing a direct role in governance. Modi's *Mann Ki Baat*, a monthly programme on All India Radio (AIR) where he delivers a talk, is another special platform for connecting with citizens, getting to know their views and acting on their proposals. The exercise has brought some great ideas to the government and has also given Modi the image of a reformer as he frequently takes up issues of social change and awareness in the programme—the Beti Bachao (save the girl child) campaign, for instance.

Yet another step that exhibits the government's concern for citizens is the new law to tackle the problem of bankruptcy—the Insolvency and Bankruptcy Code, 2016. In the old system, when a businessman or his company went bankrupt, the first dues to be cleared from the sale of his property were to the secured banks, followed by the dues to the government in the form of pending taxes. Under the new law, the dues to the employees will be cleared first and then those to banks and the government. The possibility of creating deliberate defaulters is almost foreclosed under the new law. Now the entire process of clearance of dues will have to be completed within nine months, in place of the previously stipulated four years. A government-appointed regulator will oversee the process of selling the property and clearing the dues. The new law is also expected to have a positive impact on the problem of bad debts and spur private-sector investment.

Fiscal management under Modi and Finance Minister Arun Jaitley is perhaps at its best in many decades. Wasteful spending has been arrested; inflation and fiscal parameters such as fiscal deficit and current account balance are under control like never before. That the budget size has increased from around ₹16.55 lakh crore in 2013–14 to around ₹21.50 lakh crore in 2017–18 is proof of India's improving financial health. This has enabled the government to increase outlays for infrastructure and social infrastructure. The government has removed the categories of planned and non-planned expenditure and replaced them with capital and revenue expenditure to create a clear and effective link between the government's earning, spending and outcome. The earlier distinction also left room to camouflage wasteful spending.

But one success of the government—to be precise, of Modi and Jaitley—that virtually leapfrogs over all other financial achievements of the government is the GST, which is on the verge of becoming a reality. If Sardar Patel is the symbol of India's political integration, Modi will go down in history as the main contributor to the nation's financial integration. Nripendra Misra, the prime minister's principal secretary who has played a role in translating Modi's thoughts into action, says: 'What is remarkable about the prime minister is that he has the sagacity and the perseverance to turn his vision into reality. GST is a great example. Plus, his vision for good governance stands out because there is socioeconomic agenda behind all his decisions.'[1]

There have also been dissenting voices on the Make in India campaign to push economic growth in twenty-five major economic areas, on how it could have been executed better. But the fact that India has emerged as the number one global destination for FDI has been possible only because of two factors—the 'Make in India' idea of the prime minister with emphasis on the advantages of doing business in India, and his fifty-odd foreign visits, designed to leverage the country's economic growth and to ensure its rise as a commanding power.

A sharply visible streak in the schemes undertaken by Modi is an unrelenting resolve to cleanse the delivery system so that the fruits of development reach the last mile. In the process, Modi emerges as the man who is changing the paradigms of governance. If good governance now features most prominently in India's political and electoral parlance, overriding narrow considerations of caste or community, the credit has to go to Modi. In that sense, the election win of 2014 was a watershed moment. From that election were reborn figures like Akhilesh Yadav of the Samajwadi Party who took the cue from Modi and made development and good governance his pet themes, curbing his father's old-fashioned, destructive politics based only on matters of caste and community. Even the Bahujan Samaj Party's Mayawati has been talking more about development and less about caste.

A monumental shift is also visible in India's approach to foreign relations, particularly with the US, as also with China, Pakistan and other neighbours. The former inertia, hesitation and meekness in foreign policy replaced with bold, visionary and innovative diplomacy. The defence sector too is changing under the new dispensation. It is overcoming the paralysis that had afflicted it for a long time till 2014. However, much more needs to be done in the defence sector as the pace of development remains slow despite a new vision which is not translating into results as quickly as one would have thought.

In April 2014, when it was almost certain that Modi would become the prime minister, I gave an interview to journalist Sheela Bhatt, who is now the editor of political affairs at the *Indian Express*. The interview was on my first book on Modi's governance in Gujarat, titled *Centrestage: Inside the Narendra Modi Model of Governance*. I had made some interesting predictions about what Modi would do if he came to power. One of these predictions was that the favour-driven culture of Delhi will get a rude shock if Modi became the prime minister. That is what has exactly happened.

Modi's unprecedented step of breaking the nexus between politicians, bureaucrats, corporate houses and high-profile middlemen can be traced back to his origins. He is one of the first prime ministers of India who has not been reared in Delhi's

Lutyens culture. He truly comes from the margins of India. Even icons of the Bharatiya Janata Party, like A.B. Vajpayee and L.K. Advani, in spite of coming from humble backgrounds, had been politically reared in Delhi and therefore weren't outside the influence of the Lutyens milieu. What is remarkable about the Modi regime is that it is national pride, long suppressed by alien ideologies and appeasement politics, which is now playing a role in bringing about change. There is a genuine attempt to invoke national pride in attaining national goals in a systematic manner, something that has rarely happened since Independence. As part of his plan to invoke national pride in diverse sections of the society, Modi is also trying to highlight the alternative narrative of the history of India's freedom struggle by giving recognition to those whose contribution remained unrecorded or had been downplayed despite their sacrifices.

Thirty-seven-year-old Viral Desai, a medium-scale textile-processing-unit owner in Surat, aptly sums up how Modi generates pride by creating a level playing field where even the smallest can realize their potential. While running his textile processing unit, the completely apolitical Desai had been doing a commendable job of protecting the environment and saving energy. This was in 2010 when Modi was the CM of Gujarat. One of the many enthusiastic officers posted by the Modi administration in the industries department at Surat came to know about Desai's work for the environment and forced him to apply for Gujarat's top award for environmental protection and quality in the state's MSME (micro-, small- and medium-scale enterprises) category. When Desai won, he received the award from Narendra Modi himself at the 2011 Vibrant Gujarat Summit at Gandhinagar.

Says Desai: 'I was just thirty-one years old then, and so while giving me the award, Modiji asked me twice whether I had won the award. He wanted to know if I was receiving it for someone else. When I told him it was me who had won, he told me to keep it up, holding my hand. That push changed my life. Thereafter, my company has won environment awards at the national level, beating some of the biggest names in the business. Due to the recognition I got from him and his administration, I have turned a big philanthropist out of a new give-back-to-the-society feeling. I organized one of the biggest-ever cancer medical camps recently for 40,000 tribal women. I also remember having written a letter to him telling him he will symbolize a new era for India one day. I think that has come true.'[2]

There are visible qualities of sixty-six-year-old Modi that make him unique in many ways. He is the first prime minister who has touched 450-odd districts among the 688 districts in India as a *pracharak* of his parent body, the Rashtriya Swayamsevak Sangh (RSS), and later as an office-bearer in the national organization of the BJP and then as Gujarat's chief minister. In most of these districts, he has stayed at least overnight. That makes a big difference when it comes to understanding the problems of the country as the prime minister. Perhaps no other prime minister of India had such a close view of the country before occupying the august chair. The experience gave him both a macro and a micro view of the nation's problems and a sense of the country's strengths and weaknesses. Such a view is sometimes much more useful while taking precise decisions on crucial matters as a leader than reports prepared by experts in air-conditioned chambers.

At another level, between 1990 and 2001, when he became the chief minister, Modi had visited the Unites States every two or three years, staying each time with families of non-resident Indians (NRIs), mostly Gujaratis. Those who hosted Modi then have fond memories of him. These are interspersed with remarkable episodes giving indications of his future rise. For example, Boston-based Kanchan Banerjee, an RSS volunteer once and now a businessman and publisher, recalls how Modi refused to accept a gift on his 1994 visit to his home in Boston. 'As a pracharak, I can't accept gifts,' he told Banerjee's family.

When repeatedly pressed, he asked for something that could help him in his work. Modi's choice left Banerjee startled—the latest model of a laptop that even Banerjee hadn't used. Banerjee says: 'That gave an idea of his level as an emerging leader and his futuristic approach besides, of course, his techno-savvy attitude.'[3] Modi went to the US first in 1990 under the US state department's International Visitor Leadership Program, which had identified him as an emerging leader. Once exposed to the US system, he started visiting the US regularly to study it.

Perhaps Modi's exposure to the diverse shades of rural India as well as to the US convinced him that the fruits of development in the form of schemes and programmes won't reach the last man unless a delivery system clogged with corruption and nepotism is cleaned up. This view matched those of the late prime minister Rajiv Gandhi, who had made an honest admission in 1990 that made for a sad commentary on the Indian system. Gandhi had said then: 'I tried my best to break the unholy nexus but ultimately only 15 paise reached the last man when I released ₹1 from Delhi.' It seems as if Modi made that historic statement by Rajiv Gandhi his guiding principle when he took oath on 26 May 2014. According to a reliable estimate, the transparency and accountability that Modi has brought into the administration by using technology and wiping out middlemen are helping India save a whopping ₹1 lakh crore or more annually. This amount was earlier going to waste because of corruption and unwarranted expenditure.

A close look at Modi's strategy for making changes in core governance and putting the country back on track reveals that it is a fourfold plan, driven by his primary aim of clearing up the choked delivery system. These are the chief features of the plan:

1. Strike at high-level corruption by stopping corporate houses from playing a part in policymaking
2. Select honest bureaucrats

3. Use technology to bring transparency in governance
4. Make the citizens partners in development by reaching out
   to them directly and limiting the role of middlemen

To understand the importance of the new era led by Modi, which he calls the making of a new India by 2022, one has to take a close look at India's history in the past five decades. The story of India's degeneration in governance starts from 1980, when Indira Gandhi came back to power after suffering a massive defeat in the 1977 Lok Sabha polls. That she was ditched in that election by her most trusted man, Dalit leader Babu Jagjivan Ram, played big a role in changing her political priorities. So, when she returned to power in 1980, she made personal loyalty, rather than merit and quality, the main criterion for selection. This, according to old political observers, is the starting point of the corruption that tainted India's public life and subsequently governance. Once the disease affected politics, it also spread into the bureaucracy through the Congress, which was in power then. Soon it started shaping the middlemen culture in the governing corridors of Delhi and later entered the state capitals.

Along with this downfall, the nation was also being treated to a populist model of poverty-alleviation that aimed at securing votes rather than the actual uplift of the poor. By the beginning of the current century, this model was fully entrenched and had become a powerful vote-catching device, particularly in the hands of caste-based regional parties. 'Throw freebies and buy votes' virtually became the motto of Indian politics. Waivers of farmers' loans and power dues—to mention a few of these populist measures—became part of the political system. Against this backdrop, what is significant about the Modi government's efforts at poverty-alleviation is its refreshingly new approach based on an empowering model—one that is largely unburdened by freebies and meaningless subsidies. The aim is to provide social security to the poor through well-thought-out insurance schemes, cutting the flab and corruption of worthless subsidies so that the money saved could be used to cover more BPL families and reduce poverty.

These measures are apart from schemes of financial inclusion, like the Pradhan Mantri Jan-Dhan Yojana and the Pradhan Mantri Mudra Yojana, and in sharp contrast to the UPA government's schemes, such as its loan waiver of ₹60,000 crore in 2008, for which the country paid a stiff price. Clearly, 'Garibi Hatao' has so far either been a vote-catching slogan or a promise based on the distribution of freebies at the expense of the public exchequer. The present attempt to remove poverty stands on an enabling model that helps the poor become self-sufficient. Minimum subsidy for the lowest rung of the poor in areas such as health is a necessity in a relatively impoverished country like India. And the Jan-Dhan bank accounts for the poor have been integral to Modi's scheme of things. The direct transfer of subsidy to the beneficiary with no go-betweens is possible only because of the Jan-Dhan bank accounts.

If one assesses the Modi government with an open mind, one can't help but think that the foundations of a new order are being laid that will ensure a cleaner delivery system, taking the fruits of development to the last citizen. His efforts for transparency coupled with visionary long-term governance measures match his promise of a new India in the time to come. The prime minister's model of governance stands out for two things. One, a never-ending commitment to policy-driven governance where there is no place for ad hoc decision-making. And two, a firm resolve to bring the poor out of the BPL category. On the foreign diplomacy front, India finds itself in the strongest position in the international arena, thanks to Modi's policy of leveraging the country's strengths. If there were some questions regarding Modi's approach to China and Pakistan, he has answered these by largely isolating Pakistan and by boldly giving China the same pill that it has been prescribing for India all these years. Modi has, for the first time, given India the confidence that it can take on China in spite of being a weaker nation in terms of resources and military strength.

Significantly, there are clearly defined areas in which China appears visibly scared of India—India's galloping FDI backed by its richer talent pool and a better technology, especially in space technology, besides the growing India–US ties, and the edge which India is expected to have in manufacturing due to low labour costs as compared to China. This is in contrast to the feeling of being a lame duck that Indians had about themselves while facing China earlier, notwithstanding that country's open and increasing support to the terror originating in Pakistan. But few can deny that Modi is turning into a man of history in the international arena as he becomes the most watched leader apart from Xi Jinping and Donald Trump. In a way, the situation was given to him on a platter as there is almost nobody in the world who has Modi's international appeal, not even Jinping. The ovations and the respect he has received during his visits to fifty-odd countries so far is proof of that.

There had been accusations about Modi's diplomacy not giving the desired results in the neighbourhood—in Nepal, Sri Lanka and the Maldives—which were seen as tilting towards China. But here too his diplomatic tactics have borne fruits as these tiny but strategically crucial nations are either veering towards India again or maintaining the right balance while dealing with India and China. And this is apart from Modi's China- and Pakistan-centric successful counter initiatives in countries like Iran and Afghanistan as well as in central Asian countries, and his dynamic foray into the Middle East, where even Wahhabi Saudi Arabia, a strong Pakistan ally, has recognized Modi's growing importance by honouring him with the Arab nation's highest award.

The relationship Modi is forging with the US, cutting across that country's web of diplomatic calculations, is also new in the history of India's diplomacy, notwithstanding the achievement of Manmohan Singh, the previous prime minister, in carving out a nuclear deal with the US. The way Modi capitalized on India's strength during his June 2016 US visit, which took the US Congress by storm and instilled the fear of isolation in the heart of Pakistan, and even China, left the world powers impressed. India may not have got a seat in the United Nation's Security Council as yet, but it is no more the sulking and supplicating entity. Rather, it is fast emerging as a nation that is well on its way to playing its own significant role in the world agenda on climate change and many other key issues. Indians as well as NRIs living in powerful western countries intensely feel this change in India's image.

The BJP's foreign policy hand and party general secretary, Ram Madhav, who played a key role in broadening the foreign policy vision of the RSS before entering the BJP, says: 'The most confident note that any Indian prime minister had ever struck echoed in the first joint India–US statement, issued by Modi and Obama during the Indian prime minister's first visit to the US in 2014 when Modi emphasized "the priority India accords to its partnership with the United States, a principal partner in the realization of India's rise as a responsible, influential world power".' Madhav says, 'This was the first time that an Indian prime minister was talking so strongly about its global role. It signified a new confidence in our nation's global approach.'[4] However, Modi now faces the fresh challenge of the new US President Donald Trump's protectionist policies taking a toll on Indian jobs in the US. However, according to all indications, the prospect of Trump heavily relying on India while tackling China makes Modi's task less burdensome than it looks at the outset.

When it comes to connecting with the Indian diaspora, the Union external affairs ministry has seen a revolution under Sushma Swaraj. Thanks to her proactive approach in solving the problems of citizens and NRIs, particularly in the war-ravaged Middle East, the embattled NRIs are seeing India as some kind of a deliverer. Her moves are in keeping with Modi's vision of turning the NRIs into brand ambassadors of India. In the process, the plan floated by Atal Bihari Vajpayee of bringing India closer to the NRIs through celebrations like the annual Pravasi Bharatiya Divas is progressing by leaps and bounds.

But back home it is still a tall order. India is a complex republic where people are ruled in three different ways—directly by the state government concerned, by the Centre in matters like income tax, customs and other taxes, and jointly by both the Union and state governments in a third area. Therefore, there are three lists on the governance agenda—the state list, the Union list and the concurrent list, where both have a say. So it is next to impossible for any government at the Centre to bring instant changes in the lives of the people. But the Modi administration is creditably setting high standards of innovative governance that will ultimately percolate to the states, no matter which party is in power there.

Apart from this, it is giving its best in areas where it has a full role to play and laying the precise foundations of cooperative federalism. An example of this is to be found in Modi's monthly experiments on the platform of Pragati (Pro-Active Governance and Timely Implementation), where he reviews stalled Centre–state projects and national programmes through video interactions with Chief Secretaries of states and Secretaries of the central departments. This monthly Centre–state direct dialogue led by the prime minister, a first in independent India's history, has achieved fantastic results when it comes to putting Centre–state projects on course, thus reducing the nation's NPAs.

In 2015, Modi had called the chief ministers for a meeting and requested each of them to share his or her best ideas on good governance so that these could be replicated across India by other state governments. Although the Congress chief ministers boycotted the meet, most other chief ministers, even those belonging to parties that did not make up the National Democratic Alliance (NDA), attended it. The exercise was modelled on a knowledge-sharing experiment Modi had conducted as the chief minister of Gujarat. He used to call dynamic bureaucrats from other states to address the Gujarat bureaucrats during the annual *chintanshibir* (barnstorming camp) so that the latter could replicate the successful governance schemes mooted in other states.

Another quality that differentiates Modi from others and establishes him as a visionary administrator is his step-by-step planning in all important areas of governance. Interestingly, his first step often doesn't reveal to his observers what his forthcoming steps would be. Usually, while taking the first step, he would have already thought of the future plan of action. A good example of this is the Jan-Dhan scheme. After nearly 27 crore poor people had opened their bank accounts under the scheme, he made those accounts a basis for launching a slew of other social security initiatives, ensuring that the government money accruing to the beneficiaries would go directly to their accounts. His vision behind Jan-Dhan was very precise: most poverty-alleviation schemes have failed in India because the beneficiaries didn't have a bank account. As a result of this, a major part of the funds sanctioned for the schemes had landed up with corrupt middlemen.

So after Jan-Dhan came his three insurance schemes under the label Jan Suraksha, with the minimum possible and affordable premium. Then came Mudra (Micro Units Development and Refinance Agency Limited), a scheme to encourage small businesses and skilled people by giving them loans ranging from ₹50,000 to ₹10 lakh. Mudra is changing the lives of innumerable people. The scheme is laudable because it provides loans without seeking a collateral guarantee. After Mudra came a few equally innovative schemes like Stand-Up India, which was meant to encourage women and entrepreneurs from the scheduled castes and tribes (SC and ST) by giving them loans ranging from ₹10 lakh to more than ₹1 crore. Before launching these schemes,

Modi had taken another step related to Jan-Dhan: he had linked the Aadhaar card to the mobile phone, thus ensuring that the benefits went to the targeted population. The prime minister says: 'When I take the first step I know what my tenth step would be. That is why my programmes generally succeed. Without a bank account in the name of the beneficiaries, all these schemes would have failed.'

Modi is absolutely correct if one goes by his Gujarat record. The improvements brought about in Gujarat's primary school sector can serve as an example of this. After becoming the chief minister, Modi first launched the girl enrolment programme by asking officers to go to villages and persuade parents to send their daughters to schools. Then came the teacher recruitment drive to meet the huge shortfall of pedagogues. This was followed by the decision to build more classrooms. After this, toilets were constructed and the provisions of electricity and Internet connectivity were extended to the schools. Finally, in 2010, a programme called Gunotsav was launched to assess the quality of education at the primary level in government schools, along with a scheme to ensure the annual health check-up of all students. The health scheme was accompanied by free treatment if cancer, kidney or heart problems were detected.

Modi's step-by-step planning is also visible in Delhi in the way he has used the Aadhaar card. First, he linked the Aadhaar card to mobile phones and then launched the insurance schemes, followed by the Mudra loan scheme as well as by Stand-Up India. His actions leading to the demonetization in November 2016 also revealed a grand plan behind it. Bhupender Yadav, a national general secretary of the BJP, who has studied Modi's style of governance and knows his priorities, says: 'For the common man, Modi is a great teacher while being a great administrator. One can get some great ideas if only one follows his personal app on a day-to-day basis and his monthly *Mann*

Ki Baat radio show. He gives realistic solutions and future perspectives for daily life.'[5]

There are also shades of a politician–cum–social reformer in Modi, as his Swachh Bharat mission has proved. Many critics question the efforts of the government under the Clean India campaign without realizing that Modi has mooted the idea as an awareness campaign for the common man in order to make it a mass movement. As time passes, it is indeed turning into a mass movement—this is indicated by the daily increase in Clean India groups across the length and breadth of the country. In keeping with his vision that seeks to achieve multiple objectives with one stroke, the Clean India campaign is linked to health and hygiene. Cleaner certainly means healthier. The Beti Bachao campaign that Modi started way back when he was Gujarat's chief minister proves his zeal for social reform. As yoga guru Swami Ramdev puts it: 'Innovative Modi has a reformist mindset and that includes social reform.'

But when it comes to results on the ground, one of Modi's problems is that he does not have adequate hands. Arun Jaitley, Nitin Gadkari, Piyush Goyal, Ravi Shankar Prasad, Venkaiah Naidu, Suresh Prabhu, Dharmendra Pradhan, Nirmala Sitharaman, J.P. Nadda and quite a few others have done a good job of handling their ministries in the context of the stiff targets Modi has set. But the number of such ministers is still not enough. Sometimes, Modi has faltered in selecting the best man for the job, an area in which he is otherwise seen as a master. For example, the selection of Mahesh Sharma as the minister of state for culture and tourism, which is an important service sector with potentials for job creation, is perceived as a mistake since more suitable hands were available.

India's tourism sector has shown significant growth during the Modi administration, thanks mainly due to the pressure from the Prime Minister's Office and the efforts of a good bureaucracy in the tourism department, but it could have still done better had Modi selected the right person to head the ministry, instead of Mahesh Sharma, a man from the medical field. Minister Jagmohan made all the difference to tourism ministry under the A.B. Vajpayee government over a decade and a half ago. Then in another instance, Rajiv Pratap Rudy, who would have been fit for tourism, was given skill development, which is another area with good prospects of job creation. Skill development remains a weak area despite the PMO's efforts to drive the sector with innovative ideas. For example, the government's schemes like allowing private industrial training institutes (ITIs) to meet the shortfall of skilled manpower, in the light of the galloping FDI in India, are falling short of their objectives because of insufficient ministerial focus. Rudy could have done much better in the tourism ministry.

In the larger scheme of things, Modi is yet to pass the test of an institution builder that is a prerequisite for becoming a nation builder. A period of little less than three years is too short a time to pass judgement on this aspect of Modi's performance. But there are people who doubt his ability on this front, influenced as they are by Modi's tendency to look for implementers of his vision rather than for people who can establish their own visions under him. No matter how much one may criticize Pandit Jawaharlal Nehru, India's first prime minister, for his failures on India's national security front, no one can deny him praise as an institution builder who enriched India with great centres of learning such as the Indian Institutes of Management and the Indian Institutes of Technology, besides cultural and other organizations. Modi will have to qualify in this area if he is to be counted among India's greats. But to be fair, Modi has shown remarkable ability to bring about changes in his attitude and approach with time in larger public interest. Maybe institution building is reserved for the next phase in his scheme of things.

On disinvestment, Modi has been cautious. He is seen to have taken only incremental measures but with due reason.

Always geared up for extracting the best for the government, Modi probably believes that he can open the disinvestment route only when he gets the best price from the bidders—which is possible when the world economy starts shaping up again. Still, however, many even among his admirers feel Modi should have gone in for meaningful disinvestment of bleeding big public-sector undertakings (PSUs) like Air India, Coal India Ltd (CIL) and Steel Authority of India Ltd (SAIL).

Says Aroon Purie, editor-in-chief of *India Today*: 'The prime minister is seen as an honest, hard-working, bold and decisive leader working in the service of the nation without the baggage of family or legacy. But he could have been done much on the disinvestment front and also tried to reduce the size of a bloated bureaucracy in keeping with his promise of minimum government and maximum governance.'[6] But to Modi's credit, he has either turned around some of these loss-making PSUs or brought about appreciable improvement in their performance, like in the case of CIL, Power Grid and Air India, so that they are no longer bleeding entities.

But despite the criticism on the PSU reform front, a precise evaluation of the Modi government's economic performance on its completion of two years in 2016, done by the *Wall Street Journal*, gave it a thumbs up.

On the twelve crucial economic parameters, the newspaper rated the Modi government 'well' or 'very well' on nine. It is a matter of pride that the government was rated highly by the world's leading newspaper in the field of economics in spite of the fact that India had faced back-to-back droughts. Had the newspaper also rated the government on transparency and innovation, then the Modi administration might have got even better marking. However, as former cabinet secretary of India T.S.R. Subramanian says: 'The Modi government has taken some fantastic initiatives in core governance. But there are two areas where it will have to work hard. One, making state governments comprehend the essence of good governance. And two, making the bureaucracy work harder for getting the best results. At present the efforts are falling short of meeting the vision of the government.'[7]

Significantly, success to Modi has also come due to his selection of honest and committed bureaucrats and a team of experts in the PMO who work overtime and with precision, to translate his vision into reality, though not without giving the impression of centralization of power at the PMO. Two carefully selected retired IAS officers, Principal Secretary Nripen Misra and Additional Principal Secretary P.K. Mishra, lead the PMO, working in the South Block even on Sundays. Union Cabinet Secretary P.K. Sinha works in close coordination with the PMO, picking up the crucial threads of Modi's vision and making a big difference.

Under the top two PMO officials, Secretary Bhaskar Khulbe and Joint Secretaries A.K. Sharma, Anurag Jain, Tarun Bajaj, Vinay Mohan Kwatra, T.V. Somanathan and Debashish Mukherjee drive the pace of the various ministries from the front. They have an imprint on almost every ministry as they are constantly driving their performances. The BJP president and Modi's confidant, Amit Shah, too has played a significant role in many ministries, thanks to his drill of keeping tabs on the performance of key ministries, as well as keeping Modi posted about his own views on the performance. In fact, Modi and Shah meet at regular intervals to exchange views on ministerial activities. Significantly, Shah not only contributes innovative ideas on governance, but also plays an important role in policymaking.

Modi has a set of officers on special duty (OSDs) who have been with him from his Gujarat days and enjoy exceptional powers in the areas demarcated to them. For example, Hiren Joshi, who has a doctorate in information technology, drives areas to do with IT and social media, in keeping with PM's vision and is responsible for the PM's excellent connect with the people, rather with the smallest citizen in the country. Prateek

Doshi, another OSD, does research in diverse sectors to come up with innovative ideas on governance. Some of the most radical ideas implemented by the Modi government have come from Doshi's research.

Modi has another interesting streak which perhaps contributes to the smooth functioning of the PMO. He seldom shuffles staff who deal with him in non-governance matters. His OSD for appointments, Sanjay Bhavsar, his public relations officer, J.M. Thakkar, and even his personal assistants, Tanmay Mehta, Om Prakash Chandel and Dinesh Thakur, who joined him when he became the CM of Gujarat in 2001, remain with him even today—an association of almost seventeen years. This streak extends even to some senior IAS officers. P.K. Mishra and A.K. Sharma were his most trusted officers in Gujarat, and Sharma has been continuously with him since 2001. The entire PMO shares one thing in common: It keeps out of the media limelight and is simply unapproachable to extraneous forces, a big plus for Modi when compared with the powers and the glamour that even the smallest of employees in the PMO enjoyed in the past.

So it is no wonder that in the Modi era, decision-making has been swift, responses to the common man's problems sharp and talent-hunting precise. A recent example of an ailing girl from Assam said everything about Modi's quality of governance. The girl suffering from a serious ailment had to be provided a green corridor from the Delhi airport to Sri Ganga Ram Hospital. Her failure to reach the hospital in time would surely end his life. Someone dropped an email to the Delhi police commissioner, with a copy marked to Modi's personal email ID, on the girl's behalf. To the utter bewilderment of the girl's family, Delhi Traffic Police was ready with the green corridor when she landed from Guwahati and managed to take him to the hospital in time. Had he reached seven minutes late, she would have died.[8]

On the international political turf, Modi's job is perhaps the toughest in the world with the kind of targets he has set against the existing challenges. His is certainly tougher than the jobs of Donald Trump or Xi Jinping, even in a scenario where the economies of both the countries are not doing too well as compared to India's. This is because one rules a country where the voters are mature enough and there are ample safeguards against corruption to enable government schemes to succeed, while the other has a one-party system to deal with, which makes his job easier.

In Modi's case, he is leading the country with the world's second-highest population, a significant part of which is illiterate and a substantial portion of which is extremely poor, with the bagful of hopes that he has generated ever since he came to power. And Modi has to succeed while working within the restricting democratic framework and without having the safeguards to ensure good governance. He failed to get the Right to Fair Compensation and Transparency in Land Acquisition, Rehabilitation and Resettlement (Amendment) Bill passed in 2015 because the opposition parties refused to cooperate. This is a reminder of the price a nation has to pay for selecting a democratic form of governance. Had the bill been passed, Modi would have been on cloud nine by now as the legislation would have spurred many developmental projects which, in turn, would have pushed forward manufacturing.

After the BJP's landslide victory in Uttar Pradesh, which with a population of over 22 crore is bigger than that of many European countries, Modi's popularity is on the way to rivalling that of India's first prime minister, Pandit Nehru. If Nehru got India a respectable place in the comity of nations, Modi too, in a short span, has taken India to a new level in the international arena on the basis of his economic policies, transparent governance and dynamic diplomacy. The similarities end there, though.

Nehru enjoyed the advantage of becoming India's prime minister after its independence from British rule and therefore had a natural golden run in the form of the people's support till India suffered a crushing defeat under his leadership in the 1962 India-China war. Modi, on the other hand, has come to power after going through the rough and tumble of modern-day Indian politics to become the symbol of people's aspirations based on true national pride, thanks to the curious mix of development, hope and level playing field he offers through his vision and commitment. And his foreign relations strategy is based on much more realistic and solid foundations than Nehru's, wherein India speaks from a position of inherent strength rather than just platitudes. The times though are different as the post-Independence period for India was a phase of intense economic struggle, even survival.

What further sets Modi apart is his ability to take risk. When the issue of selecting the new chief minister following BJP's victory in Uttar Pradesh arose, Modi and Amit Shah sprang a surprise by picking the saffron-robed Hindutva hardliner Yogi Adityanath, who has opposed the politics of Muslim appeasement tooth and nail and has also gone overboard in doing so. But Modi and Shah chose him for two qualities—unparalleled honesty and hard work. These are the very characteristics needed to lead India's largest state out of the morass of maladministration it is in right now. Of course, Adityanath has been reportedly told to keep his Hindutva instincts under control. If Adityanath succeeds in turning around the most difficult Indian state, which appears likely from the initial indications, Modi would have taken his image to a new level.

All in all, this book, woven around my talks with bureaucrats and experts, analyses the monumental changes that Modi has brought about on multiple fronts in less than three years. He has radically altered India's governance landscape by ushering in an unprecedented culture of transparency to create a level playing field, vital in a developing country. In doing so, he has made optimum use of technology to spur faster delivery of services and eject corruption from the system and drive large-scale economic, administrative and other reforms.

He has not only salvaged but also put India in a commanding position on the international front by his deft handling of key areas of governance, including foreign affairs. The dramatic near 30 per cent increase in India's budget in his third year in power is the biggest proof of how things have travelled on India's governance turf under his leadership.

In a way, the Indian prime minister is implementing the same kind of changes that the maker of modern Singapore, the late Lee Kuan Yew, brought about in his country after it broke from Malaysia in 1965, transforming the city state from a backward, malarial nation into a vibrant international hub of finance and logistics. In fact, such was Modi's reverence for Lee that he used to consult him on administrative matters and also went to Singapore to attend Lee's funeral in 2015. Of course, Modi's job is much harder given India's size as compared to the minuscule Singapore.

Incidentally, Modi's Indian inspiration for good governance is the legendary Maratha ruler of the erstwhile princely state of Baroda, Sayajirao Gaekwad. Sayajirao died before Independence but is known as the father of many social and administrative reforms that still exist today. Among other things, he was the first Indian ruler to make women's education compulsory, 110 years ago. He would have easily been in contention for the post of the first President of India in 1950 had he not passed away in 1939. Modi picked up the writings on Sayajirao's methods of governance early on as his home town, Vadnagar in north Gujarat, came under the jurisdiction of Baroda and also had a rich library, in keeping with Sayajirao's vision of having libraries in all villages and towns of his kingdom. Though Modi was born eleven years after Sayajirao's death, he could pick up the threads of the latter's reformist administrative and social traditions as these survived in these villages and towns long after India's independence.

Modi's other inspiration for the strong poverty-elimination measures he is taking is the famous BJP-RSS ideological icon Deendayal Upadhyaya, who mooted the concept of Antyodaya (the upliftment of the weakest sections of the society) as described in the ancient Indian philosophy. Upadhyaya, who truly believed in simple living and high thinking, mooted the ideological concept of integral humanism which opposed the excesses of both individual capitalism and Marxist socialism and sought to take a middle path in favour of an indigenous economic mode that puts the human being at the centre. Inspiration from the right icons makes all the difference, particularly to an administrator, and keeps adding to his vision. Take, for example, Modi's revolutionary proposal to hold parliamentary and state elections simultaneously in the country to save time, money and add to good governance. One after another elections, particularly in the states is one of the main reasons for poor governance in the country as top politicians whose performance has an impact on the nation's growth remain occupied with elections almost throughout the year. If the prime minister's proposal is implemented, it will have an unparalleled impact on the growth trajectory of India. BJP chief Amit Shah, Modi's closest confidant, says: 'I have worked with Narendrabhai in an almost unbroken line from 2001 onwards. I can clearly see that with his tireless energy, great vision and unwavering commitment to principles of good governance and public welfare marked by unprecedented transparency, the prime minister is laying the foundation of a great India that will show a new path to the world.'

Much has been said about Modi's attitude towards Muslims. But a close look at his approach reveals that his game plan is to free Muslims from the cycle of appeasement and put them on the path of progress by giving them their rightful share in the cake of development while refraining from giving in to the special demands of a section of Muslims. He is also encouraging progressive trends in the Muslim community just as he does for sections of the Hindu community. His government's bold stand on triple talaq has made a lot of sense and brought out in large numbers the woes of the hapless Muslim women who have been abandoned by their husbands for extraneous reasons, using the triple talaq route for divorce.

Modi's plan with regard to Muslims met with a lot of success in the 2012 elections to the Gujarat state assembly. Encouraged by his developmental work in Muslim-dominated areas, nearly 23 per cent of Muslims voted for Modi—no mean performance for a man who had been projected by his enemies as a Muslim-hater. Honest assessors who know the dynamics of the complex Indian system and recognize the missionary zeal that Modi possesses to attain his objectives can't deny that he is that rare leader who has the potential to find solutions to two of the most complex problems of modern India—poverty and Hindu–Muslim strife. Though Kashmir remains an eyesore for Modi, there is a silver lining here created by his political diplomacy. He has been able to turn around Chief Minister Mehbooba Mufti to the Indian point of view even at great personal security risk to herself. He seems to have convinced the once unbending Mufti about the honesty of his purpose—which is no small achievement.

Jadunath Sarkar, the renowned Indian historian, while analysing the life and works of the Indian warrior-statesman and emancipator of Hindus from Muslim tyranny, Chhatrapati Shivaji, in his book titled *Shivaji and His Times* had used the writings of British educationist-thinker H.A.L. Fisher and Italian statesman Count Cavour, to define Shivaji's statesmanship. Citing the two, Sarkar said, 'Statesmanship lies in correctly calculating and skilfully utilising the forces of one's age and country so as to make them contribute to the success of his policy. A statesman doesn't grumble about inadequate material for his objective. Nor does he court failure by insisting on abstract perfection impossible in his age. Statesmanly wisdom lies in taking correct stock of the material around oneself and using it suitably and skilfully to meet the grand objective. His genius lies in enlisting the greatest amount of support for his policy while weakening that policy as little as possible by his concessions besides his instinctive perception of what is possible and not possible under the circumstances.' Sarkar attributes all these qualities to Shivaji. If one looks at Modi's trajectory since his days in Gujarat, Sarkar's definition would apply to Modi too in some degree. The Indian prime minister is clearly the man to watch out for in the world arena, his few failings notwithstanding. The Modi era has just begun.

Note: All the figures in this book are taken from the ministries concerned and the MyGov portal of the Ministry of Electronics and Information Technology (www.mygov.in/). Most figures are up to December 2016, while some are of 2017.

The Relevance of
Marching with a Billion Today

For a non-fiction writer—especially one who analyses the political scenario—there is no greater satisfaction than seeing what he writes coming true in real time.

Though published in May 2017, this book on the prime minister's vision and initiatives in governance assumes a special significance today for the nation and its citizens after Narendra Modi's return to the helm following BJP's thumping victory in the 2019 polls. This is perhaps the only book that takes the reader comprehensively into the foundations of core governance that were laid as soon as Modi assumed office. The groundwork done by his team led to innovative, pro-people schemes and an unwavering commitment to the two interlinked phenomenon of poverty elimination and transparency—correcting the ills of the past as embodied by late prime minister Rajiv Gandhi's candid statement in 1985 that, of every rupee minted, 'only 15 paise reaches the end beneficiary'.

With a view to tackling this, we have seen Modi making deft use of technology to take the rate of delivery of government welfare schemes from below 50 per cent when he came to power in 2014 to over 80 per cent and even 90 or 95 per cent in certain cases. There has been an unprecedented last-mile delivery of schemes with skilful use of technology and an unflinching commitment to changing the destiny of the nation. It allowed BJP president and now Union Home Minister Amit Shah to deftly woo the electorate by capitalizing on the idea of fair governance. The curbing of the culture of nepotism and cronyism is what impressed the masses who were convinced that corruption had become a part and parcel of their lives.

Indeed, after political pundits predicted in December 2018 that Modi's popularity was on the wane, his schemes were ineffective and that his party would secure about 200 seats in the Lok Sabha polls, I started a survey of my own to find out how taxi drivers across India viewed Modi. I visited five Indian cities between January and April 2019, apart from Delhi where I stay, and tried to gauge their mood. They all declared somewhat unanimously that they would vote for Modi because his schemes were reaching the poor. The Direct Benefit Transfer (DBT) made the greatest impact. Before DBT came into effect it was taken for granted that one would have to grease the palms of government clerks whether one was claiming subsidy or pension. No wonder then that DBT played a most pivotal role in Modi's victory. It turned out to be a certificate of the new-found transparency among the people.

This book traces five main features of Modi's governance: transparency; delivery; use of technology and innovation; ability to create pride in the citizen to enjoin his latent energy with the developmental journey of the nation; and finally the remarkable shift in national security and foreign policy from a doe-like stance to a confident one based on India's inherent strength (as discussed in in the chapter 'India and the World').

The great political thinker and revolutionary Veer Savarkar had predicted the 1962 Indo–China war in 1954, saying, 'After what China has done to Tibet kowtowing to the Chinese would whet its appetite. I won't be surprised if China feels emboldened to swallow Indian land tempted by India's weak-kneed approach.'[1] His words proved true eight years later. That China has recently given in to international pressure in the United

Nations to declare Masood Azhar a terrorist is the culmination of a Savarkarian shift that Modi has brought about in both our national security and diplomacy in the past five years, albeit many new challenges have risen that will test his diplomatic skills and sagacity. The book describes the strong stance that Modi took against China by befriending and even delivering military help to countries like Vietnam who are locked in a tussle with China over the latter's attempts to dominate the South China Sea and his firm stand in the Doklam stand-off.

After the unprecedented Balakot air strike in February 2019 on terror camps of Jaish-e-Mohammed in response to the killing of forty-two Indian jawans of the Central Reserve Police Force (CRPF) by JEM terrorists at Pulwama, one can easily say that Indian security and foreign policy vision has started acquiring the depth of Chanakya and the deftness of Chattrapati Shivaji after nearly seven decades of a defensive stance marked by what can be described as self-flagellation, except during the tenure of Indira Gandhi when India experienced a robust transformation for a few years.

All the five defining factors of his governance whose initial implementation is described in depth in this book played a key role in Modi's landslide victory. For example, the chapter 'Digital-techno Revolution in the Making' describes how the government's adoption of technology is opening a new chapter in curbing corruption in delivery of schemes at the ground level by getting rid of middlemen. In this, Modi's Jan Dhan scheme played a stellar role. The scheme opened bank accounts for 35 crore people, mostly from the poor sections of society or the middle class, ensuring direct transfer of money due from the government to the citizens in their bank accounts in different verticals, from pension to subsidies and insurance money. Only 2.50 crore citizens were receiving money in their bank accounts from the government when Modi came to power. That figure now stands at a mindboggling 55 crores.

Another great technological innovation has been the use of geotagged photographs in the monitoring of schemes and their last-mile delivery as part of a new app-based concept. This initiative was yet to be introduced when I finished my book in the beginning of 2017 but there were indications of the introduction of new tools to monitor implementation of schemes at the grass roots. Geotagging is one of the biggest innovations as it requires the personnel responsible for implementing a scheme to not only deliver the benefit but also take a picture with the beneficiary. A prime example of this is the prime minister's housing scheme for the poor in which pics of the beneficiary with his home are taken thrice and posted on the specially designed app. This has brought about a sea change in delivery. Housing schemes are seeing 95 per cent delivery, a record in independent India's history and proof, if ever it was needed, that an assault on poverty has begun in the country and that this is a government that will walk the talk.

The book also describes the revolution the government brought about soon after taking over through the selection of honest and intelligent officials. This was done by a 360-degree inquiry and has made all the difference to the implementation of government's welfare schemes. I believe that for schemes to reach the last mile, bureaucrats have to be transparent. When Modi came to power, 90 per cent of officials at the Centre had outstanding personal appraisal reports (PARs), including almost all officers from the central services, many of whom were subsequently suspended or dismissed on corruption charges after Modi's arrival. This included secretaries and one chief secretary of state, who went to jail in a corruption case. It is apparent that there was no difference between a bad and a good official as officers scratched each other's backs in writing the PARs.

Modi went about addressing this in a planned manner. First, he dismantled the decades-old transfer posting industry of officials in Delhi by removing the role of middlemen in postings and setting up a machinery for the purpose under the leadership of his additional principal secretary, Dr P.K. Mishra. Next, he institutionalized selection by introducing the 360-degree criteria under which a secret team of officials makes a 360-degree inquiry about every official, checking on his integrity, efficiency and aptitude before marking him fit for posting in Delhi.

I have also covered extensively two experiments of the government that have had a deep impact on governance. The first one is a government web platform called 'MyGov' which marks a revolution in people's participation in governance whereby ministries invite suggestions for its various schemes from the people urging them to go to this platform and then implementing the better ones. Hundreds of suggestions by common people have been implemented across ministries, which has created a sense of participation among the citizens in the journey of the nation.

Another experiment in innovation is 'Pragati'—a monthly platform on which the prime minister, with his officials, takes up delayed Centre–state projects and review of Central schemes in states with state chief secretaries through video conferencing. No prime minister has ever interacted with state chief secretaries, and this experiment has proved to be a master stroke as it has brought on track over Rs 3 lakh crores worth of Centre–state projects, many of which had become Non-Performing Assets (NPAs).

The book also takes a broad look at the massive work in infrastructure that began in 2014 across verticals like roads and highways, railways, shipping, power and rural electrification of thousands of villages seven decades after independence. Another area it looks at in brief is legislative reforms that the government took up, like modifying the Insolvency and Bankruptcy Code to plug all the loopholes in it to stop manipulation by powerful people and making it fair.

However, water distribution and conservation is one area in which the government needs to concentrate as India is sitting on a powder keg of water crisis. Another related sector, agriculture, will have to be paid more attention in order to dispel the impression that the Modi government is urban centric and pays less attention to core agriculture.

Marching with a Billion along with *Centrestage* (2014), another book of mine on Modi's thirteen years as chief minister of Gujarat, has become more relevant today for anyone trying to get a peek inside Modi's mind. The reason is that after coming to Delhi, Modi proved the sceptics wrong by demonstrating much greater administrative ability than he had shown in Gujarat. One of the major elements that marks the Modi era is the changed parameters for evaluating governance. The barometer is no longer the fluctuations of the Sensex but the extent to which benefits of good governance have reached the poor and the common people.

When I wrote *Marching with a Billion*, Modi had been in power for barely two-and-a-half years and it was too short a time to make a comprehensive statement about the road it was treading. However, I did make one saying that the 'Modi era might have begun'. There is no denying today that it has indeed begun in the right earnest.

Interestingly, in August 2017 when as a speaker at a seminar of economists and thinkers I spoke about the firm foundation of good governance that the Modi government was laying, I found myself almost alone in my view. Last week the organizer of the seminar admitted that I was correct that day and most others had erred in judging the impact of Modi's governance.

Marching with a Billion is a ready reckoner on the governance model of the Narendra Modi government and is even more relevant now.

Uday Mahurkar
July 2019

1

We, the People

The Social Pitch

Ramesh Babu, aged thirty-four, a bangle-maker of Andhra Pradesh's West Godavari district, is a relieved man. He is visibly happy. He seems to have found relief after a long struggle. It is true in Babu's case. In 2011, he had taken a loan of ₹30,000 at 10 per cent compound interest from a local moneylender. When told about the high interest rate, semi-literate Babu couldn't comprehend that he was walking into a trap. He was only concerned about expanding his trade so that he could earn enough for the family and live a decent life.

Five years later, at the end of 2015, Babu was on the verge of committing suicide. The reason: he had paid over ₹1.5 lakh in that five-year period, with the principal amount still dangling over his head. In spite of his hard work, he could never earn enough to clear the interest and the principal amount at one go. Just when the depressed Babu was thinking of ending his life to free himself from this endless agony, a friend told him about the prime minister's Mudra loan scheme to encourage small businesses like his. The loan could be secured without much paperwork and without a collateral guarantee, and at

1

a low interest rate. Seeing a ray of hope, Babu immediately rushed to the local Vijaya Bank and told his story to the bank officials. Moved by his plight, the officials, briefed properly by the government about the purpose of the scheme, came quickly to his rescue. Within days, Babu had a bank loan of ₹50,000. The first thing he did after getting the money was to pay off the moneylender's principal amount. Today, not only is he doing good business but he has also become the brand ambassador of Mudra in his area.

The story of Devendra Pal, a roadside tailor of Nisai village in the Farrukhabad district of Uttar Pradesh, is of a different kind. He had rarely ever gone to a bank in his life. He never had a bank account because he never had the necessary documents to open one. And since he didn't have a bank account, his saving habits were also poor. After the Union government launched the Jan-Dhan scheme for opening bank accounts for those who didn't have them by relaxing the rules, the IDBI bank officials in Pal's area organized a camp as per directions from the government. The poor people of the area were called to the camp, where they were helped in opening the accounts. It was for the first time in independent India that bank officials were going to the poor. The history till then had been of the poor chasing the bank officials. After taking Pal's details, the officials opened an account for him. The man who had never saved any money has over ₹12,000 now as savings in his bank account.

It's the same with Nabisha Begum, a domestic help from Managiri near Madurai. Her husband is a daily-wage labourer and they have two kids. They never had saved any money. After her account was opened by a bank in a camp in 2015, this family too has saved ₹19,000 in a brief span of time. The savings have triggered off a new kind of dynamism in Nabisha. Now, while still working as a domestic help, she also sells flowers and makes extra money. 'It has changed the way we live our lives,' admits Nabisha.

Both Jan-Dhan and Mudra define the method the Modi government has chosen to tackle poverty. India's figures when it comes to wealth creation and other economic parameters might have improved, particularly after the reforms of 1991, but the poverty levels haven't come down correspondingly. In this context, the two schemes, along with many others that the government has launched in the last two and a half years, demonstrate an empowering and enabling model to remove poverty. These steps are in sharp contrast to the empty 'Garibi Hatao' slogan of the past that was accompanied by loan waivers offered at the cost of the public exchequer with an eye on votes alone. That policy was always in danger of turning the poor either into laggards or freebie junkies. Some of the schemes might have been well intentioned but were doomed to failure because they had no connection to the ground realities.

Modi's biggest asset has been that he has seen India at the grass-roots level as a commoner in his formative years. Coupled with his sharp intellect, this has enabled him to identify problems and find solutions for the common people. His enthusiasm to create a level playing field where millionaires, billionaires and the common man all get the same treatment from the government has made him come up with schemes that bridge the gap between the rich and the poor, the privileged and the underprivileged.

Jan-Dhan emerged as the biggest symbol of financial inclusion and a tool of poverty alleviation. That the scheme in which the banks were virtually told to chase the poor and open bank accounts in their names has led to the opening of 27 crore new bank accounts and savings worth over ₹80,000 crore deposited in them by the poor is also a comment on the administrative priorities that the country's leaders had in the past. Of course, a part of the savings should be credited to the attempts by the people to turn their black money into white by using the Jan-Dhan accounts following the prime minister's demonetization stroke. But even if the true figure is a little more than ₹60,000 crore, it is no negligible amount for people who simply didn't have a bank account two years ago.

The absence of bank accounts and the lack of the facility of direct benefit transfer (DBT) to the accounts of the poor in case of government schemes have helped middlemen eat up the subsidies. Almost seven decades after India became independent, and forty-eight years after the nationalization of banks in the name of 'Garibi Hatao', as much as 42 per cent of the Indian population didn't have a bank account when Modi took oath on 26 May 2014. Today, over 99 per cent have been covered. The lack of bank accounts makes poor people ineligible for all kinds of loans. Even wages have to be collected by them in cash—this leaves room for exploitation by middlemen, who often work hand in glove with lower-rung government officials.

Not having a bank account also meant that no interest was earned on the money saved, howsoever small the amount. On the flip side, it was a loss to the government as a significant number of these bank-account-less people did have the capacity to save but had no bank account to keep the money in. The money was prevented from entering the economy. Besides, in scores of Indian villages, the poor people with no bank accounts have been akin to playthings for moneylenders and chit-fund operators. So Jan-Dhan deals a body blow to these 'unofficial' bankers. The absence of bank accounts also meant that the poor remained disconnected from the government's insurance schemes and the DBT route that the government is increasingly choosing for transferring subsidies.

Right from the day Modi took over as the prime minister, his vision was clear: ending the *dalal* (middlemen) raj in the subsidy structure was necessary for poverty alleviation. And for ending the dalal raj, bank accounts were the key as they could be used for transferring money directly to the beneficiary. So when Modi launched the Jan-Dhan scheme soon after taking over as prime minister in 2014, he had already thought of the future methods of alleviating poverty and empowering the poor using bank accounts. His later initiatives like Mudra, Jan Suraksha and the crop insurance scheme could have succeeded only after Jan-Dhan. Had there been no Jan-Dhan, most of these schemes would have remained only on paper, as they had been in the past.

Voices from across India prove what difference the Jan-Dhan scheme is making. Forty-one-year-old Ramadevi Prakash Chandra, the wife of a small grocery shop owner with three children in Nawar Kheda village in Uttarakhand, is a good example. The family has an income of over ₹5000 but didn't have a bank account. An IDBI Bank official managed to open her account in the Goulapaar branch, to make Ramadevi one of the few in the landlocked village to have an account. Ramadevi says, 'I get a feeling of empowerment. Sharing my experience, I have convinced quite a few in the village to open bank accounts.'

The same kind of voices can be heard on the Mudra scheme. Twenty-four-year-old Gurjit Singh, living 500 km away from Nawar Kheda in Punjab's Faridkot, is elated. Mudra has changed his life altogether. From a daily-wage-earning carpenter who earned just over ₹2000 a month, he is now making ₹15,000 as an entrepreneur and living a life of dignity and peace, thanks to a Mudra loan of ₹50,000, which enabled him to start his own shop. Take the case of thirty-six-year-old Saudarani Mohanty, a graduate. For her too, Mudra has come as a lifesaver. Divorced from her husband in 2014, she had no means of earning a livelihood for herself and her son. She addressed her problem by deciding to make garments at home on a sewing machine and sell them. When she was struggling, she learnt about the launch of Mudra. She went to the local UCO bank branch and secured a loan of ₹50,000. The loan has enabled her to take a big stride in her fledgling business. Today she earns ₹15,000 to ₹20,000.

The objective behind Mudra is to extend loan from ₹20,000 to ₹10 lakh to small businesses without seeking collateral guarantee, which is the cornerstone of the loan-giving business in the public as well as in the private sectors. Government records reveal that over 6 crore people have been given loans so far, totalling ₹2.24 lakh crore under Mudra in about two years. The beneficiaries include ground-level small-business people like flower sellers, vegetable vendors, boutique shop owners, tailors, ironsmiths, button-purse makers, women doing embroidery and laundrywallas. These people are individual entrepreneurs. But there is another class of beneficiaries who are eligible for a higher category of loans. They can employ three to four people and, therefore, become job providers.

Mudra has created an ecosystem wherein people who have skills but no resources to set up their business can get financial help. It is also enabling those with already established businesses who want to grow but don't have the money to invest in expansion. After almost two years of the launch of the scheme, the payback rate by the beneficiaries is more than 98 per cent—which is a measure of the strong relation established between the government and the common people after Modi's arrival and is a proof of his belief that once a government reposes trust in the people, the latter seldom betray. A source close to Shaktikanta Das, the Union economic affairs secretary, says, 'It is because of Mudra that there is no hue and cry over joblessness in the country in the context of slow manufacturing.'

By coming up with innovative entrepreneurial schemes like Mudra, Stand-Up India for entrepreneurs from the SC/STs and women, besides Startup India, Modi has changed the definition of job creation, which so far was largely restricted to private-sector and government jobs. He has rightly understood that joblessness will remain a problem as long as people are not empowered to become job creators and remain job seekers. In a way, this has been the only proven model to create sufficient jobs. Modi says: 'Many of the surveys that project the job scenario in the country are unreal. For these surveys skip schemes like Mudra which are about job creation through self-employment.'

Jan-Dhan took off right from the day it was launched, thanks to the firm guidelines issued to the banks and the administration to remove all impediments that came in the way of opening the accounts. The managements of various banks held camps to open bank accounts for all those who didn't have one. A major concession was made when it came to providing residential address proof, without which no bank account can be opened. For those who didn't have an official address proof in the form of Aadhaar card, Voter ID card or a job card for the Mahatma Gandhi National Rural Employment Guarantee Act (MGNREGA), a local officer issued a character certificate with an address in the name of the person for whom the accounts had to be opened. Soon the account was ready in his or her name. 'This was a great mindset change for the bureaucracy reared on a colonial set of rules, regulations and conventions,' remarks Hasmukh Adhia, the financial services secretary.

The fact that the Modi model for the poor is of an enabling nature and not dole-based is proved by just one example. When the Jan-Dhan accounts were opened, the government remitted ₹5000 in these accounts. Many observers thought that this was a freebie. But no, the amount was a loan to the beneficiaries that they had to use and return within a specified time frame. If not used within that period, the money went back to the government treasury automatically. As a bureaucrat working in the PMO reveals: 'His pro-poor approach is highly refreshing and distinct from the past. He is in favour of meaningful subsidies of enabling nature to the poor but at the same time doesn't want to give them the impression that they should expect freebies from his government.'

The way banks went chasing people without accounts for enrolling them had an exact parallel in Modi's drive to enrol girl students in rural schools when he was Gujarat's chief minister between 2001 and 2014. During that drive, the entire Gujarat bureaucracy went to villages for two days every June to convince parents to send their daughters to schools. It was discovered during the programme that one of the reasons for parents refusing to send their daughters to study was the lack of separate toilets for girls in schools. Eventually, the government launched a parallel drive to build toilets for girls in all schools. The enrolment rate for girls climbed from 62 per cent to 100 per cent and the dropout rate came down from 3.5 per cent to 2.6 per cent. Many of Modi's Delhi initiatives are embedded in his first innings as an administrator in Gandhinagar, where he had his schooling in the business of running a government. He came out with flying colours in the final round.

Modi's insurance scheme under the umbrella of Jan Suraksha for the poor has also proved to be a master stroke. Modi believes that for the best talents to emerge from the weaker sections of society in the service of the nation, it is important that they don't suffer from a sense of insecurity about their future. So the first step in bringing up the poor, as per the Modi model, is to build their confidence by removing uncertainty with schemes of financial inclusion like Jan-Dhan, followed by moves like Mudra and Stand-Up India to create a level playing field for them.

Under Jan Suraksha, the Modi government provides insurance of different types to the poor at affordable rates. The scheme has met with popular approval. The Pradhan Mantri Jeevan Jyoti Bima Yojana, which offers a cover of ₹2 lakh, is available at an annual premium of just ₹330, which is less than ₹1 per day. Earlier, a ₹2 lakh insurance scheme invited a premium of more than ₹5000 a year. The second scheme under this label, covering accidental death, or full or partial disability, has a premium of just ₹12 per year—which is less than 5 paise a day. This scheme, in routine course, would have called for ₹900 as annual premium. In case of accidental death or complete disability, the insurance holder gets ₹2 lakh, and in case of partial disability, ₹1 lakh.

Modi took a two-pronged approach to make this scheme viable, which he thought was a must for strengthening the social sector. While aiming at low-premium insurance policy schemes, he also had to make sure that the schemes weren't an unaffordable liability for the insurance companies. So, as a first step, his government increased the FDI in the insurance sector from 26 to 49 per cent in March 2015 to create a cushion. It then launched Jan Suraksha in May 2015. Before the scheme was introduced, only 16 per cent of the population, or roughly over 20 crore people, availed of the insurance schemes. With Jan Suraksha, the cover increased to include around 13.50 crore people in less than two years. The beneficiaries are all from the poorer classes.

Yet another step of the government involved the offer of social security to the unorganized sector in a manner that was effective. This was based on Modi's belief, developed in the course of his travels in the country, that unorganized workers like domestic helpers, drivers, vegetable vendors, newspaper sellers, cobblers and roadside vendors have to face great difficulties after retirement due to the lack of a steady income and savings. So he floated the Atal Pension Yojana for different age brackets. It was designed very imaginatively.

The pension of ₹5000 per month under the scheme starts when the beneficiary reaches sixty but the monthly premium to be paid by him or her is linked to the age at which he or she enrols for the scheme—between eighteen and forty years. For an eighteen-year-old, the monthly premium is just ₹210 but for a forty-year-old, it is ₹1454. The beneficiaries of this pension scheme in the unorganized sector are people with low income, who are not familiar with concept of saving money for

the later years of their lives. Almost 37 lakh poor people availed
of the scheme within twenty months of its launching—not an
unimpressive number in a country with low awareness levels
among the disadvantaged sections of society.

The Modi government's empathy for the common man also
extends to the health sector, where it is moving with messianic zeal
to make medicines and treatment affordable for the people at large.
The prime minister has shown his determination to come out with
a new law to break the doctor–pharmaceutical company nexus
which results in undue profits to the doctors and the companies and
makes medicine unaffordable. In a first in India's recent past, Health
Minister J.D. Nadda capped the prices of 700 medicines to make
them affordable. A slew of other measures is being taken. Like his
government's historical 2017 decision to cap the price of life-saving
coronary stents used in cardiac surgeries at ₹30,000, almost 85 per
cent less than the ongoing price in the market, thus giving a great
relief to poor cardiac patients and exposing the exploitation of
patients in India's medical market.

But the scheme which has the potential to establish Modi as
the messiah of the poor is the Pradhan Mantri Ujjwala Yojana,
a venture of the Ministry of Petroleum and Natural Gas to
equip 5 crore BPL families, who cook food on *chulhas* (earthen
ovens), with LPG connections. Interestingly, a debate has been
going on in the country for years over whether there should
be a subsidy on LPG connections or not. The reason behind
such a debate was that the subsidy had no relevance for the BPL
families in India as these families didn't have LPG connections
in the first place. None amongst the past leaders ever thought
of providing the poor with subsidized cooking gas. During his
days as a pracharak in the rural areas, Modi had observed how
the poor contracted lung diseases as a result of cooking on the
chulha. When he came to power, the issue had been playing
on his mind. A World Health Organization report saying that
nearly 5 lakh people die in India every year due to health

complications arising out of the use of unclean cooking fuel strengthened his resolve. But the financial disciplinarian in him was also thinking of ways to meet the expenses.

To settle the issue, Modi chose his favourite 'patriotic route'. He has a typical way of enlisting public support for his schemes by creating a sense of pride in the people. So in a function of the Ministry of Petroleum and Natural Gas in Delhi in March 2015, he appealed: 'Let the well-off leave subsidy on LPG gas in an elder brotherly sacrifice for the poor and contribute to the nation's progress.' In less than eight months, as many as 1 crore people gave up their LPG subsidy in response to Modi's call. Dharmendra Pradhan, the Union minister for petroleum and natural gas, was also leading this from the front. One patriotic appeal did what no government regulation could have done. The government decided to transfer the saved LPG subsidy to the bank accounts of the truly eligible through DBT. Lakhs of bogus subsidized LPG connection holders were wiped out from the official subsidy rolls as a result of DBT. These two moves alone are saving the exchequer over ₹21,000 crore annually and making it possible for the government to provide cooking gas to 5 crore BPL families.

Modi's desire to create an enabling model instead of a freebie-based one is visible in the case of Ujjwala too. The non-subsidized gas stove and cylinder cost ₹3200 per set. When the scheme was announced, many thought that the offer came free, while the fact was that the government was giving 50 per cent subsidy, not 100 per cent. This wrong initial impression created confusion among freebie seekers, who were inquiring the government of the reasons why people who got new connections were being asked to pay ₹1600 for the gas stove and subsidized LPG cylinder. Things settled down in a matter of a few weeks. The problems of delivery to the interior areas of the country were surmounted by the government through smart planning. The implementation of the scheme has been a grand success. Against a target of extending LPG connections to 1.5 crore BPL families by March 2017, the petroleum minister had covered a whopping 1.94 crore families, thus exceeding the target by 44 lakh. That covered over 9.50 crore people from among India's most poor at five persons per family. The target is to cover 5 crore families by 2019. For those few who cannot pay even ₹1600 at one go, the petroleum ministry has offered the option of paying the amount in easy instalments.

The Modi government's empowering vision is no less visible in the agriculture sector. The government has focused on small farmers. What is noteworthy in this context is the innovative crop insurance scheme for farmers where only 2 per cent of the insured amount has to be paid as premium in the case of kharif crops and 1.5 per cent in the case of rabi crops. This premium earlier was usually over 20 per cent of the insured amount and was subject to a number of impractical conditions, which made crop insurance a wild goose chase for poor farmers. Now hailstorms, which occur very often in north and central India, are covered under the scheme so that insurance is easily available to the ryots if their crops are damaged.

Many in the corporate community privately accuse the Modi government of arrogance and insensitivity. They seem to have been provoked by the strict actions of the income tax authorities and angered by the government's attempts to eliminate the role of corporate houses in policymaking. They think that in order to woo the poor constituencies, the prime minister is deliberately being harsh on them. 'Businessmen are virtually being seen as criminals these days in Delhi,' says a middle-level industrialist who has known Modi for long. But Modi believes that he is cleaning up the system by not letting corporate houses play a part in decision-making. The nexus between the administration and corporate houses has been exposed in the many scams that marked the pre-2014 era. The corporate bigwigs have taken a lot of money from the system by taking the illicit route. The phenomenal increase in the size of the Union budget from around ₹16.55 lakh crore in 2013–14 to ₹21.50 lakh crore in 2017–18 also gives a fair idea of the amount of money being saved by the Modi government by curbing corruption and wasteful expenditure. There has been an impressive increase in the collection of direct and indirect taxes.

A New, Empowering Approach towards Dalits

In a highly politicized country like India, rhetoric can be the antithesis of facts on the ground. This is seen nowhere more clearly than in the way ideological rivals of the party in power at the Centre use the issue of Dalits to cast aspersions on the ruling government, citing certain unfortunate incidents. In reality, few governments in the past have tried to empower Dalits as much as the Modi administration has. The Startup India scheme for creating entrepreneurs from among Dalits and tribal groups is one part of the Dalit empowerment story. Another involves the stringent amendments brought to the Scheduled Castes and Tribes (Prevention of Atrocities) Act, 1989. Common offences committed against Dalits in certain parts of the country that were not under the purview of the old law have been made punishable under the amended law.

The list of offences against Dalits that have been made punishable or more severely punishable than before is long— tonsuring of head, moustache, or similar acts that are disrespectful towards SC/ST members; garlanding with chappals; denying access to irrigation facilities or forest rights; asking someone to dispose of or to carry human or animal carcasses, or to dig graves; using or permitting manual scavenging; marking out SC/ST women as devadasis; atrocities perpetrated in the name of witchcraft; imposing social or economic boycott; preventing SC/ST candidates from filing nominations to contest elections; hurting the dignity of a woman from the SC/ST communities by removing her garments; forcing a member of the SC/STs to leave their house, village or residence; defiling objects sacred to the SC/STs; using words, acts or gestures of a sexual nature against members of the SC/STs; and not allowing Dalit marriage processions. While the punishments for these offences have been made more stringent, the compensation to victims of certain offences has been increased fivefold.

In his endeavour to empower Dalits, Modi has an enthusiastic supporter in Milind Kamble, a famous Dalit businessman from Pune who heads the Dalit Indian Chamber of Commerce and Industry. The Stand–Up India scheme of the Modi government that offers a loan between ₹10 lakh and ₹1 crore for SC/ST borrowers and women entrepreneurs was originally Kamble's suggestion. He calls it Modi's great gift to the entrepreneurial Dalit youth of India, who can now set up businesses with the loans. The scheme, which was launched in April 2016, has set a target of helping over 1 lakh entrepreneurs in the first phase from the categories for which it is meant. The response to the scheme has, however, been slow due to the social conditions prevailing in the country. Less than 20,000 individuals had been covered under the scheme by the end of 2016. Kamble says that the number has to be considered along with the fact that the Mudra scheme, under which 6 crore or almost 5 per cent of India's population has already been covered, includes a number of Dalits and tribal people.

Kamble precisely sums up Modi's vision for the poor when he says that Mudra and Stand–Up India are the biggest-ever financial- and social-inclusion measures of independent India meant to empower the downtrodden and take the relationship between the government and the poor from one of patronage to that of partnership. 'I see a different India some years from now when it comes to the uplift of the Dalits and the downtrodden. Economic parity is a great leveller. It will automatically neutralize distinctions and discriminations based on caste and other extraneous factors,' says Kamble, who finds that Mudra is working very well at the ground level.[1]

But there is something even more remarkable about Modi's inclusive approach to the Dalit issue. Take, for instance, the way B.R. Ambedkar is being projected by the NDA government and compare it to the way he has been presented in the past. All along, Ambedkar had been sold as a leader of the Dalits and one of the makers of the Indian Constitution. But the Doordarshan programme to mark the 125th birth anniversary of Ambedkar on 14 April 2016 presented a more rounded image of Ambedkar that encompassed many new facets of the great leader. The show highlighted Ambedkar's views on many areas, including economics, industrialization, the importance of technology and women's emancipation. It thus showed him as a leader of all sections of society.

Gaurav Vallabh, professor of finance at XLRI, Jamshedpur, says: 'Ambedkar's rupee exchange determination theorem is relevant even in today's economic context. He was for opening up the economy and encouraging the private sector in the 1950s. He emphasized on science and technology and industrialization as being essential to progress and development. All these things are coming true. It is unfortunate that these aspects of Ambedkar are ignored.'[2] Observes Kishore Makwana, a Dalit writer from Gujarat: 'Keeping Babasaheb separated from certain parts of the society is politically beneficial to some because he will be acceptable to one and all in that case and will lose his political exclusivity that some people want for their political benefit.'[3]

Modi's empowering approach was evident at the event in which he inaugurated the Dalit Indian Chamber of Commerce and Industry in Delhi in December 2015 and awarded five enterprising Dalit entrepreneurs. Dalits present on the occasion broke into applause when he said, 'We want to create job creators out of Dalits, not job seekers.' He explained the economic and industrial ideas of Ambedkar, stressing that the latter was much more than a Dalit leader and a maker of the Indian Constitution. His speech on the occasion was in a way landmark. Modi said that when people talk about their rights they should also talk about their duties towards society. He added that he was happy to note that the Dalit entrepreneurs present on the occasion were talking not only about their duties but also about fulfilling them. It won't be an overstatement to say here that the era of appeasement is receding and a new era of empowerment is beginning to take shape.

2

India First

A Digital-techno Revolution in the Making

Less than a month after Narendra Modi took oath as prime minister on 26 May 2014, he called a meeting with officials from the PMO to share with them his digital-techno vision of governance. Modi, who has always been ahead of his times in adopting the latest technology, told the officials that he wanted to link people to digital technology like nowhere else in the world. Stressing that these weren't empty words, he said that he would like to lead from the front by adopting the best options himself.

Just as England led the Industrial Revolution in the eighteenth century, India might lead the digital revolution now, thanks to a series of moves made by the Modi government, including the digitization drive, which started in November 2016 after demonetization. The success of the Unified Payments Interface (UPI) designed by the government as a digital payment tool that makes cumbersome digital transactions unbelievably easy points to the bright future of India on the digital front.

The latest technology has been Modi's priority from the day he took over as the chief minister of Gujarat on 7 October 2001.

Modi declared 2004 as Gujarat's e-governance year. To mark the occasion, he delivered a significant speech. Laying the state's roadmap and delivering a loud message to the state bureaucracy, he said: 'I believe e-governance is the bedrock of efficiency, transparency and quick delivery in governance. I want the entire state administration under e-governance cover without loss of time.'

In Delhi, Modi began his digital-techno march as soon as he had addressed the PMO. In July 2014, he launched his novel, people-centric digital initiative MyGov, which is a platform for various ministries to invite suggestions from people on specific topics, debate them and implement the good ones. This was the first time in India's history that a government was using the digital path to give a chance to every citizen to play a role in policymaking.

Results prove that MyGov has been a meaningful experiment. Out of the lakhs of suggestions that have come on the MyGov platform since 2014, there are some great ideas that have been mooted by the commonest of people. These have been implemented or are in the process of being implemented by various Union ministries. More than 2.50 lakh village panchayats have been consulted on the new national education policy through MyGov—such grass-roots-level consultation on policymaking on such a large scale has rarely taken place anywhere else in the world.

The Core Digital Vision and the Challenges Ahead

What is the Modi government's core digital vision? The prime minister believes that the country has to overcome the urban–rural digital divide if it is to move forward. The bridging of this divide will prevent the migration from rural to urban areas that is happening at an alarming rate at present. He believes that access to technology is essential at the grass-roots level if people in the rural areas are to be provided with faster and adequate access to education, and to health and monetary benefits, without which the urban–rural divide can't be closed. Leapfrogging technology, Modi believes, is vital for inclusive growth.

Modi thinks that India will become part of the digital revolution when hardware (e.g. smartphones) is easily obtainable along with local digital infrastructure in the form of Net accessibility and user-friendly apps. Fortunately, India is moving fast towards smartphone availability, an area in which the country has done extremely well after Modi's arrival on the national scene. But a lot more has to be done. Only a third of the 108 crore mobile phones in India are smartphones. The Modi government's electronics policy aims at enhancing local smartphone production to bring down the cost and make them affordable for everyone.

The growth rate of smartphone manufacturing is most impressive, with India leading the smartphone market at the international level, outpacing China in 2016. Till 2014, mobile phones used to be imported or made in fully imported plants in India. After the introduction of the government's new policy, which waives duty if mobile phone parts are imported and the phone is assembled in India, seventy-two new units, representing a dozen and a half foreign and Indian mobile-manufacturing companies, including Samsung, LG, Micromax, Foxconn, Intex and Lava, are being set up—forty-two of these are making mobile phones and the remaining are making phone components. The Taiwanese manufacturer Foxconn had come to India in a big way. The multinational corporation (MNC), which is the third-largest information technology (IT) company in the world in terms of revenue, has already started production. This is creating 60,000 direct and 60,000 indirect jobs in the country.

The latest figures of mobile-phone production demonstrate the change that is coming. In 2014–15, India made a little more than 6 crore units of mobile phones. In one year, the figure jumped by 83 per cent to 11 crore units in 2015–16. In value terms, the figure is even more impressive. From ₹19,000 crore in 2014–15, the value of the mobile phones manufactured in India has touched ₹94,000 crore in 2016–17—almost a fivefold increase in over two years.

According to Arvind Vora, CEO of Gionee India, the Indian subsidiary of the Chinese mobile company, the Indian mobile-manufacturing market is set to expand by leaps and bounds in the next five years. Handsets worth ₹1.47 lakh crore are expected to be produced by next year, out of which ₹1.27 lakh worth would be smartphones. In the next five years, this is expected to grow by ten times to over ₹14 lakh crore worth. Such massive expansion will simultaneously play a big role in the missions of Digital India, Make in India and Skill India. On the other hand, he says, this will bring the supply chain to India, which is significant because at present only a few of the 700 spare parts of a smartphone are made in India, like the battery charger. Says Vora, a founder member of the Indian Cellular Association: 'Modi's vision is commendable. It has made all the difference to my industry.' Under Make in India the Modi government waived the 12 per cent duty on mobile manufacturing if the manufacturers made the phone by importing spare parts and assembling them here to make the phone instead of fully importing the manufacturing plant. In digital infrastructure too, the government has made great strides although issues like call drops and non-availability of broadband facilities in key areas persist. The previous UPA government had laid lines of a meagre 358 km of optical fibre in the last three years of its rule. In contrast, the Modi government has already laid 1.77 lakh km of optical fibre line in the country in less than three years.

The number of village panchayats connected by the optical fibre network has jumped from around 4000 in 2014 to 78,000 at the beginning of 2017—a near twentyfold rise. The number of village panchayats in the country is around 2.50 lakh—this means that almost 27 per cent of the panchayats already stand covered.

A few of the connections, however, are not operational, because they are yet to be linked to the service providers. The revenue generation from the IT sector also gives an idea of the growth. Against $43 billion or ₹9.02 lakh crore in 2015–16, the highest ever, the revenue increased to $163 billion in 2016–17. The IT exports also increased from the highest-ever $108 billion in 2015–16 to $112 billion in 2016–17. Intel, the American MNC and technology giant which is partnering with the government in implementing the Digital India vision, is confident that 60 per cent of rural India would be broadband-connected by the time the present term of the Modi government ends in 2019. Internet subscribers in India have more than doubled since 2014, from 20 crore to 50 crore. Partnering with Intel in spreading digital literacy, the IT ministry has trained nearly one crore people, mostly youths, a substantial part of them from rural areas, in digital skills. Intel is also running a programme with the government for coming up with technological solutions to people's problems, with a focus on rural areas. Says Saurabh Kumar, an Indian Revenue Service officer in the office of Ravi Shankar Prasad, the minister for information technology: 'The ministry's digital push is all-encompassing as India marches on the path of digital growth. Things are changing very fast.'[1]

Intel is developing digital hubs in community service centres in 100 villages to gauge the impact. It then plans to replicate the model across India with necessary changes. The name of the project is Ek Kadam Unnati Ki Aur (One Step towards Progress). If the government's grand digital plan is not implemented in the right manner, all the money and hard work is bound to go down the drain. Intel's managing director in South Asia, Debjani Ghosh, says: 'We have to ensure that the access of this technology in rural areas is used for productive purposes. So, we have to see that the focus shifts from entertainment to productivity.'[2] Adds Sandeep Aurora, the Indian marketing head of Intel: 'We need a 360-degree approach on this. Therefore, we are pushing this technological change in an imaginative manner. In this, we are involving women in a significant way as in many cases they are found to be more mature in productive use of technology once taught about its core importance. They can become trendsetters.'[3]

As this digital revolution spreads, there are areas of concern as well. The biggest is about the coordination between the various departments. The government's departments seem to work in silos and not in harmony. The upshot is that the speed of execution slows down, although it is much faster than before. Ghosh admits: 'Clearly, the gaps between various departments will have to be closed with greater coordination. The enthusiasm is there in most departments but a coordinator is needed. Today when a broadband line is to be laid, different departments have to be reached out to for things like electricity and water. Maybe we need a one-window clearance system where all departments fall in line once a decision is taken.' She hastens to add in the same breath: 'The Modi government plans are very well laid out with all the details in place. And there is sincerity and enthusiasm when it comes to approach. The future is very bright on the whole.'

In keeping with his phased approach in reaching a goal, Modi is driving this digital-techno revolution step by step. The first step of the Union minister for IT, Ravi Shankar Prasad, was to strengthen the digital infrastructure. Next, he sensitized all the departments regarding the ways to share information— apps, websites, phones—thus preparing the bureaucracy to interface with the people when information would be shared in respective domains. Modi's OSD for IT, Hiren Joshi, has also played a significant role in preparing the ground on the basis of Modi's digital vision.

Modi began by first floating MyGov and then setting up his own Narendra Modi app in 2015. Simultaneously, he popularized the existing apps and the interactive government websites by improving connectivity and delivery of services.

One of his government's biggest successes is bringing on track the website of the Indian Railway Catering and Tourism Corporation (IRCTC) that issues online railway tickets. The IRCTC website had often been a nightmare for ticket buyers because of connectivity problems, which stand resolved now, thanks to a technical solution.

The App Revolution

Modi has launched an app revolution. When he took over as the prime minister, there were less than four dozen apps of the Central government. That figure had crossed 200 in 2016–17. The app revolution started with Modi's own app, which is a storehouse of the latest information about the schemes, policies and progress not just of the PMO but also of the government. The prime minister's app was developed by a set of six youngsters drawn from different engineering colleges. On the one hand, the work infused a sense of pride among the participating youngsters because they had designed the app for a person no less important than the prime minister of India. On the other hand, it cost the PMO nothing in terms of money. It would have cost a whopping ₹30–40 lakh had Modi hired a professional company to do it. The experiment also confirmed Modi's faith in the youth of the country.

Along with Modi's own app, it was the Garv mobile app of the Ministry of Power, launched in 2015 and meant for tracking in real time the electrification of 18,000 villages, which played a major role in encouraging other ministries to join the app-creation drive. The app experiment not only helped achieve good governance but also had a positive side effect. It put the bureaucracy on its toes.

The Garv app also helps track down officials who are handling the job of electrifying each village with their phone numbers. Because of its unique features, the Garv app became

an instant hit not just with the common people and digital
experts but also with analysts and media commentators. The
prime minister popularized it in his speeches in India and abroad
and also on his social media network.

This had a ripple effect. A number of ministries came up
with their own apps with interesting features, and the power
ministry took the experiment further in December 2016 by
launching the Garv-II app to provide to the common man real-
time data of electrification for all the villages in the country. The
normally reticent Union agriculture ministry, which was under
attack from critics in the first phase of the Modi government for
what many saw as its slow pace, launched as many as four apps
after the launch of the Garv app. The Kisan Suvidha app enables
farmers to get the latest information about weather, temperature,
humidity and rainfall. The Pusa Krishi app gives information
about seeds, new methods of agriculture and varieties of crops
developed by the Indian Council of Agricultural Research.
It also suggests methods to tackle pests and adopt conserving
cultivation practices and the latest farm machinery. It connects
farmers with the existing scientific knowledge so that they find
solutions to their particular problems. A call centre caters to the
app, thus facilitating the flow of information.

The third app in this category is the AgriMarket app developed
by the in-house IT division of the Union agriculture ministry
that gives the farmer the best prices for his products within a
radius of 50 km from his location and protects him from distress
sell. The Crop Insurance app is part of Modi's dream project
for farmers. It is for farmers suffering damages on account of
unexpected weather conditions and other factors. It links farmers
to the crop insurance system to enable them to understand and
get the benefits in the event of crop damage. Equipped with the
facility of geotagging an image, a farmer can upload a picture of
the damaged crop and send it to the crop insurance bureau, so as
not to leave any doubt about his claim.

The app also gives complete information about crop insurance, including the premium for notified crops, based on the area, the coverage amount and the loan amount. Radha Mohan Singh, the Union agriculture minister, says: 'These moves are part of our efforts to meet our target of doubling the farmers' income by 2022. We believe that dissemination of precise information, particularly scientific information, is key to solving many of the problems of the agriculture sector. The earlier we succeed in covering the last-mile farmer under this vision, the greater will be the growth of the agriculture sector.'

The impact on the ground of the agro apps has been remarkable. The apps are easy to operate and provide valuable information to the farmers. A farmer like Ashok Sahu, from Gotada near Bundi in Rajasthan, would vouch for the effectiveness of the apps. Educated up to the tenth standard, Sahu grows mustard, maize and wheat on his 12 acre farm. Sahu uses an Android-based Lava mobile phone. In mid-2016, he learnt from a friend about the usefulness of the Kisan Suvidha app in getting the best rates for his produce as well as weather predictions. He installed the app on his mobile phone. A month later, he was quite impressed with the app, which he found handy and informative. 'I have found it very useful for anticipating weather conditions. I have also been observing the best *mandi* rates on it keenly and I think it is helping me in that too,' Sahu says.

Dipak Kumar Dev, an engineer from a farming family, now working in an Indore-based IT company which makes apps for private companies, says: 'We are developing a special agro app on order from a big farmer in Punjab. But in our exercise we are relying heavily on the Kisan Suvidha app because it is aptly designed for the average farmer. Its categorization is superb and the content in Hindi is easy to understand. It spearheads the Modi government's app drive in the agro sector.'[4]

The agro apps clearly demonstrate Modi's vision for the farm sector based on the dissemination of scientific knowledge and precise information. He had tried this experiment successfully in Gujarat too by launching a series of innovative knowledge-sharing programmes using the latest communication technology to ensure that scientific and precise knowledge relating to agriculture reached every farmer. The government's country-wide soil health card scheme for farmers, which enables them to assess the quality and nature of farm soil, use fertilizers accordingly and also change the crop pattern, if needed, for getting better returns, has its genesis in the test run of the soil health card scheme in Gujarat under Modi.

Modi's agricultural plans based on science and technology were one of the key factors behind Gujarat's average of 9 per cent growth during his thirteen-year rule in the state, although the rain gods too had been favourable towards him. Modi's Krishi Mahotsav in Gujarat saw a *krishi rath* (a mobile exhibition—literally, chariot of agriculture) accompanied by an agricultural scientist and a senior agricultural official going to each tehsil of the state every year in the summers. The experts interacted with the farmers and helped them with scientific information to solve their problems.

After the agriculture ministry, the Union health ministry joined the app drive. First came the Anmol app that gives details of the health ministry's various schemes according to one's eligibility. This was followed by the e-Rakt Kosh app, a reservoir of information for those looking for blood donors in ordinary as well as emergency situations. It connects the user to all the blood banks of India and also to banks in the respective states and gives the benefit of donor identification to organizers of blood donation camps. It's a geotagged app and is useful to find donors and banks around one's location in emergency situations.

Then came the sensationally labelled India Fights Dengue app. It creates instant alerts regarding the spread of the dengue-causing mosquito, which breeds at a high rate during the monsoon. The app lists the preventive and curative measures for dengue.

One of the most imaginative apps has been the Swachh Bharat Clean India app of the urban development ministry that is playing a key, but a less-known, role when it comes to involving the people in the Swachh Bharat drive. The app has two sections. The first section aims at building up a movement for ensuring cleanliness by celebrating public participation in a spirit of patriotism. The app calls upon people to post their work in the form of pictures, specifying the time frame within which they had to complete the task.

People register their support for the Swachh Bharat drive by posting the pictures of their programmes in colleges, schools, corporate and media houses, housing societies and public places. In many cases, the pictures posted are of two states—before and after—which gives us an idea of the amount of cleaning done. As per government records, thanks to the app, people have given over 1.25 crore hours to Swachh Bharat so far. The voluntary participants in this drive belong to diverse groups— from school and college students to housing society members to corporate employees and even the Chhatrapati Shivaji lovers in Maharashtra who have been on a spree to clean Shivaji's medieval forts under the Swachh Bharat banner. The other section of the app deals with the government efforts towards a clean India.

The Ministry of Road Transport and Highways under Nitin Gadkari isn't lagging behind. It has done a yeoman service by using technology to bring transparency and efficiency, in the true spirit of good governance. Most important, it has broken into the cartels of raw-material providers. Two of its experiments are noteworthy—the INAM-Pro portal (which will soon be available in app form) and the e-PACE app. The INAM-Pro brings on one platform raw-material providers and users, who here would mean the government which might be implementing road projects directly or through a Public Private Partnership model. Its biggest benefit is that it has stopped the cartelization of cement producers and distributors and the resultant artificial increase in cement prices. INAM-Pro has broken the monopoly of a few in the cement industry and made cartelization difficult by bringing together all the 4000 cement suppliers across India in one portal. Now there is competition among the cement dealers and, therefore, no cartelization.

The e-PACE app is about transparency in road-building and ensuring a high standard of construction by giving people the chance to monitor the quality and post their views. It enables real-time tracking of road projects wherein one can know how far a given construction project on a highway has progressed and whether the reality on the ground and the claim of the quality of work on paper tally. If one finds a mismatch between the claims of the agencies which have built a certain road and the actual condition, one can post the relevant data on the app.

Gadkari says: 'We are committed to effecting grass-root changes in the road-building sector by using technology with the aim of bringing transparency and competition.' The other is a portal of his ministry, the Infracon, which brings infrastructure consultancy firms and key personnel in the road engineering and construction sector on one platform. It has the credentials of the chief personnel in the field and has links to the Aadhaar card and the DigiLocker (another imaginatively designed Modi-government app that enables you to digitally store your eligibility certificates and documents so that you don't have to carry them physically with you for submission or verification) for validation. Nearly 40,000 consultancy firms and 2400 key personnel are registered on the app. Agencies under the ministry can receive technical proposals through Infracon. This greatly reduces the paperwork and brings transparency while speeding up the process of evaluation of technical bids—all at the click of a button.

The Union power ministry is not far behind either. It has brought about significant changes by developing an app that has put an end to the politics of electric power in the country. Till recently, it was common for a ruling party in a state to blame the government of another party at the Centre for a short supply of power. The former would usually insinuate that the Centre was deliberately refusing to sell power to the state to defame the state government in the public eye and derive political mileage. The Modi government too has faced such allegations after coming to power. Modi's own Gujarat government had made such allegations against the UPA government in the past.

The power ministry's Vidyut Pravah (electricity flow) app enables one to know on his or her mobile phone the availability of power in the nation's power exchange system and also the rate at which it is available at various corners of the country. Using the app, farmers, domestic users or factory owners can track the availability and unit price of power in their region. They can question the state government on why it is not providing power and ask it to buy from the Centre's exchange system. Pratyush Singh, a tech-savvy professional in the power sector, says: 'It is a good example of how a blame game has ended with the imaginative use of technology.'

The National Scholarship portal (which will be converted into an app later) of the Modi government makes all the central government scholarships available at one place. Thanks to the app, a student has all the scholarship options—whether of the Ministry of Human Resource Development, the Ministry of Social Justice and Empowerment or the prime minister's fellowship programme—available on his or her palm. It is a one-stop solution to the problems of identifying and completing the scholarship process, starting from submission to verification and sanctioning. The public rating option in the app shows that 75 per cent of the people who have used it found it excellent, very useful or useful. Currently, the app covers eighteen central scholarships and seventy-six scholarships from the states. As many as 1 crore students across India have used the app. Tasnima Fatima, a fourth-year student of pharmacy from Hyderabad and the daughter of a government employee, says: 'Thanks to the National Scholarship portal, applying for scholarships has become much easier. Every uploaded document is e-verified. No need to physically go and apply with loads and loads of papers.'

But one of the best examples of how an app can ease problems of services and delivery from the top to the grass-roots level is the revolutionary Umang (Unified Mobile App for New-Age Governance) app launched by the prime minister in 2016 to solve all problems of delivery of government services across diverse areas. The all-purpose app has details of 200 government services, from passport, land records and income tax to DigiLocker, health services, etc. Sandeep Shah, a sharemarket dealer of Gujarat, says: 'It is a revolutionary kind of digital inclusion. It enables you to access anything that is being offered in the name of government services including school board results, train tickets and even registration in the public distribution system (PDS). It aptly symbolizes the Modi government's deep digital vision.'

Then there is the Himmat app of the Union home ministry that enables distressed women to reach out to the police when faced with danger. If a woman is being attacked, she can alert the police by pressing a button on her mobile phone after installing the app. The government has gone a step further and amended laws to ensure that every phone manufactured in the country has a geotagged panic button.

The Idea of Digital India and the Aadhaar Card Pathway

Modi's ideas behind his Digital India mission are simple. The plan aims at connecting every person in the country with his respective area of interest. If you are a manufacturer, you get information about the market; if you are a farmer wanting to sell your produce, you get the opportunity to do so at the best possible price in the country via the digital path. Any person can use the service provided by the app—you can be a carpenter, a jeweller, a furniture-maker or even a teacher wanting to serve society in your free time. The Vidyanjali app of the HRD ministry offers options to teachers who want to teach children in their free time as a social service.

What is unique about the Modi government's multidimensional digital-techno vision is the way in which it is linking the Aadhaar card (under the Unique Identification Authority of India) to the delivery of government services. The idea had been mooted and implemented by the previous UPA government led by Manmohan Singh, with Nandan Nilekani of Infosys fame playing a spectacular role. The system of DBT of subsidies to the beneficiaries in certain schemes had also begun in the last stages of the UPA rule. But it is the Modi government that has converted something that began as an organ to weed out illegal Bangladeshi immigrants into a multifarious tool by making it the core of transparency, efficiency and activities connected with the government.

The Aadhaar card has already been used by the Modi government as a DBT tool to remove ghost-account holders of subsidized LPG, to bring transparency in many other schemes like the MGNREGA, to award scholarships to meritorious students. According to an estimate of the Union finance ministry, the DBT as a delivery tool of subsidy schemes is saving around ₹60,000 crore every year for the exchequer. Now the plan is to use it for faster delivery of passports and link it to land-record holders to give them crop insurance after accurately evaluating the damage done to crops. Plans are also afoot to connect it to the voting system to bring about an error-free voter identification process that removes duplication. The ultimate aim is to make it a platform for realizing the government's dream of delivering its services to the people digitally and without pilferage. Ravi Shankar Prasad, the minister for information technology, says:

'The Aadhaar card is being converted into the most powerful tool of good governance.'

The long-term vision is to make government entitlement of all kinds available to the people on the basis of what, in administrative parlance, is being called the JAM trinity—Jan-Dhan (bank accounts), Aadhaar card and mobile phones. This will make governance easy and less time-consuming. The progress has been phenomenal. Around 113 crore Aadhaar cards issued in the country have been linked to over 43 crore bank accounts in less than three years. The number of Aadhaar cards registered in 2014 when the NDA took over was just 63 crores.

Digital India isn't about government workings only. It is also about the government playing the role of a facilitator in encouraging private players to reach their targets. A fine example of the government's role as facilitator can be found in the Startup India scheme, which enables one to start a new company in a day with active digital help from the government. If one is eligible and ready with the required certificates, one's company gets registered online in a matter of hours.

Amit Paranjape, an IT innovator based in Pune who runs a company called ReliScore, says: 'All governments these days talk about digital vision, which is easy to talk about but difficult to implement. But with almost half of its term left to go, the Modi government has a lot to show; there is no dearth of sincerity on its part though, which augurs well for the future.'[5] Many moves of the government have impressed Paranjape. One of them is the initial plan of the government to improve cities by using technology in the Smart City plan. The progress that the government has made on the UPI, which is part of the plans of the Reserve Bank of India to ensure secure online payment for e-commerce and other activities, is another.

Paranjape is also appreciative of the technology drive of the minister for road transport and highways, particularly Gadkari's plan for e-tolls on highways that would reduce traffic congestions at toll-collection plazas. One of Modi's grand successes involves the use of the digital platform to interact with ordinary people through experiments like MyGov and the sensitization of ministers to the use of technology.

Towards Paperless Governance

There has been a lot of noise about paperless governance. But that had remained mostly in the realm of empty talk. The DigiLocker is an initiative to fill up those meaningless words with some substance. It is another experiment carried out by the IT ministry to save people the hassle of carrying documents and spurs the administration in the direction of paperless governance. The stakeholders in this experiment are three—citizens, issuers and requesters. Citizens could be students or working in the public or the private sector. Issuers could be government agents like the registrar, income tax authorities, educational institutions, RTOs or private entities. And requesters could be passport offices, employers, universities—entities requesting secure access to e-documents stored in the repository.

Once you register yourself on DigiLocker, there is no need for you to present your official documents, whether you are appearing for an interview, sitting for an examination or standing in a queue to avail yourself of a government scheme. You just have to feed all your original documents digitally in the locker and give a one-time password (OTP) for your locker to the authorities, who then check all the documents by entering your locker. The facility can be used to store URLs of the e-documents issued by government departments and personal documents like university certificates. It also reduces the administrative expenses of the government.

The locker registration is linked to one's Aadhaar card. Having a mobile phone number is also necessary to register with DigiLocker. The DigiLocker has been designed to provide security to physical documents and access to government-issued documents. Divided into various sections, DigiLocker is easy to operate. Launched in July 2015, the DigiLocker experiment is gradually becoming popular. Over 43 lakh people have registered on DigiLocker in less than three years, and over 63 lakh documents have been uploaded so far.

The government can also issue documents to the applicants through DigiLocker. Government agencies have issued over 165 crore documents to 43 lakh people through DigiLocker. Currently, the facility is accessible through a portal but soon it will also be accessible on mobile phones through an app. Bhuvanesh Jha, a Delhi-based psychologist working with IBM, says: 'My academic certificates as well as my work experience certificates are all stored in DigiLocker. I have been encouraging my friends to learn to use it given of the fact that India is currently facing an identity crisis.'[6]

Technology to Solve the Problems of the Farming Sector

For years, Indian farmers have faced the problem of scarcity of urea and fertilizers during peak periods, leading to a lot of rancour in the farm sector. But much of this scarcity has been artificially created since the quota of urea usually gets diverted surreptitiously to the industrial sector, where it is useful for certain purposes. The UPA government had found a novel way to tackle this 'smuggling' of urea. The solution it found served a dual purpose—coating the urea with neem oil made it unfit for use by factories and also added value to the urea as fertilizer for use in agriculture. However, the implementation of this scheme was tardy during the UPA regime.

Modi took up the implementation of this scheme in March 2015. It was completed in November 2015 in all urea-manufacturing plants across India. The eight months were used to make technical changes in the plants for getting the neem-oil coating on urea.

The move is saving, according to a rough estimate, ₹11,000 crore annually for the nation, as pilferage has been controlled.

In many ways, Modi's technological plans are an extension of his activities in Gujarat during his thirteen years there as the chief minister. For example, he introduced a biometric system for withdrawal of subsidized ration from the PDS and used voting cards to remove 16 lakh bogus-ration-card holders from the list, thus bringing down the number of ration-card holders in Gujarat from 1.25 crore to 1.09 crore and saving a huge amount of money for the state. It was a step that needed courage because it had strong political repercussions for the BJP at the ground level, for most of the beneficiaries of the bogus-ration-card racket are political entities of all parties and the so-called small-time social workers.

The Grey Area

The problem of call drops stood corrected to an extent by the end of 2016, after becoming a menace for mobile-phone users. But that seemed only like a temporary relief as the problem has surfaced at regular intervals, to the great discomfort of the phone users, due to the reluctance of telecom companies to spend on infrastructure to support their networks. In fact, the call drops problem has been like a broken spoke in the wheel of the Modi government's Digital India initiative. In the first year, the government struggled to get telecom companies to invest in infrastructure commensurate with the connections they had issued. The government hoped that strengthening the infrastructure would help tackle the problem. Though the government succeeded in forcing the service providers to erect as many as 80,000 towers across India, that wasn't enough.

Then the Telecom Regulatory Authority of India (TRAI) came up with a radical solution of imposing fines on every call drop, a step that the government thought would force the companies to invest in infrastructure. But the companies challenged the move in court and won the case. Following the court order, the government redoubled its pressure on the service providers since the call drop issue had begun to make people question why, with its vast resources and writ, the government was not being able to get over a problem affecting the entire nation. Sunil Parekh, an Ahmedabad-based expert on Indian industry, says: 'After the court judgement, one felt the customers were in for a dark period. But the government has retrieved the situation substantially using its strong hand with the companies. The call-drop problem stands partially curbed. But there has to be a permanent solution to the issue.'[7]

The companies wanted the per-unit rate to be increased so that they could have larger margins and invest in infrastructure. But TRAI doesn't allow them the hike because it believes that the profits accruing to the companies at the present rates are good enough, as indicated by their balance sheets. Some of the operators started value-added services to raise revenue but the experiment didn't succeed against Google, Amazon and Flipkart in the online market.

Clearly, call dropping is one area where the nation's phone users, in spite of the government's restricted role here in the presence of TRAI, are desperately seeking a permanent solution from the Modi administration. However, the grey areas in the government's digital march are few. Its successes are far greater. The government seems to be heading towards a digital-techno revolution that the country couldn't have hoped for till a few years ago. Modi's digital vision is firmly in place.

3

Transforming India

Governance as an Agent of Change

In 2010, Nitin Gadkari, the then BJP president, requested Rajeev Chandrasekhar, a member of the Rajya Sabha, leading entrepreneur and founder of Loop mobile (formerly BPL mobile), to prepare a vision document for the BJP till 2025. The Illinois Institute of Technology–educated son of a former air force officer was given the task because of his brilliance—his ability to think out of the box and his capacity to see things in the Indian context. The thirty-three-page document was, according to many partymen at that stage, a masterpiece when it came to envisioning India in 2025, provided that the nation was put on the path of good governance. The document pointed out a list of goals to be achieved by 2025. It included accountable, transparent governance, removal of poverty through job creation, and an empowering model, instead of a dole-based one, that would sustain high economic growth surpassing China's, a fivefold increase in per capita income, 24/7 power supply and a development structure centred on people's participation in policymaking.

As Gadkari made way for Rajnath Singh as party president in 2013, the document perhaps got lost somewhere among

the official files at 11, Ashoka Road, New Delhi. Much later,
almost three years after the BJP-led government came to power,
it would seem as if a blueprint has been made to achieve the
vision expressed in that document. Prime Minister Narendra
Modi, then Gujarat chief minister, had perhaps never read
this document—even if he had seen it, he probably just had a
cursory look. But the steps he is taking are very precisely the
ones mentioned in that document titled 'BJP Vision 2015:
Transforming India: Empowering Indians for an Assertive
India'. Today Modi calls it the march towards a New India by
2022, the seventy-fifth year of India's independence.

Whether it is reforming the bureaucracy or breaking the
stranglehold of middlemen in the system in the case of government
contracts and postings; whether it is turning around the infrastructure
sector or opening up the attractive self-employment sector to tackle
joblessness; whether it is people's participation in governance or
taking the benefits of development to the last beneficiary; whether
it is ending the decades-old domination of corporate houses
over policymaking or innovation in governance, Modi is clearly
rebuilding the core ethos of administration after several years marked
either by misrule or ineffective rule. An unstinted commitment to
public service marks this new ethos.

The barometer of good governance is not the stock markets
any more. The markets don't go up and down when an honest
bureaucrat is placed in a high position. In the Modi era, things
are no longer about short-term gratification. Stock markets
might take a longer time to go up but the people's index must
rise swiftly in this new era. There is a marked shift from business-
driven governance to citizen-driven policies. Even reforms in
the 'flying' aviation sector are consumer-driven.

Modi is slowly changing the narrative that Delhi has
followed all these years under different governments. Delhi was
a place where anyone with big money could gain entry into the
musty corridors of power. Today even the richest person can't

buy that kind of connection with his money. With the right connections he can certainly reach the top echelons but only through a system based on transparency, or, to go a step further, on principles. More than that, leading by his own example, the prime minister is changing the story of a typical Indian leader. He is not easily accessible, no matter how powerful the person seeking to get to him is, and simply not amenable to influence. It is next to impossible to get him to change his views on core issues once he has taken what he believes to be the correct stand.

In one sense, Modi is a believer in absolutism. But it is the absolutism of a benevolent leader wanting to be unbending in his approach for public good. There is no grey area here. Neither is there any chance of a policy paralysis in his case. He has zero tolerance for corruption. He seems to be virtually saying: 'I won't dilute myself by playing the politics of pragmatism.' That appears to be in his political DNA. Perhaps he knows that in the politics of pragmatism lies the seeds of compromise on good governance. One can't make him change his mind once he has taken a decision he thinks is perfect, whether that 'one' is a media baron, a top-ranking intellectual or a top politician of his own party. In the process, the capital of 'settings and adjustments', as Delhi is known in local parlance, where people with money could get anything done till a couple of years ago, is still reeling under the shock it got when Modi took over. Suddenly, all the channels of reaching the top by practising the art of palm-greasing have disappeared.

The transformation that is taking place in core governance at the ground level is fast in many areas and relatively slow in some, but it is something that can't be denied. Progress might be tardy in areas like education and health, and not as fast as many expected at NITI Aayog, which has replaced the Planning Commission and is writing a new chapter in cooperative federalism, but there is none of the policy paralysis that afflicted many previous governments. Rather, new and bold ideas are being planted. They are having a noticeable impact on the nature of governance in a country where things move slowly and bold ideas take time to take root. Chandrasekhar says: 'The sheer number of innovative ideas that are being successfully tried and the high level of commitment to principles of good governance indicate that a new era has begun. If at all there is a flaw, it is in the presentation of the achievements before the people. It could have been better.'[1]

Modi's great vision and its fulfilment are well demonstrated in the area of science and technology. In 2004, while inaugurating the LNG terminal at Dahej port in south Gujarat as the chief minister, Modi told an audience of professionals, industrialists and bureaucrats: 'Like handsome road highways, I dream of highways of optical fibre lines. If there could be optical fibre lines along the railway lines why can't we have them on the sidelines of the highways?' His government in Delhi, at a halfway point now, has implemented what he had envisioned as the chief minister more than a decade ago. Against just 358 km of optical fibre line laid in the last three years of the UPA government's rule, the Modi government laid a mindboggling 1.77 lakh km of optical fibre lines in the country in a little over two and a half years. When Modi took oath, only 4000 village panchayats in India were broadband-connected. The figure stood at 76,000 in February 2017—a stupendous performance by any yardstick.

On the social platform, Modi's arrival signals the recognition of the ones who didn't breed in the 'English' atmosphere and so were considered lower down despite talent and ability. This is also a big development for a nation where a minuscule minority taking pride in speaking good English has held sway. A good example of this is Manish Baradia, a small documentary film-maker who studied in a Hindi medium school in an obscure Rajasthan town, on whom Modi relies significantly when it comes to projecting his governance through films. Baradia is still not very comfortable with English but has an eye for perfection and the quality to match Modi's sharp vision. Some of the best high-profile ads that the government unleashed following demonetization, telling people to go for digital transactions, were made by Baradia's company, Moving Pixel.

Baradia's talent was identified in 2001 by Modi back in Gujarat. And he continues to deliver for Modi professionally even now—a big deal considering the impression that it is difficult to work with Modi for a long time because of his high expectations on quality as he continues to raise the bar. Says Baradia: 'Modiji gives inspiration to all those who felt neglected because they were not bred in a particular atmosphere. After having interacted with him for over sixteen years now, I call him a Living University given his knowledge on diverse subjects from photography, yoga, literature to household things and agriculture and his eye for perfection.'[2]

Five transforming initiatives successfully implemented by the Narendra Modi government that are listed below show how the narrative of governance is changing after several decades.

1. A Silent Revolution

MyGov is ushering in a new era of participatory governance that could change the way people look at development

Rajendra Surendran, a worker in a private company in Coimbatore, always had ideas for improving the services provided by the Indian Railways (IR). One of his favourite ideas, which had been playing on his mind for quite some time, was of clean, reservation-less, superfast trains that anyone could hop on to without having to book a ticket in advance. He got the opportunity to offer the suggestion early 2016 on the Modi government's digital platform, MyGov, where ministries invite suggestions from common people by engaging them in debates and then implement the doable and innovative ones. He gave his inputs in response to the invitation made on MyGov by the Union Ministry of Railways to propose new ideas. To his utter surprise, it was accepted. Railway Minister Suresh Prabhu unveiled India's first reservation-free Antyodaya Express in February 2016.

Fifty-seven-year-old M. Krishnamurthy, an accounts manager in a private company in Hyderabad, is close to retirement. He has never been as happy as he is now. A suggestion made by him is set to revolutionize the banking system for rural people, particularly for the poor in those areas. In the MyGov debate on the 2015 budget, he had suggested that since most villages across India don't have a bank but have access to post office branches, the latter should be converted into loan-less, simple savings banks. The post office bank, he suggested, won't get involved in moneylending but will work as a simple payment bank and offer a usual rate of interest on the money kept in it. He gave the proposal because he had seen many villagers trusting slimy chit fund operators with their money in the absence of access to banks and then losing it.

The idea was considered by the finance ministry and by the Department of Posts (DoP). After a careful scrutiny, the government accepted the proposal and incorporated it in the 2015 budget. In spite of the gigantic scale of the task, action on it has been swift. By 2016, all the 25,000 post offices in India had opened banking sections, 1100 of them even ATMs. By the end of 2017, all the rural post offices in the country, numbering around 1.20 lakh, will have banking facility.

Take another example: A Bangalore-based professional, Mukesh Bhaiji, suggested in a 2016 budget debate that the idea of DBT of government subsidies to the bank accounts of beneficiaries—which had erased ghost accounts and middlemen from subsidy structures like those of the LPG—should also be applied to the fertilizer subsidy. His argument was that the volume of subsidy in fertilizers was much more than in other subsidy items. DBT, he said, would stop pilferage and save government money. Union Finance Minister Arun Jaitley accepted the suggestion. The government has already started a pilot project in many districts and is on its way to replicating it across India. Once rolled out, it could save big money for the government.

In yet another example, in 2015, the Union Ministry of Tribal Affairs decided to develop an authoritative syllabus on the medical knowledge of tribal communities. It was to be on the ways in which local herbal remedies could provide a cure for many ailments. The suggestion came from Richa Abhyankar, a twenty-seven-year-old girl from a simple Maharashtrian family who works as a subeditor in the English-to-Sanskrit and Sanskrit-to-English dictionary project of the Deccan College Post-Graduate and Research Institute in Pune. Abhyankar's proposal was inspired by her grandfather, who had managed to learn the herbal cures for crucial ailments from the tribal people of the north Konkan area in Maharashtra. This was her second suggestion which was accepted by the government through MyGov. Earlier, she had received an appreciation certificate from the government for suggesting the name Shram Suvidha for a portal of the labour ministry. Abhyankar's idea was accepted after an online competition organized by MyGov. Today she intensely feels that she is a part of the government. As Abhyankar puts it: 'MyGov has given me the feeling that I am part of a democratic government. It's a wonderful move which is making people a part of participatory governance.'[3]

The potent pathway of participatory governance

MyGov was Modi's first major announcement after he took over as prime minister. It came in July 2014. It was mooted much before his other known initiatives like Jan-Dhan, NITI Aayog and Swachh Bharat. In its ultimate aim of making development and good governance a mass movement, the idea has travelled far and wide since then and emerged as a massive platform for incorporating common people's ideas in the story of India's progress. Close to 300 ideas coming from ordinary people, some of them extremely important, have been implemented or are in various stages of implementation by a wide spectrum of Union ministries. In the process, MyGov has created over 40 lakh dedicated followers, who regularly suggest ideas on good governance.

The interest it has generated is marked by the fact that over 11 crore people have visited the MyGov site since it was floated in July 2014. And about 13 crore people, or more than one-tenth of India's population, saw the videos that the various ministries posted on the website to mark their achievements on the completion of the Modi government's two years in office. The figures show the reach and expanse of this experiment aimed at giving people a role in the government's policymaking. It also points to a positive change in governance.

Most important, the experiment is changing the way the government has been run since Independence. Krishnamurthy's suggestion of converting post offices into savings banks is path-breaking, to say the least, and has an impact on the whole of rural India. Abhyankar's proposal of making a syllabus on ancient tribal medicinal practices is no less significant, given the fact that researchers have found great healing qualities in the secret medical traditions of various forest-based tribal communities in many countries, from Malaysia, Indonesia and Australia to the US and nations of Latin America and Africa.

The new system of engaging people is not limited to just inviting ideas. The emerging platform is also being used extensively to help the government decide on important policy matters on the basis of the majority's opinion. Some of these decisions have had an impact not just on India but also on the entire world. The government's final stand to remain Net neutral is one example. This topic had invited intense debates. India emerged as a world leader on the subject by framing clear-cut guidelines on Net neutrality. The issue was being debated on the sidelines in 2014. The government took it up and encouraged a freewheeling discussion on the topic in MyGov, which was floated only two months later.

It turned out to be one of the biggest-ever debates on a digital platform regarding something to do with the government. It hit a level of frenzy on 14 August 2014 when as many as 3 lakh people either joined the debate or visited the website, bringing the firewall on the website almost to a breaking point. Among the participants in the debate were many celebrities, television figures, activists, members of Parliament and active netizens, including the parliamentarian and business tycoon Rajeev Chandrasekhar and the entrepreneur-journalist-publisher Nikhil Pahwa. Eventually a total of 72,000 people expressed their views on the subject. A vast majority was in favour of Net neutrality and this helped the government reach the final decision.

MyGov has an interesting history. It was born in Modi's mind at a function in Delhi in 2007, when he called for turning development into a mass movement with people's active participation. He compared it to the public awakening brought about by Mahatma Gandhi, who had suggested making khadi on the spinning wheel. This simple idea had made lakhs of people join the freedom struggle. While explaining the objective behind MyGov, the prime minister said: 'What was a movement of mainly lawyers became a mass movement in no time with the introduction of spinning wheel. Similarly, people at the grass roots have had little say in the process of development all these years. MyGov is making development a mass movement.'

Some of the most interesting suggestions influencing governance have come from the MyGov platform. Once ideas are put forward in MyGov on discussions generated by various ministries, they are analysed, pruned, collated and then sent to the ministries along with the summary and complete data for perusal and implementation. For example, in a discussion started on the website by NITI Aayog on bridging the gap in the health sector,

Suchitra Raghavachari, an avid contributor on MyGov and a medical imaging expert from Chennai, suggested that the Aadhaar card be tagged with the digital health smartcard. She said that this will reduce paperwork for professionals on the move and help the poor who don't have the space to keep medical files safely at home. Besides, she said, this would make the task of claiming medical insurance a one-stroke job minus suspicion of an individual. The power of the suggestion was proved during the 2015 Chennai floods in which lakhs of people lost their documents. Those having Aadhaar cards found that their crucial data was safe.

NITI Aayog has accepted her idea and is now working on its implementation. Raghavachari, who had been mentioned by Modi in one of his monthly *Mann Ki Baat* radio talks, says: 'Till MyGov was launched, common people didn't have any direct role in public policymaking. What's more, MyGov has a brilliant team for collating incoming information and data. Plus, MyGov is not an urban phenomenon. With increased connectivity, rural people are participating with almost equal enthusiasm.'[4]

Sometimes suggestions are not accepted formally but they succeed in triggering a debate leading to important decisions. An instance of this is an idea given by one Neerav Sheth. He suggested that the government should come up with an animal insurance policy, which, he said, would earn an income for the government, provide employment to veterinary doctors and insurance staff, besides benefiting animal lovers. His suggestion was not accepted but it resulted in Arun Jaitley, the Union finance minister, announcing the animal wellness programme. This is a concept very dear to Modi. During his chief ministership of Gujarat, his government would regularly organize health camps for cattle, which were treated like human beings.

Under the scheme, an animal health card called Nakul Swasthya Patra will be given to the owner for each of his livestock (the focus is on cattle) and emergency animal helplines will be set up. The programme envisages a national animal database and a unique identification card for cattle. The card aims at helping dairy farmers keep a record of their livestock. It would keep them updated on the dates of vaccination and also on insemination exercises for cattle. It would help owners fight animal epidemics, which are known to wipe out cattle populations or to make them invalid in the absence of immediate solutions.

Good suggestions continue to pour in on MyGov, more than two and a half years after its inception. One Jan Basha Shaikh of Hyderabad came up with a very inclusive suggestion for the railways. He proposed designing a light kit for the gang men working on the sidelines of railway tracks who move about with heavy iron equipment on their bodies. The idea was aimed at reducing their burden. The railway ministry accepted the suggestion and a light kit is being designed for the men. It will benefit 1.75 lakh gang men of the IR. Some innovative ideas have also come for Modi's favourite concept, Ek Bharat Shreshtha Bharat (One India, Great India), under which he seeks to bind India through cultural exchanges among various states by creating sister states on a rotational basis.

A fifty-year-old professor from Mumbai, Aniruddha Pal, suggested that a joint assembly session of the partner states should be held, while one Sanjay Shridhar from Chennai pitched the idea of exchanging mobile state museums among partner states. The museums would contain one state's cultural and sovereign items of merchandise and move around selling them in the sister state. The discussion on Ek Bharat Shreshtha Bharat was organized in the form of a contest. Out of the 60,000 ideas that came up, thirty were selected and appreciated with a certificate by the prime minister.

A platform of creativity in the service of the nation

One of the most important aspects of MyGov is selecting logos for government schemes. It also invites ideas on specific subjects by organizing online competitions with prize money, as in the case of Ek Bharat, Shreshtha Bharat. The logos of Digital India, Swachh Bharat, the new national education policy and India Post Payments Bank were selected through competitions. The excitement of Rana Bhaumik, aged thirty-one, knows no limit. An assistant manager in the Delhi office of an IT company, Bhaumik won a prize of ₹1 lakh in 2015 when his logo design was selected, from among 826 submissions. Apart from the prize money, he got a certificate of appreciation from the prime minister.

Bhaumik had voted for the Communist Party of India (Marxist) in the last Lok Sabha polls. He has become a Modi supporter almost overnight. He says that MyGov has opened an entirely new window for many talented people like him at the micro level whose creativity had no meaning for the government till now. As he puts it: 'The story of this country is that the voice of the common man has never reached the government in these seven decades. MyGov has changed that. Modi is known for innovation and this is his government's greatest innovation. For me Achhe Din have come.'[5]

Nawaz Shaikh, the son of a daily-wage earner who is now doing his PhD in science at a Pune institute, is yet another example of an individual empowered by participatory democracy. The logo he designed was selected for the new education policy, which has been formulated after three decades. Even the PMO's mobile app, which has directly connected citizens with the office, was developed through a competition on MyGov. 'By taking the competition route for selecting PMO's app, the government saved lakhs of rupees which would otherwise have gone to a private firm for developing the app,' says the director of MyGov, Akhilesh Mishra.[6]

Gaurav Dwivedi, IAS, who is the CEO of MyGov, says: 'Governance comprises policies, programmes, feedback and implementation. MyGov is a unique platform that allows people to participate in all these four aspects of governance.'[7] Vidyut

Thakar, a veteran political analyst from Gujarat with a deep understanding of Modi's style of functioning, avers: 'Creating pride among the people and, as a result, a win–win situation for the ruled as well as for the rulers is Modi's underlying theme. It's an innovation in Indian politics.'[8]

Optimum use of technology for the common man through competition

MyGov started one of the biggest exercises in digital innovation on behalf of the Union Ministry of Science and Technology to create apps or hardware/software products that would reach each and every person. The competition was titled Intel Science Innovation Challenge, with the American MNC Intel as the government's partner. The ministry earmarked ₹1.50 crore for twenty teams to enable them to research and develop people-friendly applications. It also supported them with mentorship by expert bodies like the IIMs and Intel for business, technical, marketing and financial assistance. The twenty were selected by a reputed jury following presentations by fifty teams on their proposed projects.

Each of these twenty teams was given ₹2 lakh for developing prototypes of their proposed projects. These twenty presented their prototypes before a select jury. Out of them, ten were selected and given a further grant of ₹5 lakh each to develop their final models for the ten specific subjects they had proposed. For example, Team Digital-Education-in-a-Box of Budhhadev Burman and two colleagues, Rohini Gehlaut and Sachin Jain, is developing a portable, solar-powered learning ecosystem that can host a digital classroom in the middle of nowhere without the need for electricity or a building. This instrument is sure to revolutionize education in the backward areas.

Then Pune-based Sonali Tripathy, Pratit Jain and Prateek Jain of Team Embryo (3315) are developing a cerviscope to help hospitals tackle the lack of early screening methods for stage-0 and stage-1 cervical cancer. The device also addresses the lack of trained gynaecologists on the subject. It will be an affordable image-based screening device to detect cervical cancer. But more interesting is the app that Team Hardarshak, comprising Chennai-based Aniket Deogar and P.R. Ganapathy, is developing to enable interested people to know what government schemes they are eligible for. The app is also expected to create job opportunities for people who will help individuals identify schemes with this app and avail themselves of the benefits. Burman says: 'MyGov is writing a new chapter in this country when it comes tapping the potential of science and technology for the good of the common man. It is extracting the best from the society. This is possible because there is an element of patriotism in it due to a feeling among the participants that it is India's initiative.'

Suggestions, competitions and polls on MyGov are playing an impressive role in the formulation of major government schemes and policies. For the Smart City plan, the urban development ministry came up a with the unique idea of appealing to the municipal bodies of ninety-eight selected smart cities to ask their citizens to vote on topics related to the city concerned by organizing polls on the MyGov website. The result was overwhelming.

As many as seventy-six smart cities organized citizens' polls on specific aspects of the smart city project. Thanks to these polls, the decision-makers will be able to choose features of the proposed smart cities on the basis of majority opinion. The participation of common people in the polls showed the level of involvement. In Agra, as many as 1.32 lakh people voted. In the small town of Satna, just one poll attracted 14,000 votes. Polls were organized by throwing simple questions like 'which area of the city should be developed first and why', with three or four options as the answer to each question.

Even the proposed new education policy was thrown open for public comments on MyGov, in keeping with the constitutional requirement of giving a role to the panchayats and municipal bodies in the management of education at the school level. In response to the HRD ministry's directive, 2.50 lakh local bodies have offered their views on the proposed policy, thus ensuring consultation at the grass-roots level in making a national policy.

How the data is collated

A significant part of the success of the MyGov experiment goes to its twenty-member team of young technocrats led by CEO Dwivedi and Director Mishra that collates and researches the data to cull the best out of it for the purpose of good governance. The team is helped in its task by 200 volunteers from across India. These are researchers who do the job of analysing the data as a service to the nation. No wonder then that regular contributors to MyGov have a very high regard for the team. Prerita Chothaiwale, one of the team members, says: 'Optimum use of technology is made by our team to analyse the trends and get the best results.'[9]

According to Mishra, the first step towards analysing the inputs is to use Word Cloud to get the first impressions about the major phrases and words around which the ideas are built. Next, the volunteer teams create Idea Buckets around which ideas are suggested. Then, from every bucket, representative examples are selected. Finally, a summary of Word Cloud is made along with representative comments for each bucket and an analytical report. Reveals Mishra: 'Both the analytical report and the full data are sent to the ministry concerned for action. It's an elaborate process. In the end, when the ministry selects an idea for implementation, MyGov is told to inform the contributor.'

The full potential of MyGov is yet to be tapped. As many as half a dozen of all ministries are yet to use MyGov for ensuring participatory governance, although some of them are doing well in terms of actual performance. The ministries of health; water resources, river development and Ganga rejuvenation; tourism; and sports have used MyGov but are not so active on it. An insider says: 'Perhaps some of them feel uncomfortable in the atmosphere of public scrutiny that the prime minister is trying to create or haven't understood its real importance.' To the credit of some of the ministers, they may not have gone to the MyGov pathway but have developed their own means to incorporate public suggestions.

However, ministries like finance, HRD, science and technology, urban development and skill development and entrepreneurship have used MyGov to the optimum level for participatory governance. The registered users of MyGov are just over 40 lakh. The number should have been much more after more two and a half years. Still, the final report card of the digital platform seems to point to a golden phase in good governance.

It is significant that more than 300 ideas of the common people that have come to the website's 'Discuss' section have been implemented or are in various stages of implementation. These are apart from the competitions for logos and ideas organized in the 'Do' section. The poll section too has seen frenetic activity. Now MyGov plans to enhance the number of its registered users from 40 lakh to around 5 crore in the next three years, a difficult target but not impossible if one considers the concrete strategy it has drawn up to engage people in multiple ways in the days to come. Hiren Joshi, OSD at the PMO who supervises MyGov on the prime minister's behalf, says: 'Even world-renowned social media tools like Facebook and Twitter took time to get popular. We are confident of succeeding in our mission.' The son of an RSS pracharak from Rajasthan, the reticent Joshi is Modi's super guy on all things to do with social media.

A truly engaging platform

The MyGov website is quite user-friendly. Any average apolitical youngster or someone who is keen to follow up on issues involving governance can't refrain from engaging themself with the platform once they connect with it. The site has twelve active sections which keep changing with time and developments. On an average, two sections keep people involved in online competitions for designing logos or suggesting names for new government schemes and programmes. One section is dedicated to innovators—it asks them to come up with suggestions to transform India. Two sections call for suggestions on emerging national policies.

One section recently asked for inputs to make the coal sector more efficient while another section said, 'Revolutionise India through use of renewable energy,' thus calling upon people to submit their proposals to two crucial energy sectors that have an impact not just on the power sector but also on the green-energy scenario. Then a section titled 'Tasks' requested people to put forward innovative ideas for the PMO's mobile app. The parameter for fixing MyGov's level of engagement is the real-time figures available on the website. Over fifty popular groups have been formed on the web platform, suggestions invited for over 500 tasks and over 600 themes discussed. Over 18 lakh suggestions have come in the 'Tasks' section and nearly 34.54 lakh comments have been posted so far on the themes discussed.

From MyGov to Transforming India

MyGov was launched as a concept of participative governance in what marked a paradigm shift in the administration. As part of this experiment suggestions were sought from the people for effecting both short-term and long-term changes in key areas of governance, covering in the process even policymaking. After two years in power, Modi's next step was to share with the people in real time the information and figures about the work that the government was doing in eight key areas:

1. How many panchayats have been connected with broadband
2. How many LED bulbs have been sold by the power ministry in the country as part of its green energy programme
3. How many people got training under the Pradhan Mantri Kaushal Vikas Yojana
4. How many villages without electricity have now been covered and how many are still without electrification
5. How many people waived the LPG subsidy in favour of the poor (in response to the prime minister's appeal)
6. How many people secured loans under the Mudra scheme for small entrepreneurs
7. How many people got enrolled under the government's Jeevan Suraksha insurance scheme
8. How much money has been deposited in the Jan-Dhan bank accounts by the poor.

When a person logs on to the Transforming India website, he can find the figures relating to these eight areas of governance.

The prime minister took his vision for transforming India to a new level when he completed two years in office. He decided to ask people to rate his government in fifteen key areas through an online poll on MyGov. It was a bold move that showed Modi's confidence—the self-rating exercise could have been brought discomfiture for Modi because of the room it gave to mischief-makers as well as to his ideological and political opponents, many of whom have dreaded him for a long time. It was the biggest-ever survey in sample size compared to the ones that are done by rating agencies for media houses. Over 2.68 lakh people voted through the MyGov website or through the dedicated toll-free number.

The results were heartening for Modi. Of the fifteen parameters, the highest score was 76 per cent on proactive foreign policy and the lowest score was 62 per cent on tackling black money. The scores on road connectivity, railway modernization and the ease of doing business were around 75 per cent, and around 68 per cent on tackling corruption, Skill India, Digital India and the transparent taxation system. What was comforting for Modi was that more people from the rural areas voted than people in the urban areas. The highest traffic was from rural employment generation websites like MGNREGA. This showed that the Modi government has been able to project a positive image in rural areas on the basis of its work. The rating was done in two parts. In the first part, the voter had to respond 'yes' or 'no' when asked whether he knew about specific government schemes. The second part pertained to rating on the parameters. The exercise served the dual purpose of spreading awareness among people on government schemes and getting their opinion.

If Modi gets re-elected in 2019 to kick-start his second parliamentary innings, his initiatives in registering people's opinion through MyGov should be counted as one of the significant reasons behind his success.

2. Dismantling the Transfer-Posting Raj

Overturning a dark tradition in the corridors of Delhi

Till May 2014, the lobbies and restaurants of five-star hotels not very far from the seat of power in Delhi used to teem with familiar faces—those of liaison men, officers of the Indian Administrative Service and other central services seeking lucrative postings, and businessmen eyeing hefty government contracts. The liaison men can be better described as plain touts, powerful lobbyists or corporate fixers. In many cases, they were personal secretaries to the ministers, who were some of the point men to be contacted in the Delhi darbar for plum postings and contracts.

Today, a random survey reveals that these faces are conspicuous by their absence at the hotel lobbies and restaurants. The reason: the sources from which this structure of giving prized postings in the central government had grown has dried up now, thanks to one of the biggest exercises launched by the Modi government to end the transfer-posting raj in India's centre of power, the Delhi bureaucracy. In the process, crony capitalism has been quashed. The clean-up act has brought in honest officials in place of the ones who had come through recommendations and nepotism.

In this, the Modi government has done something unthinkable in the recent history of the nation's top bureaucracy. Modi has taken people back to the pre-1970s era of transparent postings in the Delhi bureaucracy. Since he took over, 500 officers have been posted in the bureaucracy, from secretary and joint secretary levels onwards, and around another 500 have been appointed in public-sector undertakings and banks strictly on just two criteria—honesty and efficiency, with honesty being the first criterion.

Not a single posting has been done on the basis of personal recommendation or on extraneous consideration. This is a record in recent decades. A top official in the Department of Personnel says: 'In cleaning up the musty corridors of power in Delhi, the prime minister has delivered on his biggest promise of giving clean governance by dismantling the transfer-posting industry. In doing so, he is also making a future roadmap for something similar down below in the states where things are horrible on this front. Modi rightly gauged that unless the delivery system is clean, the vision in governance can't be translated into action.'

As a crop of straightforward officers make it to the higher echelons of the Delhi bureaucracy, a new, bright side of babudom, a section of which has for long been synonymous with corruption and lethargy, is coming to the fore. The idea that for a good posting, political connections or the right relationships with middlemen were needed, stands demolished today. As Vinod Rai, the former comptroller and auditor general of India (CAG) and now the chairman of the Banks Board Bureau (BBB), puts it: 'The transparency that Modi government has brought in bureaucratic postings is exemplary. The old practice of allowing ministers to choose their key officials, in fact, destroyed the civil services because it led to massive lobbying at the ministerial level for extraneous considerations. Modi has brought a lot of objectivity by stopping this practice and demonstrating further commitment by choosing upright officers in the PMO to oversee postings.'

The roadmap: How the method of identifying transparent officers was evolved

The Modi government's plan to clean up the bureaucracy began with the selection of P.K. Mishra as the additional principal secretary to the prime minister. A retired IAS officer known for his unimpeachable integrity who was principal secretary when Narendra Modi was Gujarat's chief minister in 2001–04, Mishra was entrusted with the task of creating a roadmap for posting honest officials in the Delhi bureaucracy. The instructions to Mishra from Modi were clear: identify officers who are honest and efficient. Let personal integrity be the first criterion. The chemistry between the two helped. In an interview given many years ago, Modi had said: 'When I took over as Gujarat CM, it was Mishraji who taught me how to use a green or red pen on the file.'

In the new task, Mishra soon got two helping hands in the form of the joint secretary in the PMO, Bhaskar Khulbe, a West Bengal cadre officer, and Rajiv Kumar, an IAS officer of the Jharkhand cadre and an establishment officer (EO) under the cabinet secretary. Modi's narrative of postings with no recommendations started with Khulbe. He was a joint secretary in Delhi with no inkling that he was being posted in the PMO. One fine morning, he got an SMS from a colleague in the Department of Personnel saying, 'You have been posted in the PMO.' Khulbe says: 'I was pleasantly surprised because I had never expected it.' Rajiv Kumar was surprised about his posting too.[10]

Mishra's main problem was finding a way to track the true credentials of an officer in an age of subterfuge. A court judgement of 2008 specified that a senior officer writing the annual performance appraisal report (APAR) of a junior has to show his comments to his junior. So, a bad APAR for a junior invited the possibility of personal enmity for the senior officer writing the APAR. Few were willing to provoke hostility. The result was an explosion in 'Outstanding' APARs of officers which went up from 30 per cent to over 90 per cent. Outstanding APARs meant over 90 per cent grading in each case. So, from 30 per cent, the percentage of officials getting over 90 per cent marks went up to 90 per cent, all of a sudden. Thus the purpose of the entire exercise—to rate an officer on the basis of his performance and integrity—was lost. After a lot of deliberation, Mishra, along with Khulbe and Kumar, and later with the new P.K. Sinha, who had just taken over as cabinet secretary, evolved a method of real-time rating of officers with due diligence to overcome this obstacle.

How due diligence in selection of officers works

After an officer of the level of joint secretary, additional secretary or secretary has applied for a posting in Delhi, the cadre controlling authorities (CCA) sends the proposal to the EO, who is under the cabinet secretary but is also secretary to the Appointments Committee of the Cabinet (ACC) headed by the prime minister. The cabinet secretary is also a member of the ACC.

Then EO Kumar carries out the first step of due diligence with the help of Khulbe, under the supervision of Mishra. The exercise involves conducting a 360-degree scrutiny by making around a dozen calls in each case to an applicant's batchmates, seniors and juniors to verify the officer's integrity and efficiency. A.K. Mittal., the Railway Board chairman who is leading the mission to end the transfer-posting raj in the railways, says: 'On taking charge, I was surprised when some of my colleagues in the service told me that they were contacted by the PMO and cabinet secretariat officers to know about my real service record.'

Once an officer is cleared through this process, his or her name enters the retention pool and he or she is ready for a suitable posting. This is an ongoing process—the retained names are kept ready in advance and adjusted against vacancies. Next, the name is sent to the Central Services Board (CSB) for matching the candidate's profile with the job profiles of the posts that are vacant. Here the Secretaries of the departments are also involved, as are the EO and the cabinet secretary.

Once the name is finalized, the CSB sends it to the ACC, which clears it within twenty-four hours. Before the Modi government came to power, the process of passing the final order after the CSB had sent the name to the ACC used to take two to three months because of the overwhelming nepotism and corruption marked by pulls and pressures. Ministers and their personal secretaries were involved in a large number of cases along with invisible middlemen. These middlemen used to figure out when the file moved from the CCA to the EO and then was on its way to the CSB. Sometimes, the selected officers were sent back by the ministers even after being posted if their 'frequency' didn't meet the ministers'. The personal secretaries of the ministers were usually the ones connected with the middlemen (touts, lobbyists, corporate fixers), who wanted their men in crucial posts.

The impact of the due diligence method is visible today. There are many officers working in small places who had never dreamt of getting good postings, which they eventually got. Ashok Dongre, a Tamil Nadu cadre IAS officer who had never worked in Delhi, was picked up and given the important post of joint secretary, defence (he was transferred from there later). He did not have any inkling of this before he got the order. The case is the same with another Tamil Nadu cadre IAS officer, Anita Praveen, who is now joint secretary in the Department of Commerce. Usha Padhee, an Odisha cadre IAS officer, falls in the same category. She had not worked in Delhi earlier. Now she is joint secretary, civil aviation.

Due justice: The services of officers from the non-IAS categories are being widely and effectively utilized for the first time

One of the biggest innovations Modi has brought about lies in utilizing the services of good officers from non-IAS categories, which again is a result of the due diligence method adopted by the PMO and the cabinet secretariat for reaching out to officers of integrity, irrespective of the services they belong to. So Aniruddha Kumar from the Indian Revenue Service (IRS) finds himself as the joint secretary, power, and Amitabh Gautam from Indian Forest Service finds himself as the joint secretary, agriculture. Darshana Momaya Dabral, an officer of Indian posts and telecommunication accounts and finance service, is now joint secretary and finance adviser to the HRD ministry. The number of non-IAS officers empanelled for posting in Delhi is now nearly 100, one of the highest numbers ever recorded.

Two significant examples of such innovations in postings came in Air India and the Department of Commerce. Ashwani Lohani, a railway official, was made the Air India head. The changes he has brought in Air India are set to give results. After a long time, the loss-making airline is on the verge of making operational profit. When a railway official, Sanjay Chadda, gave a good account of his understanding of commerce as a member of the Railway Restructuring Committee under NITI Aayog member and economist Bibek Debroy, he was posted as joint secretary, commerce. P.K. Sinha, the cabinet secretary, says:

'Our single-minded pursuit is to get the best possible officers in terms of integrity and delivery wherever we can find them. The rule of thumb is merit and merit alone. Also there is much greater speed now in filling up the posts.'[11]

The meritocracy extends to appointments in banks and PSUs through a new model

The system of appointments in banks and PSUs too is witnessing a transparency not seen in many years. For making appointment in banks, a new body called the BBB was floated. Its first chairman is 'Mr Clean' Vinod Rai, the man who drew attention to the unimaginably high level of corruption in the country through his investigations into the bidding for spectrum and coal mining when he was India's CAG. The bureau members interview an applicant thrice, in batches consisting of two members, before taking a call. The Public Enterprises Selection Board has been reconstituted in a manner that leaves no room for any manipulation in appointments for PSUs. What is more, the process of making appointments, whether in the bureaucracy or in PSUs, is on a fast track. Political appointments have also been made to the banks but have been kept to a bare minimum and make little difference as the real power now lies with bureaucracy more than the political appointees.

The history of the downfall of the Indian bureaucracy is interesting. Its roots lie in Prime Minister Indira Gandhi's defeat in the 1977 elections, when she was stung by the desertion of the Jawaharlal Nehru family loyalist, Babu Jagjivan Ram, on the eve of the polls. When she came back to power in 1980, she made 'personal loyalty at any cost' the main criterion of selection for roles in politics and later also in the bureaucracy. This gave birth to a patronage raj in the ruling party that, in turn, led to the creation of the transfer-posting industry in the bureaucracy. When A.B. Vajpayee became the prime minister, he was able to arrest the decline, but only partially. Modi learnt quite a few lessons from his experience in Gujarat and put them to full use in Delhi, spurred on by the robust support that the majority had given him in the Lok Sabha elections.[12]

The flip side: Complaints of the partymen

The watertight, interference-free posting policy has not found favour with many members of the BJP because now they have very little say in the working of the government. A BJP leader, who admires Modi's clean-governance drive, says: 'Many of our leaders think that there is bureaucratic raj under Modi where even genuine party workers have little say. Those who have been posted without any recommendations obviously have their own way of working. This affects the political mandate so necessary in a true democracy.'

A senior officer, who has studied the new process evolved by the Modi government and also observed the way earlier governments have functioned, counters: 'This is an issue where the government has to make a stark choice. If the floodgates are opened for apparently some good partymen, the waters will gush in, bringing along with it filth, the percentage of which is much more. What's more, every effort is being made to post honest officials in the system, which takes care of the fears expressed.'

3. Reforming the Bureaucracy, Part II: Administrative Reforms Unparalleled

The Modi govt has sent shock waves by introducing modern HR practices in the selection of top officials

Many who have seen Prime Minister Narendra Modi's functioning at close quarters in Gujarat as well as in Delhi will vouch for the fact that his reign in the national capital is turning out to be better than his innings in Gandhinagar. He is showing greater wisdom, application and the ability to implement than ever before. This is transforming things. The reforms his government is carrying out in the bureaucracy are sure to change the character of the central services and bring in a new era of good governance, though this may happen gradually in phases.

After dismantling the transfer-posting raj, he has laid out an elaborate plan to choose quality manpower from the all-India services for specific areas of governance by changing the parameters of selection of officials at the topmost level in Delhi. This has been achieved by bringing in key human resource inputs based on an international study that will make it impossible for non-performing and corrupt officials to reach the highest rungs. The step, which faced massive resistance from vested-interest groups in the bureaucracy, sent shock waves in a system in which the I-scratch-your-back-and-you-scratch-mine tendency had made a mockery of merit-based selection.

Many governments in the past had talked of bringing in administrative reforms in the all-India services. Manmohan Singh, the former prime minister, was at one time very serious about it. He even called for presentations on the subject from the Ministry of Personnel, Public Grievances and Pensions but couldn't make much progress on this issue. Rather, in his tenure, selections became even worse as political lobbying became the chief qualification.[13] Modi's strong steps in this area are driven by two realizations: one, without giving credence to merit in the bureaucracy, he won't be able to achieve the stiff targets he has set for his government; and two, merit and integrity in the Indian bureaucracy, or, for that matter, in any institution, travel from top to bottom and not the other way around.

So the fundamentals of good governance have to percolate down. The second realization is perhaps a consequence of Modi's long experience in Gujarat before and after he became the chief minister. He has seen many efficient officers turn corrupt and lethargic in the second stage of their careers because their dishonest and unprincipled superiors could not inspire them. Inspiration has to come from the top. After arriving in Delhi, Modi saw how many top officials, in spite of being corrupt and inefficient, managed to get an 'outstanding' or a 'very good' rating in their APARs, got empanelled for a posting in Delhi, and ultimately even got the 'lucrative' postings in the national capital.

Four examples are sufficient to tell the story. Arvind Joshi and Tinoo Joshi, IAS officers of the Madhya Pradesh cadre who were dismissed from service following a case of corruption in 2014, had earlier worked respectively as joint secretary and deputy secretary in Delhi and had outstanding APARs. So did Subhash Sharma, the ex-chairperson of the New Delhi Municipal Council, who was charge-sheeted by the Central Bureau of Investigation (CBI) in 2004 in a land allotment case involving the Delhi Development Authority. Sanjiv Kumar, a Haryana cadre officer, was involved in a textbook scam—he was convicted by the CBI. Even Neera Yadav, the former chief secretary of Uttar Pradesh who had to go to jail for the Noida flat-allotment case, had an outstanding APAR.

The new method of selection was first applied in mid-2016 to a 1980s' batch of forty-two officials from the UPSC whose names had come forward on the basis of good APARs from a group of about 100 officials. Nine were rejected for reasons of lack of delivery and integrity. Surprisingly, most of these officials had outstanding APARS. The rejections of nine of these officials in empanelment jolted the country's bureaucracy and sent stern signals regarding what was to be expected in the future while looking for appointments in Delhi. As an officer involved in the exercise put it: 'There is a premium on competency and honesty for the first time in the history of all-India services.'

The new criteria of selection: A paradigm shift

The government applied the new method of selection after conducting an elaborate study on top-management selection practices in the administration based on human resources feedback as prevalent in the US, the United Kingdom and New Zealand, apart from companies like General Electric, McKinsey & Company and the Tata Group. The study, done by a special team guided by an young and energetic OSD in the PMO, Pratik Doshi, who has been with Modi since his Gujarat days, found the New Zealand government's method of selection to be the best and the most advanced. The study pointed out that the system of bureaucratic selection in the US hasn't undergone any major change in the past two decades.

In the old system, an experts committee (EC) of retired officials of integrity at the Centre had the power to make minor changes in the APAR of an officer while recommending candidates for empanelment for the post of joint secretary and additional secretary, departmental secretaries and chief secretaries at the Centre. The EC suggested changes if it found that certain facts did not match those on ground. Under the new system based on the international study, the EC has to prepare a pen-picture of the officer wanting a posting in Delhi in a seven-page format based on a multi-source feedback (MSF) which has four main criteria:

1. Functional skills like handling of finance, regulation, technology, execution and policymaking
2. Domain expertise in sectors like economy, energy, agriculture, education and tourism
3. Behavioural competence covering features like communication skills, whether the officer is a team player, has the big picture in mind, has long-term vision, has humility and empathy

4.   Integrity check to verify whether the officer has moral and intellectual, as well as financial, integrity

The new system also lays down the ways to conduct the MSF. Its requires the EC member evaluating a candidate to speak to one officer each who has worked as his senior, his junior and in his peer group and get feedback on him from them on the four components, with the promise of maintaining complete secrecy about it. A fourth feedback has to be procured from a person who has dealt with the officer as a customer in an interface with him. Then the member has to record this data in a seven-sheet format with names of the four persons interviewed. In the end, he is supposed to say whether he just recommends the candidate or strongly recommends him. This enables a complete and precise picture of the candidate to emerge, bringing out not only his overall personality traits but also the specific jobs he is most suited for in Delhi.

Of the nine officials from a 1980 batch, one IAS officer who was rejected for the empanelment is a highly competent officer who has worked in Delhi. He was rejected on the feedback that was received about his personal integrity. Another officer was good on integrity but was very poor on delivery and leadership qualities. A third officer got rejected because his motivation levels were found to be low—which would have posed a problem, given the way the Modi government has turned most postings into high-pressure jobs.

All in all, a message has been sent regarding what lies ahead of officers when it comes to postings in Delhi. It has put the entire bureaucracy on guard. Those who thought they had no chance of showing their work at a good post in Delhi as they had no connection with the patronage network in the country's capital are naturally rejoicing. What has bolstered the government's we-mean-business image is the fact that one of the officers rejected was a close relative of a senior official in Delhi.

In 2015, the PMO and the cabinet secretariat examined the APARs of 1000 all-India service officials, including IAS, IRS, Indian Police Service, Indian Postal service, and seven services of the railways, empanelling 700 of them. 'With the new criteria of merit and quality being applied now, the figure of 700 out of 1000 could now come down to 500. Fortunately we already have a good talent pool, or else we would fall short of officers. But the gain is of the nation in the form of quality,' reveals an officer involved in the new exercise.

The old method and its dark side

The old method of empanelment by the EC was simple: take the annual grading done on the scale of 1 to 10 for each officer for his service in the first sixteen years, make an aggregate and prepare the sum total. The EC was allowed to moderate the final tally based on the feedback on the officer who had applied for empanelment. It was permitted to marginally increase, or even decrease in some cases, the final tally if it was not satisfied with his marking as compared to his image. A professional in the PMO who played a key role in formulating the new selection criteria following the international study, says: 'The whole process was not positive selection but negative disqualification. In one way, it was elimination rather than selection.'

The system miserably failed to distinguish between the good, the average and the bad, because as evaluating senior officers invariably gave a 90+ per cent (outstanding) grade to those who applied for empanelment in a you-scratch-my-back-I-scratch-yours culture. So, merit-based rating had been lost in the maze of nepotism, favouritism and a lack of sense of duty to the service. The system was also exploited by some states, which allegedly ensured that most of its IAS officers were purposely given outstanding grades so that they became eligible for postings in Delhi to safeguard the state's interest but naturally at the cost of merit.

There is a long story behind this old system that sacrificed merit at the altar of extraneous influences. Till 2006, an old system prevailed wherein the senior officer had to evaluate his junior's performance in terms of grading in which there were three options: outstanding, very good and good. There was a semblance of fairness in this. But this system was destroyed by the court, which passed an order in 2008 that the senior officer writing the APAR of a junior officer will have to show it to him. Most officers didn't want to make an enemy in the services by writing a negative APAR. Thus started the dark phase, wherein, to avoid bad blood, most officers started giving outstanding APARs to juniors in what was apparently a you-scratch-my-back-I-scratch-yours culture. This contributed to bad governance.

It is to Modi's credit that he saw through this dark area early on in his innings. He was aware of the problem when he took over. But instead of confronting the system head on, he decided to bring changes in a phased manner. First, he dismantled the transfer-posting raj in Delhi. With the arrival of P.K. Mishra, Modi's former principal secretary in Gujarat, the PMO and the cabinet secretariat had already became unapproachable for favour-seeking officials, thanks to the good and unbending officers handling the selection process. A checking of the due diligence of candidates to be empanelled in Delhi was introduced for the first time in the history of the Indian bureaucracy. The officers, while performing the selection exercise, were required to make informal inquiries about the candidate before empanelling him.

Now in the second phase of the exercise, that can be labelled 'Reform II in the Bureaucracy', a stronger dose has come in the form of formalization of due diligence on the basis of modern human resource selection methods culled from the best practices in the world. This is one of the biggest administrative reforms in all–India services in six decades. P.K. Mishra says: 'The new method of empanelment and posting will change the essential character of the services when it comes to result–oriented work. All those who want merit to be the only criterion of selection should cherish it.'[14] Indeed, studies show that there have been cases where good officers have ended up becoming cynics when they were rejected for top postings in Delhi just because they had no access to the Delhi patronage network. They were left to rot in insignificant posts.

Along with Mishra, the cabinet secretary, P.K. Sinha, the joint secretary in the PMO, Bhaskar Khulbe, and the EO in the Ministry of Personnel, Public Grievances and Pension, Rajiv Kumar, played a key role in introducing the new method, braving opposition from a section of the bureaucracy that wanted the old method to continue. But the study on the new principles of selection was done by professionals from Modi's core team of researchers that made several presentations before resisting officials in the Ministry of Personnel, Public Grievances and Pension. Ultimately, the latter were convinced.

There is, however, another side to the MSF-based system of appointment of bureaucrats in Delhi. Even some relatively good officers have got rejected in the matter of empanelment because of this new system of raising questions about the feedback that comes through due diligence. An officer who was apparently rejected in spite of being eligible, says: 'The overall exercise to assess suitability and talent of an officer through MSF is the need of the hour. But internal rivalry in the matter of due diligence can, at times, lead to a false feedback. Some correction has to be brought in the due diligence exercise.'

The PMO is going for meritocracy across the board in a bid to improve the delivery system at all levels. Parallel reforms are carried out in the selection process of chairmen, managing directors and directors of banks that too was a part of the patronage network before Modi came. The bank scams that have repeatedly hit the country and robbed the poor nation of thousands of crores, is, in fact, rooted in the nepotism and corruption prevalent in bank appointments. The biggest example is of the absconding liquor magnate Vijay Mallya, who owes crores to various banks, which continued to give him credit in spite of his defaults in paying the earlier loans. Modi wants to make sure that the banks don't create new Mallyas.

During previous regimes, even appointments in state-owned banks, in the form of directors, were a matter of nepotism or political favour. The PMO and the cabinet secretariat are transforming the database of the personnel department by integrating different sets of databases. But more crucial is the fact that the method of writing the APARs, which remains the primary basis of selection even after the introduction of the MSF system, is being changed and made more meaningful.

Need for the same transparency in political appointments

The controversial and unseemly appointments of Gajendra Chauhan as the chairman of the Film and Television Institute of India, of ex-cricketer Chetan Chauhan (now a minister in the Uttar Pradesh government) as the head of the National Institute of Fashion Technology and, earlier, of Pahlaj Nihalani as the chairman of the Central Board of Film Certification, show that the Modi government isn't practising due diligence in the matter of non-bureaucratic appointments. These appointments have jeopardized the future of the respective bodies. What made the normally compulsion-free Modi to clear these mismatching appointments is a matter of conjecture. Clearly, the Modi government has to be more careful while making political appointments.

4. Grievance Redressal

A new beginning from the PMO

In his book, *Shivaji and His Times,* historian Jadunath Sarkar has tried to find logical reasons for the stupendous rise of the Maratha hero Chhatrapati Shivaji. The son of a simple *jagirdar* (nobleman), he became an independent sovereign titled Chhatrapati, who caused the history of his life to be written in seven different European languages. He eventually became an international figure before leaving the world in 1680 at the age of fifty-three. Sarkar says: 'Shivaji's initial rise came from the moral support that he gained among the common masses on the basis of his image of a firm dispenser of justice. His dominion spread through conquered hearts which an honest administrator alone can achieve among a simple and rustic population. Shivaji succeeded because he was people's hero as King.'[15]

Narendra Modi seems to be treading the same path if one takes a close look at his approach and strategies. The efficient public grievance system he has set up at the PMO that has no parallel in the past is an example of his kind of functioning. K. Kasturi, a domestic helper in the home of a professional in Chennai, is just one among thousands coming from marginalized backgrounds who have got justice through the direct intervention of the PMO.

Kasturi has a new spring in her step these days. It is all because of empowerment. In March 2015, the lady landed up at a branch of the State Bank of Travancore with a request that a Jan-Dhan account be opened in her name. In south India, the poor identify the Jan-Dhan account as the 'Modi scheme for the poor'. She used this phrase, which the clerk couldn't comprehend. He opened a normal bank account in her name. The illiterate Kasturi remained unaware of what had happened. After a few months, when her employer Rachit Shyam, who had advised her to go for the Jan–Dhan account, found that the bank had opened a regular account in her name, he asked her to go to the bank again and repeat the request. But now the bank officer told her that the scheme had ended and it was not possible to go forward with this. Shyam himself went to plead but got the same reply.

On 22 January 2016, Shyam lodged a complaint with the prime minister on the portal www.pmindia.gov.in, explaining Kasturi's case. It worked like magic. To the utter surprise of Kasturi and her employer, the former got an urgent phone call from the bank manager on the third day, asking her to visit the bank immediately. Kasturi told him that she can go only after 7 p.m. as she was on duty in the morning hours. To her astonishment, the manager told her that he will wait. She reached the bank at 7 p.m. and the manager opened her Jan–Dhan account. Kasturi felt zapped. Shyam says: 'This is real empowerment of the poor and signifies good governance. Kasturi just can't believe that a manager would wait for her. Such a thing was unthinkable in the past.'

Back in Delhi, eighty-six-year-old Roshanlal, a retired *havaldar* (sergeant), has the same feeling. After having moved from Sonepat to Delhi in March 2014 to live with his son Pravin Jain, he found that his request to the pension department to move his account from Sonepat to Delhi had got stuck somewhere in the circuitous lanes of officialdom. He stopped getting pension as the department concerned continued to pass the buck from one person to another. The standard reply was that his file had been lost.

When he didn't get any pension for a whole year, an exasperated Roshanlal posted a complaint to the PMO on 21 August 2015 with the help of his son Pravin thinking that 'a people's prime minister' would come to his aid. The PMO's grievance redressal cell, which handles such complaints, forwarded it to the Department of Financial Services on 24 August. The effect was almost immediate.

On 1 September 2015, Roshanlal's pension was credited to his account with arrears. Roshanlal says: 'My problem was solved in a matter of days after we intimated the PMO. This is a true example of honest and sincere governance. We are indebted to the Modi regime.'

These two individuals are a part of hundreds of problem-struck but hopeful people across India who are getting justice through a redesigned and recharged PMO. The public grievance redressal scene at the PMO has undergone a complete change. Against just a lakh of petitions that came to the PMO when the UPA government was in power, the number of petitions coming in is now over 6 lakh a year, thanks to the promise Modi made to the people.

The transformation is better reflected in the fact that now people get a response from the authorities in about two days, as opposed to the period of seven or more days of waiting that one had to undergo earlier. The task of sending a faster response in spite of a sixfold increase in petitions is being handled by the same fifty-member staff of the PMO's public grievance wing. This is a miracle of sorts, brought about by an imaginative use of technology and also by a new, missionary zeal displayed by the PMO in serving the common man.

How did this transformation take place? It is directly linked to the reforms brought about in the style of the PMO's management at the behest of Modi. 'The transformation of the grievance redressal system is, in fact, rooted in the transformation of the management style of the PMO itself through process re-engineering,' says Anurag Jain, joint secretary at the PMO.[16] The winds of change started blowing perhaps on Modi's very first day in South Block on 27 May 2014, when he went on a round of the PMO, met his staff and observed things for himself.

What caught his attention was that around twenty personnel of the PMO's fifty-member-strong public grievance wing were sitting in Rail Bhavan due to a paucity of space in South

Block, while some areas in South block were loaded with unwanted waste. Modi took time to do the precise appraisal before applying his mind to a transformation. The process of re-engineering began over six months later when a complete report and execution plan based on modern management techniques, accompanied by the use of technology, was laid out to ensure smoother functioning and quicker results. The steps also took time to implement because Modi wanted to reorganize things in such a manner that the government could take inspiration from the PMO when it came to grievance redressal.

The execution began with a bang. Almost two lakh files were checked and over a lakh of these, which should have been disposed of many years ago, were removed as waste. Among these were files dating back to the 1960s. These were thrown away, along with loads of broken furniture. The total waste amounted to six truckloads. The unwarranted stuff occupied 2000 sq. ft of space while almost half the staff of the public grievance wing sat in Rail Bhavan. As soon as this space was freed, the public grievance wing was moved to South Block to join the rest of the staff.

Modern techniques were adopted to effect this transformation. The swim lane mapping method was used to track the journey of petitions from arrival to disposal. This revealed the exact time a petition took to move at every stage. It also created a way to fix responsibility for any delay in disposal. But the biggest step that effected a change in disposal of petitions was the creation of an online petition platform linked directly with the prime minister on his website. Petitions sent to the PMO were integrated with the centralized public grievance redress and monitoring system (CPGRAMS), an online cell administered by the Department of Administrative Reforms and public grievances for many years. This was part of the planned evolution of the Central Mail Management Unit and redesigning of the PMO, ensuring that all mails landed up in the same place.

The new system made the entire process go online. Any delay in reacting to the public petitions to the PMO was now identifiable. Earlier, the facility of online petition filing was not available at the PMO: the petitions received as emails were downloaded and processed as physical petitions. The old system resulted in massive file work and made follow-up very difficult. Today it is possible to track the end result of each petition in the minimum possible time. According to Ambuj Sharma, under secretary at the PMO, the disposal rate of petitions is as much as over 80 per cent now. Hemang Jani, a young technocrat and a member of Modi's team at the PMO in 2016 who also played a role in the redesign, says: 'In his very first Independence Day speech the PM had stressed on the need for changing government processes for optimum results. The transformation at the PMO is a result of that vision.'

The use of technology has ensured a series of new features when it comes to online complaints, their tracking and response. Now applicants can not only track the status of their petitions but can also send reminders. They can also see the reports of the action taken by the government organizations and departments in relation to the petitions. Petitioners now get SMS alerts in case of a delay in the disposal of petitions because of some unforeseen event. Another great feature of the new system is the periodic analysis of the nature of complaints which helps in policy decisions.

For example, there was a peculiar rule for the Jan-Dhan ATM card holder. According to it, if he didn't use the card within the first forty-five days of opening his Jan-Dhan account, he won't get a particular health insurance facility under Jan-Dhan. The PMO got a series of complaints on this. In response, the period was extended from forty-five to ninety days. The analysis of complaints regarding the railways also led to a major change in policy decisions that has come as a relief for train commuters. Till a year and a half ago, if an e-ticket did not get confirmed, the refund could be availed of only through a written application to the railway reservation authorities. Now the refund money goes directly to the bank account of the person who had booked the ticket. Policy changes were also effected in the integration of the Aadhaar card database from the point of view of health services and in the Department of Posts following the examination of certain complaints.

However, being more responsive has also meant that the PMO is sometimes being taken for granted by irresponsible citizens. The load of frivolous petitions has increased. Many of these are ones that ask the prime minister to intervene in judicial matters even after the Supreme Court has given its final verdict. One petitioner, for example, kept on sending negative emails to the prime minister for several weeks just because the PMO had turned down his impossible plea that the Supreme Court of India be asked to set up a constitutional bench to hear his case of property dispute. And this after his curative petition had been dismissed. Anurag Jain says: 'These are hazards of the profession. We just take them in our stride.'[17]

The sense of satisfaction on the face of twenty-eight-year-old Shashi Kumar, a Dalit helper in the railways' workshop at Sabarmati in Ahmedabad, tells the story of the transformation at the PMO. A resident of a small village in Saharanpur district in Uttar Pradesh, he had appeared for an examination for Group D (helper/peon) workers in the railways in 2013. He had passed all the tests. However, in the final verification round, he was rejected on health grounds. He found this untenable. He petitioned to the PMO on 10 December 2015 on the advice of a friend who had told him that an application to Modi could get him justice. It had the desired effect. After a fortnight he was called by railway officials and his appeal was heard. On re-verification, his complaint was found to be valid. Kumar joined the Ahmedabad workshop in January 2016 with an appointment letter in hand. Kumar says: 'I certainly believe people when they say this is a government that really works for the common man.'

The reform of the public grievance management system is the main offshoot of the makeover, but there is also a series of new features in the redesigned PMO. The installation of LED lights in South Block is saving monthly energy bills to the tune of ₹1.50 lakh. Tendering has been made online as also inventory management for stationery. One of the biggest changes is in the management of the Prime Minister's National Relief Fund, where the sanction of funds for applicants in the area of health has been made faster, priority-based and more considerate. A personal letter from the prime minister now goes to the applicant when the fund is sanctioned, and a prior intimation of the sanction reaches him through SMS. Modi knows that he has to inspire from his own doorstep if people are to believe in his plans for good governance. And that is what he is doing.

5. The Agriculture Innovation

Removing middlemen using the digital route

In the first year of Narendra Modi's new innings in Delhi, the buzz was that not much was happening on the agriculture front. The drought conditions prevailing across India, accompanied by farmers' suicide, seemed to add to the atmosphere of despair. But, as it turns out, a lot of things were happening silently in keeping with the prime minister's promise to double farmers' income in the country by 2022. In that one year, a foundation of a new method of approaching problems of agriculture was being laid.

A new electronically operated trading portal, the National Agriculture Market (NAM), has been created. This can fetch the farmer the best possible price for his produce. This is in contrast to the earlier exploitative conditions centred on private mandis, where middlemen walked off with huge cuts on the sale of crops, leaving low profits or even losses for farmers. It was a market dominated by powerful cartels of crop buyers. NAM, launched in April 2016, is slated to be connected eventually to 585 pre-identified agricultural produce market committees (APMCs) of farmer's cooperatives across the country by 2018. The progress on this has been very swift after the success of the pilot project involving twenty-one mandis.

By the beginning of 2017, business worth over ₹800 crore spread over 250 APMCs in ten states has already been conducted through the portal. It involved over 2 lakh farmers and over 650,000 traders across India. Connecting with NAM through phone or internet and finding the best buyer gives the Indian farmer the quickest possible pick-and-choose option on the largest possible scale. It gives an advantage to the buyer too, to a lesser degree, when a particular produce is in shortly supply and farmers are quoting very high prices. So the initiative will work both ways, protecting not only the interests of the farmers but also, in some cases, of the buyers.

The NAM experiment, which is part of Modi's push for a national digital grid, will make a difference even to those farmers who are not victims of the private traders' cartels and use the APMC route for selling their produce. Though an ideal system, the APMC framework at the moment is highly compartmentalized. It restricts benefits for both farmers and buyers. It is handled by the states according to certain regulations in which a state is divided into several market areas. Each area is administered by a separate APMC, which imposes its own marketing rules and fees that end up fragmenting the markets and obstructing the flow of agricultural commodities from one area to another, besides causing multiple levels of mandi charges. This results in high prices for the consumers without a corresponding benefit to the farmers.

NAM aims at bringing about uniformity, streamlining procedures across integrated markets, removing the mismatch of information between buyers and sellers, and ensuring access to real-time prices based on actual demand and supply. The online system is integrated at the levels of the state and the Centre. Modi and his reticent minister for agriculture hope that this will inject transparency into the auction process, with the prices available to the farmers matching the quality of the produce. At the same time, this will secure the interests of consumers so that they get reasonable prices.

The Small Farmers' Agriculture-Business Consortium is operating NAM as the implementing agency with technical support from a strategic partner. All the designated 585 cooperative mandis or APMCs will be covered by NAM by 2018. The Department of Agriculture, Cooperation and Farmers Welfare (DACFW) is meeting the expenses of the software and its customization for the states. It is providing the service free of cost. DACFW is also giving a grant as a one-time fixed amount subject to the ceiling of ₹30 lakh per mandi (other than to private mandis), for related equipment/infrastructure in the 585 regulated mandis and for the installation of the e-market platform.

NAM is among multiple measures mooted by the Modi government for harnessing the energies of farmers, particularly the small ones, and increasing their share in the gross domestic product (GDP). It also addresses a national problem by getting the best prices to the farmers. The problem of the flight of farmers from agriculture to other vocations has assumed dangerous proportions in the past few years due to a downslide in agricultural incomes caused by a number of factors. The migration of farmers to urban centres has added to the pressure on cities. 'NAM is an important element when it comes to the government's ambitious target of doubling the farmer's income by 2022,' says Prof. Ramesh Chand, a member of NITI Aayog and an expert who is playing a key role in setting things on the right track in the agriculture sector. According to Chand, the thrust on agriculture has never been so strong as it is under the Modi government. 'Things are changing very fast in the agro sector,' he says.[18] Economist Surjit Bhalla agrees: 'A new era has begun in India's agro scene, thanks to well-thought-out policies.'[19]

According to Chand, the focus has to be on a new transformational approach to agriculture based on a mix of easy access to modern scientific techniques and the farmer's own native wisdom. 'We are working towards a business model which will veer the farmers away from the subsidy model. Studies have showed the growth rates of crops that get subsidies is less than those which don't. But we have to harness the native entrepreneurial skill of the Indian farmer. The government is not only encouraging the concept of contract farming to neutralize the impact of low holdings but also contract marketing by farmers.'

Interestingly, the results of NAM were visible even in the pilot project in the form of a series of examples of how farmers were getting good prices for their produce. Muddam Malikarjun, a small maize-growing farmer owning three acres in Athmakur Mandal of Telangana's Warangal district: 'The e-action at NAM greatly benefits small farmers. With no middlemen in between they are getting good prices.' Malikarjun got ₹100 more per quintal when he sold 40 quintals of maize through the NAM portal at the Warangal APMC. Surendra Singh, another small farmer of Goyanda, a village in Rajasthan's Kota district, has the same opinion about NAM. Owning 1.5 acres of land and holding 8 acres on lease, he sold his *chana* (gram) through a NAM auction at the Ramganj APMC, two months after NAM was launched. He got ₹6750 per quintal as against the ₹6300 he would have received if had sold it through a private mandi—a clean profit of ₹450 per quintal.

His product first went through a laboratory test at the APMC to determine its quality. Then there was an e-auction for it. Singh said: 'NAM appears to be a great experiment of the Modi government, particularly for the small farmers.' Even medium-level farmers like Jashwinder Singh, who owns 28 acres in Shahpur village in Haryana's Ambala district, is very hopeful about NAM. 'I got ₹180 per quintal more when I sold my sunflower through a NAM auction,' he says excitedly. For those who don't have access to the Internet, NAM portals have been set up outside the APMCs, where it has been taken up as a pilot project.

The success of the project, however, depends a lot on the level of involvement of the state governments. Fortunately, the scheme is such that whichever party's government is in power in a state it will be attracted to NAM because of the benefits it offers to both farmers and buyers. To Modi's credit, his government, in spite of having tepid relations with the Congress and some other opposition parties, has kept core governance involving states and the Centre free from acrimony, in the true spirit of Team India. This is best demonstrated by the impressive progress of many of the prime minister's schemes like Pragati, which seeks to expedite stalled Centre–state infrastructure projects. NAM undoubtedly presents a bright future for the depressed Indian farmer.

The Grey Area

One of the important aspects of Modi's vision for transforming India is skill development. It supplements FDI, in attracting which India has outpaced all nations, including China, after Modi's arrival. The reason: while investing in India, skilled manpower is important to foreign investors. Many foreign players refuse to invest in countries with an inadequate skilled labour force. However, Modi's skill-development initiative is yet to exploit the full potential available on that front because of a disconnect between his vision and the Ministry of Skill Development and Entrepreneurship led by Rajiv Pratap Singh Rudy. An uncooperative and insensitive bureaucracy at the skill development ministry has done much damage to the implementation of the scheme in the ITIs.

Over 1500 new ITIs set up by private entrepreneurs have been denied affiliation although they had matched all the parameters demanded by the ministry when it invited applications in January 2016. The ministry threw a spanner in the project by introducing a new rule as a precondition for affiliation. The rule came after the private promoters had already set up the ITIs, spending huge amounts of money in the process. This attitude of the ministry is in sharp contrast to the skill-development-training scenario in developed and developing countries. China has nearly 1 lakh mini industrial training units while even a small country like Germany has 1 lakh normal-sized industrial training centres. In comparison, India has just 15,000 ITIs.

Even the department for creating skilled manpower out of the SC/STs and the disabled, that was transferred to the skill development ministry from the Ministry of Social Justice and Empowerment, has very little to show in terms of achievement. The department was doing very well when it was under the Ministry of Social Justice headed by Thawar Chand Gehlot in the first eight months of Modi's tenure. It had trained an impressive 8000 hands in various skills at that time. The problem does not lie with Modi, who has dogged determination. It lies in the failure of the skill development ministry to live up to his vision. Modi is totally focused on skill development. On his November 2016 visit to Japan, he forged an agreement that would facilitate the training of Indian hands in skill development in Japan in certain areas. But few can deny that skill development is one of the areas in which the Modi government needs to improve its performance.[20]

4

Collective Responsibility

Team India and Team Modi

In 2015, the railway ministry received a unique proposal from the Union power ministry headed by Piyush Goyal. It proposed a rationalization of the coal linkage with power plants. The railways plays a major role as the transporter of coal to the government's power generation units. In effect, the proposal meant a cut in the railway tariff and a huge loss to the railways, to the tune of over ₹2000 crore annually. But it also meant greater savings for the nation in terms of a reduction in power tariffs. Officials of the railways' traffic department were against any concession. They argued that the railways ministry should not bear the cost of bringing down the logistical charges of another ministry. In most governments in the past, the officials would have prevailed. But they were in for a surprise when Suresh Prabhu, the railway minister, took a different view. When briefed about the advantages the nation would get in the event of rationalization, Prabhu said: 'If the move is drastically bringing down the power cost in the country then railways would bear the loss as it is the nation which will benefit.'[1]

The step helped the power ministry's National Thermal Power Corporation (NTPC) Limited alone save ₹8000 crore annually. The benefit is passed on to the consumer. Prabhu gave yet another example of his positive approach when he removed the service charge on railway e-tickets in keeping with the Modi government's policy to encourage people to adopt electronic payment systems. The annual loss to the railways on this account was around ₹150 crore to ₹200 crore. But Prabhu said that this was a small price to pay to get the nation moving towards digital payments. And this happened much before the prime minister undertook the digitization drive after demonetization.

It is not only Prabhu who follows the Nation First policy. The Modi cabinet is filled with ministers like him. Piyush Goyal's power ministry has offered to electrify 25,000 km of un-electrified railway tracks in the country and recover the cost in five to seven years from the savings that the railways will make from the switchover to electric from diesel engines. In another move, the power ministry has suggested to the urban development ministry that power plants should set up large sewage treatment units within 50 km of the plants in cities or towns. The power plants should use the water treated by these sewage processing units. In both the cases, pilot projects are on the anvil. Nitin Gadkari, the Union minister of road transport and highways, is particularly known for making no distinction between BJP-ruled states and states ruled by other parties while pursuing highway projects. This has earned him the praise of chief ministers, even from opposition parties. These are the defining qualities of both Team India and Team Modi. The Modi cabinet ministry hasn't refrained from taking decisions detrimental to it politically in the short run but beneficial for the nation as well as for the government's image in the long run.

The government gave evidence of its India First approach as soon as it took over in May 2014. The issue in question was the unfulfilled promise that the previous UPA government had made to the state governments on value added tax (VAT). After the introduction of VAT in the country, the UPA government had promised the states in 2008–09 that it would compensate them for VAT-related losses in instalments from 2010 onwards. The promise was not kept, perhaps because of the financial pressure the government faced as a result of political decisions like the ₹60,000-crore loan waiver to farmers and other unproductive schemes. There was no way left for the government to keep the fiscal deficit under control except by cutting planned expenditure and the states' share of revenue. When the NDA government led by Narendra Modi took over in 2014, it found that the fiscal deficit left behind by the previous government was alarming. In spite of all odds, Modi and Finance Minister Arun Jaitley took the bold and patriotic decision to fulfil the UPA's promise of compensating the states for VAT-related losses in three yearly instalments, in a spirit of cooperative federalism.

The sterling step warrants appreciation, notwithstanding the fact that the Centre needed to bring the states on board on the issue of the goods and services tax (GST). The underlying message: certain things should be above politics when it comes to protecting national interest. The first examples of Team India can be found in India's recent history. Pandit Jawaharlal Nehru took all the parties together while forming independent India's first government. When Nehru made an offer to his sworn political rival, Dr Shyamaprasad Mukherjee, the Hindu Mahasabha leader, the latter asked for some time to decide on a response. Then Mukherjee made a trunk call to the party's chief patron, the great revolutionary leader Veer Savarkar, in Mumbai to seek his permission. Savarkar replied in the affirmative, saying that there can't be any objection to his joining the government, even if was headed by their greatest ideological opponent, Nehru.[2] In yet another instance of the spirit of Team India, Nehru invited the RSS, his sworn ideological enemy, to participate in the Republic Day parade in New Delhi on 26 January 1963, in appreciation of the support RSS volunteers had given to Indian soldiers on the war front in the 1962 India–China war.

Unfortunately, however, the tradition faded as years went by and narrow political gains took precedence over the concept of a national team. For that matter, even governments didn't work as a team. The UPA government led by Manmohan Singh had one centre of power in P. Chidambaram and one outside the ministry in Sonia Gandhi. Even the A.B. Vajpayee government was not free of power centres. In that BJP government, the saffron bodies of the RSS kept on intervening in core governance. Sometimes, governments that otherwise worked with a sense of oneness couldn't take advantage of the team spirit. The reason: portfolio distribution was often inefficient. For example, two adjacent departments were often given to two different ministers for reasons of political expediency.

Consider the UPA cabinet, which left office in 2014. In that government, the power, coal and new and renewable energy portfolios were all under different ministers, whereas, for smooth functioning, all of three of them should have been under one minister. In the UPA, power was under Jyotiraditya Scindia, new and renewable energy under Farooq Abdullah and coal under Sriprakash Jaiswal. In the Modi government, all three are under Piyush Goyal and are being run smoothly. Apart from Goyal's efficiency, the connections among the three departments has also made a difference. The power sector is one of the main clients of coal and the performance of renewable energy naturally gets enhanced when it is clubbed with power. The net result: all three ministries are doing very well.

The placing of commerce and industry under one minister, Nirmala Sitharaman, made eminent sense too. The two departments are related. Santosh Vaidya, joint secretary in the new and renewable energy department, who has worked in the PMO both under Manmohan Singh and under Narendra Modi, says: 'The results of ministries and departments working in close coordination are quite visible today.' The Ministry of Commerce and Industry also plays a key role in the functioning of the Ministry of External Affairs as trade and commerce have assumed greater importance in the age of Modi at the level of international diplomacy.

Earlier, it was often the case that one department didn't know about the workings of another department. This often resulted in delays due to the lack of coordination. One of the major changes that Narendra Modi brought about after taking over was to hold coordinating meetings of officials of major departments. The process of holding these meetings went on for several days before he was convinced that each department had a gained an understanding of the workings of the remaining departments, particularly the mutually related ones. This has given excellent results. Clearances have been faster when demanded by one department from another. Today, when there is a delay in the transportation of coal by the railways, and this threatens to affect power generation, it takes just one phone call from Coal Minister Piyush Goyal to Railway Minster Suresh Prabhu to get an extra train to make up for the delay.

These are examples of the functioning of Team Modi. There are equally strong examples of the Modi government's Team India spirit. Telangana Chief Minister K. Chandrashekhar Rao, an ideological rival of the BJP, declared when Modi went to Telangana to inaugurate an irrigation project in August 2016: 'I have been in public life for forty years. I have seen the present Union government's functioning for the past two years. And I can say with authority that this is the first government which is totally corruption-free. The credit goes to Mr Modi.'[3] A little later, he also praised the government's Team India spirit. He thanked Nitin Gadkari, the minister for road transport and highways, for Telangana's high-quality roads and connectivity, adding that 'the speed of road-making in Telangana was greater than the national average'. He also appreciated lauded Piyush Goyal, the Union power and coal minister, for making a 1200 MW power plant functional in Telangana by making coal available.

The Team India spirit is also reflected in the way the Modi government's ministers attend the global investment summits of non-NDA administrations. This is in sharp contrast to the virtual ban imposed by the UPA government on its ministers when it came to attending events of the Gujarat government at the time when Modi was leading the state.

Team India and Team Modi Are Rooted in Modi's Leadership

When the smartphone was launched in the US, many questioned its usefulness as compared to its high cost. Today, the smartphone is an empowering tool for the poorest of the poor, from the taxi driver to the vegetable vendor. Steve Jobs could see its great future but most others could not. Many examples show that Modi also has this ability to gauge the potential of something that may initially seem insignificant. He has demonstrated the ability to take people along with him on the walk towards unique goals. He has often made impossible things look possible by setting tough targets and then motivating people with his support and removing obstacles from their paths. This has earned him a robust following not just of ideologically similar people, but also of admiring outsiders. This happens only when one has the qualities of great leadership as well as vision—twin attributes that Modi has demonstrated amply. Both Team India and Team Modi have been possible only because of the prime minister's leadership qualities, which leave a lasting impression on his subordinates, notwithstanding his tough approach in dealing with his colleagues.

A remarkable example of the prime minister's visionary leadership is the International Solar Alliance (ISA) of 121 sunshine nations, a majority of them located fully or partially between the Tropic of Cancer and the Tropic of Capricorn. Modi mooted the ISA in December 2015. The organization has its headquarters in Gurgaon in India. Germany, France, the US, Brazil and a host of other nations joined the game-changing project that aims to tap solar energy on an unprecedented scale by upgrading technology. The emphasis is on mutual cooperation for research and development in order to tackle climate change and reduce the dependence on fossil fuels in an age in which nuclear power generation has raised safety issues and hydropower generation the problem of human displacement. In less than a year, the framework agreement of the ISA was ready and had also been signed by twenty countries. The alliance showed that there is a visionary leader in Modi who can think on a grand scale to transform the world. Closer home, it had a deep impact on Modi's followers, including his own ministerial colleagues, as well as on those belonging to the opposition.

The move was based on Modi's vision of solar power that he had boldly demonstrated in Gujarat. It was in Gujarat in 2008–09 that India's solar journey started, with Modi coming up with the boldest-ever solar generation policy for private players and setting up Asia's biggest solar park at Charanka in north Gujarat. Today, if the cost of solar generation has come down to less than ₹4 and is on a par with the cost of thermal power generation in many parts of India, the credit should go largely or entirely to Modi. If he had not broken new ground and taken up the solar initiative in 2008–09, India would have been lagging behind in that area now. However, setting up the ISA was not an easy job. Modi started working on it from the day he became the prime minister. He used his diplomatic channels to achieve his aim.

He took the initiative further at the Paris Climate Change Conference of the UN on 30 November 2015 to ultimately form the ISA, which is also called the International Agency for Solar Policy and Application (IASPA). In fact, Modi was one of the architects of the successful conclusion of the Paris conference. He and then French President Francois Hollande inaugurated the ISA at the campus of the National Institute of Solar Energy (NISE) in Gurgaon on 25 January 2016. India has dedicated five acres of land at the NISE campus for setting up the ISA headquarters, besides contributing $26 million to the ISA campus fund for covering its running costs in the initial five years. Plus, $400 million is being raised for the effort from membership fees in the first phase.

The idea behind the alliance is that member countries would help one another in research and development to bring down the cost of solar power generation. A target of $1 trillion has been set for the achievement of the goal. India has taken the lead under Modi in this initiative by targeting of 1.75 lakh MW of renewable energy capacity by 2022 and decreasing emissions by around 35 per cent by 2030. Vivek Katju, a former diplomat and Indian ambassador to Afghanistan, who was the chief negotiator during the Kandahar hijack episode in 1999, says: 'By forging the alliance Modi has shown very imaginative leadership.'[4]

The insights into Modi's dynamic leadership in foreign affairs are interesting. The prime minister's 2016 visit to tiny Mozambique, a country set to become the third-largest exporter of natural gas in the world, was the first by an Indian prime minister in thirty-four years. It centred on pulse imports, rather an unfashionable item in high diplomacy. Pulse imports, however, were among the top items in Modi's priority list. The reason: the malnutrition affecting India's poor is also linked to the shortfall of 6 million tonnes in India's pulse production. This leads pulse prices to skyrocket, making them unaffordable for the poor. So by increasing the import of pulses from Mozambique from

1 lakh tonnes to 2 lakh tonnes in the next five years, India will be targeting its malnutrition problem. The issue was left neither to the accompanying diplomats nor to the Secretaries. The prime minister himself took the initiative to make pulses a pivotal part of diplomatic dialogue during the Mozambique visit. He floated the proposal of a loan to that country to allow it to double its pulse production. This shows Modi's ability to find a solution to India's little-known but big problems. Modi's pulse initiative must also be seen in terms of the international challenge. China is already engaged in contract farming in African countries to meet its food deficit in various areas, as well as to extend its diplomatic outreach.

Sudhir Mankad, a former chief secretary of Gujarat known for his high integrity, and who has worked very closely with Modi in the state, says: 'I had a feel of his sterling leadership qualities when I worked with him. But now after what he has demonstrated since he became prime minister I think he has taken it to the next level. He was born to lead.'[5] Another former bureaucrat who admires Modi adds: 'Some of Modi's moves while reforming the bureaucracy are rather harsh. The changes the PMO has introduced in the empanelment process of central services officers including the IAS are too stiff. These could exclude even good officers in empanelment. The Union government could lose confidence of a section of bureaucracy on this account thus affecting both his Team India and Team Modi ideas.'

There is criticism of Modi's Team India spirit on some other counts too. One of them involves the attempt of his party, the BJP, to take advantage of the internal wrangling among state governments led by opposition parties to derail them in an underhand way, as happened in the states of Uttarakhand and Arunachal Pradesh in 2016. The moves go against the Team India spirit. Modi could take the ideal further by appointing eminent apolitical people not connected with the BJP and the RSS as state governors. This had been the tradition till the late Prime Minister Indira Gandhi overturned it in her quest to thrust personal-loyalty-based politics on the nation. The appointment of distinguished people as governors has its advantages for the nation in terms of the Team India spirit.

An example of this can be found in the episode of the internal rebellion in 1995 against the then BJP chief minister of Gujarat, Keshubhai Patel. The rebellion was led by Shankarsinh Vaghela, a BJP leader now in the Congress. In that episode, Naresh Chandra, the then Gujarat governor and a former cabinet secretary of India, left a good impression on political observers when, in spite of being a Congress-government appointee, he gave Patel as much time as one week to prove his majority on the floor of the Gujarat Legislative Assembly. This is a good example of how the appointment of people of integrity in Raj Bhavans impacts democratic ideals.

Two Great Representative Examples of Team India and Team Modi

1. Pragati is the ultimate symbol of Team India

Mohan Bhagwat, the head of the RSS and no spendthrift when it comes to words of praise, once told me that Prime Minister Modi is the best administrator India has produced since Independence. A monthly exercise called Pragati was started in March 2015 by Modi to review stalled Centre–state projects, programmes and policy-related issues and grievances by directly interacting with the Chief Secretaries of the states and the Secretaries of the Union departments concerned. This exercise, a first by an Indian prime minister, has produced astonishing results and gives weight to Bhagwat's words.

As many as 180 of the 350 stalled projects of the Centre in the states in key infrastructure areas like railways, roads, power and civil aviation worth almost ₹2 lakh crore that were delayed for various reasons for a period of four to fifteen years are on track again. Some of them have been completed and are operational. This amounts to more than half of the total Centre–state projects worth ₹3.5 lakh crore that were on hold when Modi took over. This is apart from the revival of two dozen projects of the states that had been stalled due to delays on the part of the Centre. The figures and the overall progress are certainly impressive in this regard. The ninety-minute monthly videoconference that the prime minister conducts under Pragati has caught the imagination of management experts. The successful experiment gives an idea of the Team India spirit he is forging.

The way Pragati is conducted every month is interesting. On the last Wednesday of every month, around 3.30 p.m., Modi occupies the Pragati room in the South Block. He is flanked by the PMO's Joint Secretaries and other officials dealing with Pragati. Facing him are three screens: the one on the left has the presentation of the project concerned, with photographs and general details; the one in the middle has the officer Modi is talking with; and the screen on the right has the Pragati portal, with a GPS-based location of the project being discussed (made available through the Indian Space Research Organization's software) along with details like causes of delay and cost escalation and also the latest comments of the respective departments/states on the project's status. On the middle screen, Modi is connected to Chief Secretaries of all the states and to a dozen Secretaries or heads of central departments whose projects are listed for discussion.

But of particular importance is a fourth screen placed slightly below these three screens. It's meant for the prime minister alone. The screen has precise details and directions for the prime minister on each project, and advice on how he has to conduct himself on the issue and whom he has to talk first. These are prepared beforehand after a careful scrutiny and research by the prime minister's team, led by Joint Secretary

A.K. Sharma and comprising Deputy Secretary Ajit Kumar and a junior officer, Mrigendra Jha. Armed with this precise feedback, Modi acts like a hands-on commander, lightly reprimanding officers when they are in the wrong or indulging in banter, depending on the need. Modi is surrounded by Cabinet Secretary P.K. Sinha, Principal Secretary Nripendra Misra and Additional Principal Secretary P.K. Mishra, besides the PMO's Joint Secretaries and officers who handle the Pragati programme, led by A.K. Sharma.

The projects to be reviewed are put on the Pragati portal fifteen to twenty-five days in advance so that the state Chief Secretaries and the Union officials concerned know that they will have to discuss and answer questions on these from the prime minister. Such is the impact of this exercise that, in several cases, the bureaucracy completes projects that have been held up for insignificant reasons by the time they come up for discussion at Pragati, less than a month after the first notice from the PMO.

The exercise has kept the bureaucracy on its toes. The PMO has made officials realize that the nation pays a cost for project delays in the form of accumulation of NPAs, even if the waste of national money does not make a difference to their own pockets. Sometimes, when bureaucrats come to know that a particular project is going to be placed before the prime minister for scrutiny, they plead with the PMO not to do so by promising that the project would be operational within a few weeks. To accelerate the speed of stalled projects, the PMO purposely puts fifteen to twenty-five projects on the Pragati portal for review in each Pragati session when the prime minister actually has time to review only ten or twelve projects/programmes. The PMO hopes that the thought of facing the prime minister himself would push bureaucrats to expedite the remaining ones.

One can cite the example of the delayed Katakhal–Bhairabi railway line of 84 km linking Assam with Mizoram. Sanctioned in 1999, it was almost complete but couldn't become operational because of opposition to the acquisition of over 5 hectares of land needed to complete the last mile of the project. Inquiries by the PMO found that one of the reasons behind the delay was also the governments' lack of priority. The project was uploaded on the Pragati portal on 15 April 2016. But before it came up for discussion on the Pragati session of 25 May 2016, it became operational. This showed the power of Pragati in pushing forward stalled development.

The Tumkur–Davangere railway line had been in limbo since 2011. The reason: the Karnataka government didn't give the railways its 50 per cent contribution after having asked for the project and agreeing to share half the cost. Modi was strict in this case. As he told A.K. Mittal, the chairman of the Railway Board, after talking to Karnataka Chief Secretary Arvind Jadhav: 'How long will this poor situation continue? Review all such railway line projects till 2014 in railway–state partnerships. If states are not interested, drop these projects.' Modi ended the discussion with a cryptic comment: 'There is one Pragati (progress) in this project. The cost has doubled from 900 to 1800 crore.' The pressure could be seen on the faces of the bureaucrats.

Among the programmes reviewed in a Pragati session there was one on solid waste disposal. The prime minister spoke to Chief Secretaries of six different states on their waste removal strategy and priorities and then took a cue from Madhya Pradesh, the chief secretary of which gave a very good account of the state's waste disposal system. The prime minister issued two clear-cut instructions to the nation regarding the future solid waste management strategy. He advised the states to use 8 per cent of plastic waste in the construction of roads as a rule. Next, he said that the making of compost from organic waste should take precedence over power generation because farmers need manure and power generation from waste is a costly affair.

Modi uses a mix of strictness and banter to keep the exercise result-oriented as well as lively. For example, in a lighter moment during one Pragati session, he asked A.K. Mittal, who is seen as one of the most-well-prepared officers in the Pragati exercise, 'Mittalji, you were the opening batsman. How come you are coming at No. 5 position now?' Once he asked the then Rajasthan Chief Secretary C.S. Rajan (now retired): 'Did your parents know that you will become chief secretary one day?' On yet another occasion, when a chief secretary was talking nonstop, Modi was quick to ask: 'Were you a college professor earlier?' In a session to discuss the delay in commissioning the Aurangabad–Boisar power transmission line, when the then Maharashtra Chief Secretary Swadhin Kshatriya said that work on the line had been stalled because of minor issues that would be solved soon to make the project operational, Modi asked: '*Aap kab tak is samasya ko swadhin karvainge*? (How long will you take to fix this problem?)' Kshatriya's reply was prompt: 'Only one tower needs to be erected. Sir, it will be done in a month.'

Some of the projects which have taken off or stand completed because of the Pragati follow-up have been quite old. The rail-cum-road bridge on the River Ganga at Patna had been delayed for more than ten years, its project costs escalating by almost five times to become ₹2900 crore. It was taken up in the first Pragati session on 25 March 2015 and the bridge is operational now. The commissioning of the gauge-conversion project on the Lumding–Silchar railway line in the north-east was delayed by almost a decade because of land acquisition problems and technical issues, resulting in a fivefold escalation in project costs, which stood at ₹3500 crore. Today, the track is functioning after the issue was taken up in the Pragati review.

The PMO conducts the exercise in a spirit that is free of political colour and in keeping with the idea of cooperative federalism. The proof of this are the letters of non-NDA ministers to the prime minister, requesting him to consider their stalled projects under the Pragati exercise. For example, former Uttar Pradesh chief minister Akhilesh Yadav had the Lucknow Metro project discussed under Pragati, thus getting some pending clearances for the project and spurring its woefully slow speed. The Union cabinet also helped the Lucknow Metro project get external loans. Alok Ranjan, a former chief secretary of Uttar Pradesh, observes: 'Pragati is a perfect review model for spurring stalled projects and examining national programmes. It is advantageous to both the Centre and the states. What is great about it is that the states get to place their views directly before the prime minister. The exercise is innovative and also effective.'

The idea of Pragati was mooted by the PMO after Modi viewed presentations from the 55 ministries soon after taking over as prime minister. Every presentation had to be done in just twenty slides, based on the guidelines given. But each session took two or more hours to end as Modi fired off question after question regarding each slide. After these presentations, Modi identified three major areas of infrastructure—energy, transport and digital.

During the exercise, he found that the delays in many projects were due to problems in the land acquisition process, a lack of interdepartmental and interstate coordination (often rooted in ego clashes), the absence of priority caused by a lack of vision and often just simple lethargy. A.K. Sharma, the joint secretary in charge of Pragati at the PMO and Modi's trusted officer since the Gujarat days, says: 'We found that delayed projects placed a lot of stress on the economy in the form of NPAs and escalating project costs and the aimed benefits not accruing to the targeted people. But there was no proper system of monitoring these projects so that they could be put on track quickly. A system for timely review of national programmes and policy-related grievances with nationwide consultation was also needed. That's how Pragati

was born.'[6] A thorough in-house study goes into Pragati
before the projects/programmes are uploaded to the portal for
all stakeholders to see. This is done about two to three weeks
before the actual session. The Pragati exercise is prepared
under Sharma's supervision on the basis of reports from state
governments, Union ministries and departments. The reports
of the Ministry of Statistics and Programme Implementation
and various project-monitoring groups also play a role.

The finalized agenda is uploaded on the Pragati portal for
scrutiny by all stakeholders. That's where the real activity on
the projects starts. After the monthly Pragati exercise is over,
the minutes are sent to the e-Samiksha portal of the cabinet
secretary for the necessary follow-up. Pragati is yet another
gift from Modi's bag of innovative and effective governance,
conducted in a true Team India spirit.

*2. Transforming India campaign on Twitter: A Modi innovation using
a simple hashtag is keeping the ministers and the government machinery
on their toes*

Ram Vilas Paswan, the Union minister for consumer affairs, food
and public distribution, had just 21,400 followers on his Twitter
handle in April 2015. Today the figure has jumped to over 2.21
lakh. It's the same story with a number of other Union ministers,
including Harsimrat Kaur Badal, Kalraj Mishra, Narendra Singh
Tomar and Thawar Chand Gehlot. Kaur's following has risen
by more than six times; and in the cases of Mishra, Tomar and
Gehlot, the number of followers has grown by two to three
times since April 2015. The Twitter handle of Radha Mohan
Singh, the Union agriculture minister, has also seen a surge in
the number of followers.

Did they employ professionals to increase their following?
No, they have become active Twitter players as part of a
unique experiment of Prime Minister Narendra Modi in

innovative governance. The exercise is aimed at achieving three main goals:

1. Keeping the government engaged with the people through the ministers' citizen-centric media interaction on administrative issues, and presenting the government as one entity in the public eye.
2. Keeping the ministers on their toes to improve their performance and, in the process, putting pressure on the bureaucracy down below to perform.
3. Affording an opportunity to himself (the prime minister) to rate ministerial performances and carry out an appraisal of the government.

Aiming at several birds with one stone

In March 2016, the PMO gave a hashtag, '#transformingindia', to all ministers with the instructions that they should tweet on it regularly regarding the outcomes and major announcements in their ministries, and also share these on their Facebook pages. It was implied that their performance on Twitter and Facebook would be monitored, and that non-outcome-based tweets like 'I met so and so person today' or 'I visited so and so place today' won't be considered for the performance rating.

Ministers were thus made to realize that only quality tweets having direct impact on governance and the people would be considered, along with the response they elicit from the common people. Two months later, Modi started a new internal practice of rating each minister on a weekly basis on their Twitter and Facebook performances, giving them scores under three heads: Positive, Negative and Neutral. A source in the PMO, however, says: 'It is a mindset-change exercise to put pressure on the ministers to engage with people on governance issues and also, in turn, bring pressure on the bureaucracy to work harder. It is less of a performance-evaluation exercise, for which there are other important tools.' A senior bureaucrat adds: 'This is an innovative stroke on Modi's part in his now familiar Chanakya-like style wherein he achieves multiple targets with just one decision.'

Win–win for all

The exercise is producing very good results for all—the government as a whole, the ministers, the people and the prime minster himself—and new facts, so far unknown, are coming into the public domain. For example, there is a general feeling that the Ministry of Tourism under Mahesh Sharma (independent charge) is doing badly. But one of his tweets in July 2016 sought to change that impression, at least partially. Sharma tweeted that 4.71 lakh tourists arrived in India on e-tourist visas in the first half of 2016, as against 1.26 lakh in the corresponding period in 2015—a threefold rise. It is a different matter that the success rate was more due to the PMO's pressure and the bureaucracy's efforts.

When Jayant Sinha, the minister of state for civil aviation, tweeted that passengers will have to pay less for cancellation charges because of steps taken by the government, he immediately got a response from one Rajiv Gupta, who asked Sinha to look into the extra charges levied by low-cost airlines like IndiGo and SpiceJet for making seats of choice available to passengers till the 20th row. Gupta was telling Sinha that more needs to be done. It was the same with Nirmala Sitharaman, the minister of state for commerce and industry. When she tweeted that the government had earmarked ₹12,000 crore for training one crore people in skill development, one G.K. Tandon replied to her saying: 'Plan is noble but keep an eye at ground level on execution by government bodies in the real spirit.' Incidentally,

Modi giving a RuPay card to a rural woman in the presence of Uttar Pradesh Governor Ram Naik (third from left): Much before demonetization, the prime minister made sincere efforts to get the common man and the poor to switch to the digital-transaction route by making a series of efforts to popularize the RuPay card of the Government of India.

Modi giving a Mudra loan to a skilled artisan alongside Finance Minister Arun Jaitley: Mudra is a symbol of both the prime minister's commitment and his innovative governance. The scheme has emerged as a pivot of self-employment in India and has played a sustainable role when the job scenario was not good and manufacturing was down.

Modi giving an LPG connection to a poor woman: Modi's Ujjwala scheme for providing subsidized LPG connections to BPL families has opened a new chapter in poverty welfare. Even after seven decades of independence, the nation's 25 crore poor used to cook on the chulha, thus inviting lung-related diseases.

Modi at a programme to encourage cashless payment along with the IT minister, Ravi Shankar Prasad (far left): The prime minister's demonetization salvo has put the country firmly on the track of digital or formal economy, and well on the way to becoming a big economic power.

Courtesy Press Information Bureau

Modi throwing open the NAM portal for farmers with the agriculture minister, Radha Mohan Singh (left), and the IT minister, Ravi Shankar Prasad (right): This is part of the prime minister's vision to eliminate middlemen from the farmers' markets and to double farmers' incomes by 2022.

Courtesy MyGov

Modi conducting a town hall under the aegis of his interactive portal MyGov: Similar to the way Mahatma Gandhi connected common people with the freedom movement by linking khadi weaving to the national struggle, Modi has connected the common man with development through MyGov and his *Mann Ki Baat* radio programme.

Modi and the minister for petroleum and natural gas, Dharmendra Pradhan (front row, fifth from right), at the 2016 Petrotech exhibition: The hydrocarbon sector has seen unprecedented transparency and innovation under Modi, leading to a level playing field.

Modi with Railway Minister Suresh Prabhu (second from left), Minister of State for Civil Aviation Jayant Sinha (in the saffron jacket) and Jharkhand Chief Minister Raghubar Das (in the blue jacket) while flagging off a train: The world's fourth-largest railway network is undergoing a pioneering transformation.

Modi flanked by IT Minister Ravi Shankar Prasad (far right) and Petroleum Minister Dharmendra Pradhan (second from left) at a function: The infrastructure ministries have seen a great turnaround under the Modi government owing to firm decision-making.

PM with his officials during his monthly Pragati exercise in South Block: Pragati symbolizes the precise transformation that Modi is bringing in governance. Modi interacts with chief secretaries of the states to push stalled Centre–state projects and review the Centre's programmes. It has made a positive difference to the non-performing assets of the country.

Modi with his ministers and officials in a meeting against the backdrop of his favourite line: The Modi government has set a good example of 'Team India and Team Modi' by working towards goals in unison. The passing of the GST is a good example and so is Pragati.

Modi with Union Shipping Minister Nitin Gadkari (second from left) and Maharashtra CM Devendra Fadnavis (right) at the 2016 Maritime India Summit: The government's ports have not just improved their performance under the Modi government in an atmosphere of global slowdown, but have also surpassed the performance of private ports in 2016–17. Gadkari has worked to a plan to make it happen in not just the shipping sector but also his other portfolio of road transport and highways.

Courtesy Press Information Bureau

Modi with BJP President Amit Shah: The party chief has been the principal helpmate of Modi in monitoring the performance of ministries and in giving useful ideas about governance, helping him take crucial policy decisions.

Courtesy Press Information Bureau

Modi at a function of his favourite project, Startup India, under which he wants the youth to realize the full potential of their talent and turn into entrepreneurs: 'Become job creators, not job seekers' is Modi's favourite theme.

Modi releasing a booklet in January 2016 on a ten-point action plan for start-ups, along with Finance Minister Arun Jaitley (right) and Minister of State for Commerce and Industry Nirmala Sitharaman (left): Guiding and motivating the youth to cultivate entrepreneurial skills has been one of Modi's priorities as a ruler.

Former French President François Hollande launching Modi's book on climate justice, *Convenient Action—Continuity for Change*, at the COP 21 Summit in Paris: The prime minister has taken the lead on climate change by floating the International Solar Alliance of 121 sunshine nations with its headquarters in Gurgaon, India. Modi's emphasis and arguments on climate change have left even nations like the US impressed.

Modi with BRICS leaders, including Russia's Vladimir Putin (bottom, second from right) and China's Xi Jinping (bottom, centre): Modi has brought about a paradigm shift in India's foreign affairs strategy through his dynamic diplomacy, putting the country in a commanding position at the world level, but managing China and Pakistan remains a challenge. He has visited over fifty countries in less than three years, thus weaving a web of Indian influence across the globe.

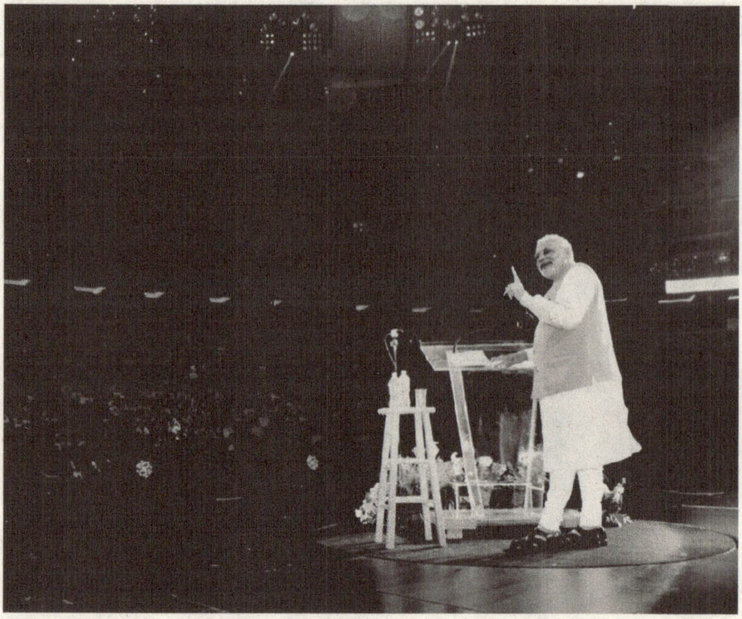

Courtesy Press Information Bureau

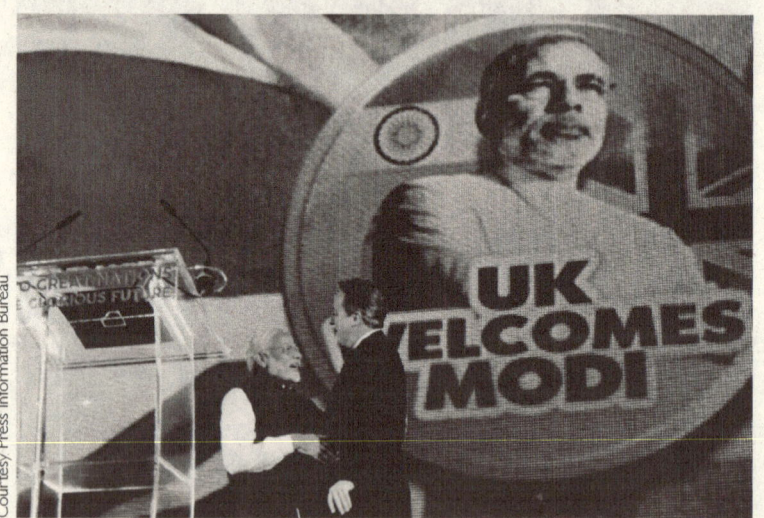

The prime minister addressing an NRI public meet at Madison Square, New York: His talk took the NRI community of the US by storm.

Courtesy Press Information Bureau

Modi addressing NRIs at Wembley Stadium in the UK: The massive crowd that came to listen to Modi by buying tickets left the then British PM, David Cameroon, impressed. Modi's NRI strategy, based on instilling in them pride for their parent country, has turned NRIs into India's brand ambassadors, thus adding to the country's soft power.

PM Modi receiving former French President François Hollande during his 2016 India visit: The two leaders played a key role in shaping the conclusion of the Paris Agreement.

Modi and former US President Barack Obama: The Modi–Obama chemistry took the Indian engagement with the US to a new level in diverse fields, particularly defence, against the hegemony of China, as India emerged as a major partner of the US in forging what could become a new world order, with India in a dominant position.

Modi delivering his address to the US Congress in 2016: The extempore speech has been seen as the best by any Indian prime minister, for its content and response as it got ten standing ovations and sixty-nine rounds of spontaneous applause from the Congressmen.

Modi with Piyush Goyal, minister of state for power: Under the Modi government, the ministries of power, coal, new and renewable energy and mines look vibrant and on track after years of mishandling and corruption. Piyush Goyal has done a result-oriented job of managing these ministries.

Modi defending demonetization at a public function after 8 November: His forceful argument to justify demonetization and the impact of his emotional appeal not only pulled him through what appeared to be a crisis in the initial period, but also showed the power of his oratory and his connection with the common man.

One of the many frightening queues outside banks across India following demonetization: There was, however, not a single public upheaval against the prime minister: This proves that when the intentions of a ruler are good, people are prepared to endure hardships. The BJP's successive electoral victories across India showed the public's support for demonetization.

Courtesy *India Today*

Courtesy *India Today*

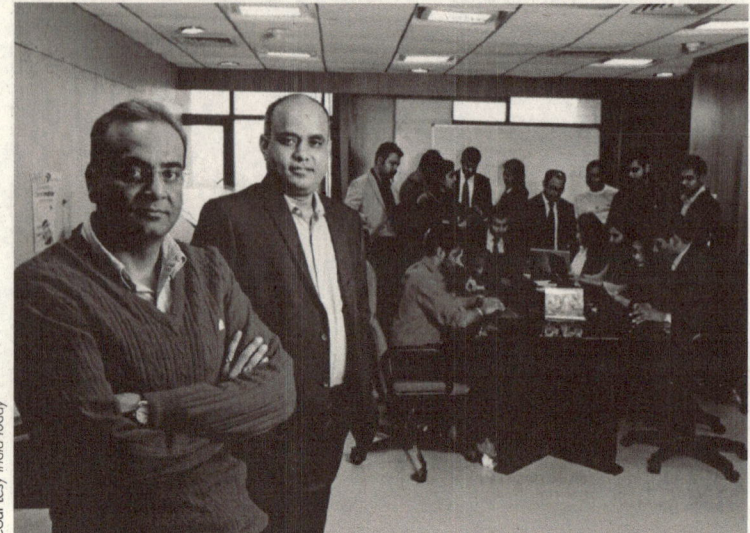

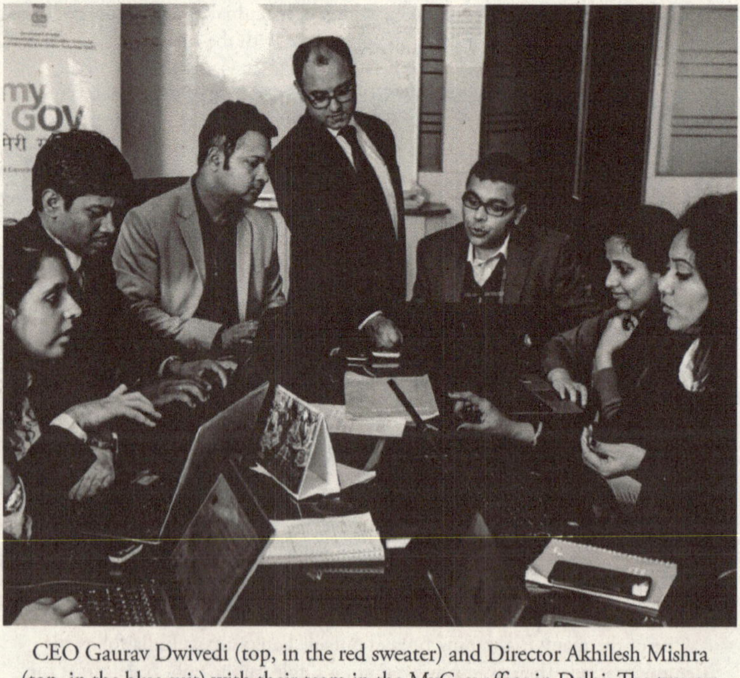

CEO Gaurav Dwivedi (top, in the red sweater) and Director Akhilesh Mishra (top, in the blue suit) with their team in the MyGov office in Delhi: The two are piloting one of Modi's favourite projects to make development a mass movement by incorporating people's suggestions into governance through the interactive platform.

Modi addressing the United Nations General Assembly in 2014: The PM's powerful address left a deep impact on the United Nations when he said that yoga was a medium to connect health with nature. The UN accepted his suggestion to observe 21 June as World Yoga Day every year. The step gave world recognition to an important part of Indian culture.

PM flanked by the minister for power, Piyush Goyal (right), and the then minister for environment and forests, Prakash Javadekar (left), while releasing a book titled *Parampara*: In keeping with its aim of making India a leader in green energy, the Modi government has set an ambitious target of achieving 1.75 lakh MW renewable energy generation capacity by 2022.

Modi's with Minister for Power Piyush Goyal (second from left) and Minister of State for Commerce and Industry Nirmala Sitharaman (far right) at the inauguration of the first Renewable Energy Global Investors' Summit in 2015: Modi has put India on top of the world climate change map.

Private promoters of ITIs protesting against the government's faulty implementation of the policy for setting up private ITIs: Skill development is one area in which the government has to do more to ensure proper implementation of policies.

Sitharaman was tweeting on a subject related not to her ministry but to the Ministry of Skill Development and Entrepreneurship under Rajiv Pratap Rudy (independent charge). She was doing it in response to Modi's direction that ministers should also tweet and share decisions of other ministries to remain engaged among themselves in a 'Team NDA' spirit.

An interesting minister-citizen Twitter exchange was the one that involved Agriculture Minister Radha Mohan Singh. He first tweeted on the steps taken by the government to double farmers' incomes in the next five years. Reacting to this, an institutional Twitter handle, Agrihub, said: 'You need to act with pro-activeness and precision to enhance farm income.' Singh responded by indicating that the government was taking multiple steps in that direction while underlining that it has launched the Paramparagat Krishi Vikas Yojana to promote organic farming.

Several tweets by ministers on outcome-based decisions show what kind of interaction the prime minister wants the ministers to have with the people using #transformingindia. In July 2016, Union Finance Minister Arun Jaitley shared the government's crucial decision to revive defunct fertilizer units in Sindri (in Jharkhand), Barauni (in Bihar) and Gorakhpur (in Uttar Pradesh), indicating the importance of the resolution from the employment point of view. Equally impactful was a tweet of Ravi Shankar Prasad, the minister for IT: '98 lakh people join digital literacy programme. Every skilled person will be e-literate too.' A meaningful tweet came from Jitendra Singh, a minister in the PMO who has the independent portfolio of the north-east: 'Government to offer venture funds to young entrepreneurs for start-ups in North-East.' Maneka Gandhi, minister for women and child development, went several steps further and posted a tweet with a graphic saying: 'Educating about food and nutrition and how to prevent malnutrition.' Power and Coal Minister Piyush Goyal trumpeted one of his big achievements: 'Annual power shortage reduced from 110 million units in 2014 to 14 million units in 2016.'

The PMO's systematic push

In keeping with his ideas aimed at encouraging competition among, Modi retweets selected high-quality tweets of his ministers. In a particular month in 2016, Modi retweeted the tweets of twenty-two of his ministerial colleagues. One of them was by Union Health Minister J.P. Nadda, who had said: 'India has been felicitated by UNICEF for eliminating maternity and neo-natal tetanus.' Such a practice has led to a healthy competition among ministers when it comes to posting achievements of their departments via Twitter and Facebook. A minister observes: 'The Twitter exercise started by the prime minister under Transforming India hashtag should be seen as great innovation in administrative reform. We as ministers couldn't ever dream that a simple hashtag accompanied by a tweeting guideline could directly impact core governance.'

Modi's hashtag move keeps the government machinery working. Knowing that the prime minister is for result-oriented tweets and is even rating their performance, the ministers are ever-agile and put pressure on officials across all levels of bureaucracy to both get work done and collect feedback. It builds a chain in every ministry from minister to secretary and officers below to the departmental head and finally to workers at the ground level. It is turning out to be a two-way communication—from top to bottom and then in reverse. The ministers have to create a structured internal feedback and monitoring system that enables them to track the progress of work on a systematic basis. After the experiment was launched, the PMO organized three one-day training sessions of ministers and their key officers to perfect the exercise. The 'dos and don'ts' on the quality of tweets were explained to them, as was the fact that a monitoring system had been organized under the supervision of the PMO through the government's suggestion-seeking portal, MyGov. All the data that get collected on the hashtag land up at the website, www.mygov.in.

A source in the PMO says: 'This experiment is basically about inter-ministerial coordination and communication and breaking silos in which the ministries used to work, besides maintaining an all-encompassing interface with the people on governance. It is administrative reform using social media tools.' Gaurav Dwivedi, an IAS officer and CEO of MyGov, says: 'More than anything else it is a live government-to-people platform for sharing the government's initiatives and allowing the people to come back with their views. It is part of the government's main aim to transform India with people-centric initiatives. It has many offshoots. One of them is self-rating as it allows people to express their opinion.'[7]

At the modest MyGov office in New Delhi's Electronic Niketan, a dedicated team tracks every minister's Twitter and Facebook accounts almost on a day-to-day basis. At the end of every week, a score sheet showing how every minister has performed during that week lands up at the PMO. The tracking shows how people are reacting to each minister's tweet and the quality of content a minister is presenting. Akhilesh Mishra, director (content) of MyGov, explains: 'The tracking shows the most trending regions and the least trending ones. These in turn indicate in which region the people are engaging the most and in which the least. The tracking also shows on which topic the people are reacting the most.' The experiment is working very well at the moment and has emerged as a symbol of the Team Modi spirit.

5

Building India

Infrastructure and Development

Highways and Roads: On the Fast Track

A.M. Naik, Larsen & Toubro Ltd's executive chairman, has the image of a performer. Coming from Gujarat's dynamic and unbending Anavil Brahmin community, he displays the typical traits of his group. Once he has set a target, he has to meet it, never giving it up midway. Larsen & Toubro has made big strides under his stewardship. But the problems of India's highways and roads sector had descended to such levels in the second term of the UPA government that even a firm man like Naik was shaken. After the NDA government took over on 26 May 2014, Naik met the new Union minister for road transport and highways, Nitin Gadkari, and made his intentions clear. He said L&T was seriously considering withdrawing from the road sector because the projects had become unfeasible due to delays and the resultant cost escalation. Naik expressed his inability to complete the Surat–Jalgaon road project, which L&T was implementing, preferring to pay instead a huge withdrawal penalty. But today Naik is smiling, and not without reason. L&T is now doing projects worth several thousand crores of rupees in the road sector because the minister has put the sector back on track.

Naik says: 'The Modi government has indeed done a very good job of removing the bottlenecks and putting the projects on fast track. Gadkari has revived confidence in India's road sector. Even banking institutions whose funds were held up are happy with him.'[1] Vikram Limaye, CEO and MD of the Infrastructure Development Finance Company Limited, says: 'The banking sector appreciates the way the government has reformed things in the roads sector with a hands-on approach, easing pressure on the banks whose funds were disentangled in the sector.'[2]

Naik and Limaye are only saying what the grand old man of India's corporate sector, Ratan Tata, told Gadkari in 1998 after the latter, as the then Maharashtra roads and buildings minister, decongested the choked Mumbai roads by taking up the biggest-ever flyover construction programme in the history of India's commercial capital and completing it on time. Tata told Gadkari: 'I appreciate your efficiency and boldness to take risk. Perhaps you are a better businessman than me.'[3] The tribute was apt as Gadkari had virtually saved Mumbai from a congestion disaster with his corporate-style, visionary approach. Tata was particularly impressed when Gadkari's ₹400-crore market capital issue floated through a state government subsidiary for his road and flyover building plan was oversubscribed by three times. Gadkari built fifty-four flyovers in Mumbai and earned the label of Mumbai's deliverer. The cost of these bridges was estimated to be ₹1600 crore. The final expenditure was only a little over ₹1000 crore. During that landmark tenure, Gadkari also mooted India's first expressway, between Mumbai and Pune.

Fast forward by two decades and it would seem that Gadkari is producing the same quality of work as the nation's minister of road transport and highways. Experience has perhaps gifted him with a sharper edge. Given the speed and accuracy of his work now, he might end up giving an equally good or an even better performance than his Maharashtra show. The work he has done is best reflected in the example of L&T. The 380-odd delayed road projects worth around ₹4 lakh crore inherited by Gadkari as legacy from a paralysed UPA government also included projects awarded to L&T. The company found them difficult to complete because of massive problems in land acquisition, forest clearance and indecision, which Gadkari is now tackling with skill.

Apart from praise from powerful private players, the turnaround brought about by Gadkari in about three years is also reflected in the figures. When he became the transport minister in 2014, Gadkari set a target of 30 km of road construction per day for two years. He had inherited a speed of 2 km per day, down from 11 km one year earlier under the UPA government. From 2 km to 30 km, the target reflected Gadkari's enthusiasm. Perhaps it also looked too ambitious, almost unreal, and therefore unachievable. But with his hands-on approach, he managed to push the speed to 16.5 km in the first year and to 21 km in the second year. Gadkari explains: 'Setting high target is often taken as a political gimmick. But in my case I purposely do it to gear up the bureaucracy with a tall vision to get the best possible results.'[4] He plans to make the target stiffer in the future as part of his performance-improvement plan.

The minister carried out a surgical operation after studying the delayed projects and the factors behind the delay. Around ₹1 lakh crore worth of old road projects which were difficult to take forward were terminated and another ₹35,000 crore worth of projects put up for rebidding. The rest were taken up for forceful execution. Now delayed projects worth over ₹3 lakh are off the ground. These include the Delhi–Jaipur project, which was delayed by three years, the Nagpur–Jabalpur project, which was awaiting completion for almost a decade due to lack of forest clearances, and the Shivpuri–Dewas and Pune–Solapur ventures. But there are many road projects that remain stalled. Among them are the coastal highway project in Gujarat touching Somnath and Dwarka, and the Delhi–Haridwar and the Dahod–Indore highways.

These seem to be jinxed projects that have simply refused to take off for years and Gadkari will have to show the best of his skills and determination to complete them. Rakesh Chawla, a deeply religious Delhi-based businessman who is a regular visitor to Haridwar, an important place for Hindus, says: 'Soon after he took as over, Minister Gadkari had promised to fix the Delhi–Haridwar road, perhaps one of the most important highways in the country for pilgrims. But the promise remains unfulfilled. The big problems have to be tackled first instead of the smaller ones.'

Problems remain but there is no tardiness on Gadkari's part. In close to three years, he has held nearly ten dozen meetings with bankers, contractors, Union and state road officials, and the environment ministry to untangle the problems that have hindered these projects. As soon as he took over, the Narendra Modi cabinet took twenty-one decisions to clear delayed and stalled road projects. The result: in the first two years of the NDA government that were plagued by back-to-back droughts, the vibrant road sector under Gadkari was a major driver of the Indian economy.

Gadkari wishes to achieve more. In the new road projects worth ₹2 lakh crore awarded under his tenure, 1 per cent of the project cost is reserved for trees and beautification—a first in India's road construction history. As many as 500 truck terminals are being planned on major highways. Each of them will have a dhaba, restrooms, parking space for 200 trucks and tyre-repair points. But the symbol of the Modi government's vision for the road sector is the Setu Bharatam project to make highways free of around 3000 railway crossings by building bridges over them with precast technology. This idea was mooted by Prime Minister Narendra Modi. A thousand of these crossings are on national highways.

As it is with the prime minister, innovation is Gadkari's hallmark. To ensure transparency in dealings and to speed up projects, he has come up with a hybrid model under which both the public and private sectors will invest in road construction but the toll collection will be done by the government. The private company will maintain the road for fifteen years and get paid by the government, which will collect the toll. Another innovative plan is to make thirty-five mega logistical parks at a cost of ₹35,000 crore outside thirty-five big cities of India that are also important business centres. Large trucks will load and unload goods bound for the particular city in the logistical park located outside the city limits on the bypass. Small trucks will then transport the goods inside the city.

This is expected to considerably bring down the transport cost and save time. The work on the project starts in 2017 and will end in three to four years. To achieve his aim of having seamless highways, Gadkari is roping in All India Radio and private radio channels to provide highway advisory services to vehicles. Radio programmes will keep drivers posted about traffic jams, accidents and amenity centres. Vaibhav Dange, Gadkari's OSD and point man in the road sector, says: 'The minister believes that the road network is incomplete without improvement in passenger convenience.'[5]

Yet another aim is to have obstruction-free toll points across the 370 toll plazas in the country. This plan is being implemented at great speed. Under this system, which is being introduced for the first time in India, the vehicle owner/driver will have to buy a prepaid card. This will get him a FASTag, which is to be attached to the vehicle. About 10 feet before the toll plaza, an imaging device will note the tag and the barrier ahead will automatically open for the vehicle. The tag will work across all toll plazas in the country. Gadkari's ministry has also identified 726 accident-prone spots on the Indian highways. Corrective safety measures are being adopted in these places at a cost of

₹11,000 crore. Gadkari has an eye for the smallest detail. Under the new rules, the cabins of truck drivers will have to be air-conditioned. Arun Narendranath, adviser to Gadkari on road transport and highways and shipping, says, 'Such a broad and long-term vision has rarely been seen in the road sector.'[6]

But Gadkari does lament a few things. One of them is his inability so far to facilitate the creation of a judicial structure that can quickly decide on road-project disputes, particularly those relating to land. 'The day that happens, our road dream will be largely free from delays,' he says. But in spite of having ambitious plans, Gadkari has a long way to go when it comes to having an infrastructure akin to that of developed countries. This is one of Modi's favourite ideas too.

The slow work on the Delhi–Haridwar highway and the coastal highway in Gujarat, which together cover the three most important pilgrimage centres of India, is not the only reminder for Gadkari that he still has a long way to go. The Patna–Gaya highway is unsafe because of the huge potholes on the road and on the sides. Arvind Kumar, a Patna-based lawyer, says: 'It is appalling because Gaya is a most important place of pilgrimage for both Hindus and Buddhists. Rather it is an international tourist spot for Buddhists.'[7] But no one doubts Gadkari's capability as a problem-solver. It is an aptitude Gadkari has been identified with ever since he found a solution to Mumbai's traffic congestion problem in the 1990s with his messianic zeal and innovative thinking.

Major Ports—From Slump to Symmetry

Gokul Agro Resources Ltd of the Gandhidham-based businessman Hitesh Thakkar has been in the edible oil import business for quite some time now. Originally from Sindh, Thakkar's family came to Gandhidham in the Kutch district as a refugee following India's partition. The family was lucky in that, around the same time, the Government of India decided to develop the Kandla port near Gandhidham to make up for the loss of the Karachi port, which had gone to Pakistan after Partition. The development of the Kandla port gave an instant platform to the Sindhi refugees to delve into and expand various businesses. Almost every major business activity in Gandhidham today is in some way linked to the Kandla port. Thakkar has been a stoic businessman. But these days an atypical happiness shines through.

The reason: the logistical cost of the edible oil worth ₹200 crore he imports through Kandla port every month has come down from 15 per cent to almost 5 per cent in 2015–16, thanks to the innovative changes in the management system introduced by the Union Ministry of Shipping to cut down the loading and unloading time of goods at all the twelve major ports it controls across India. Thakkar says: 'The change is for real. We are feeling its impact.'[8]

Before the advent of the Narendra Modi government in 2014, a vessel had to wait for three to ten days outside the Kandla port before it could be berthed. That resulted in huge demurrage charges to the importer. Now it takes just two days. Says Ravi Parmar, chairman of Kandla Port Trust: 'The cost of handling dry cargo has come down by 25 per cent to ₹60 per tonne, which is one of the lowest in the country. A series of innovative measures are responsible for this.'[9] According to an estimate, the importers and exporters of Kandla port are saving up to ₹100 crore in logistical costs annually. No wonder then that the traders of Kandla are all praise for Nitin Gadkari, the Union minister for shipping, the man behind the innovative changes in this sector.

But they are not an exception. In south India too, port users appreciate the transformation. The Tamil Nadu Generation and Distribution Corporation Limited (TANGEDCO) is one of the entities happy with the ministry these days. This corporation, which brings coal to Tamil Nadu from the mines in east India through the Paradip, Ennore and Tuticorin ports, saw savings of ₹78 crore in logistical costs in just one year, during 2015–16. The trend continues for the company, thanks to the improvement in the efficiency of these ports and the dramatic increase in their cargo-handling capacity as a result of the decrease in loading and unloading time.

The story of the twelve major ports under the shipping ministry is broadly the same. They have added a capacity of 270 million tonnes in less than three years till 2016–17— the highest in the major port sector in any given three years. The addition in the cargo-handling capacity of these twelve ports has sent operational profits soaring by ₹1800 crore from ₹3200 crore to ₹5000 crore during the period in what looks like a continuing trend. What is noteworthy is that the twelve government ports have registered a rise of 6.9 per cent in cargo handling in 2016–17 as against a mere 3.7 per cent rise by the private port sector, showing that the government's ports have eaten into the share of the private sector. The increase in efficiency has saved around ₹3000 crore in logistical costs for the clients on account of faster loading and unloading following the tightening measures by Gadkari. Small wonder then that the Kandla traders and companies like TANGEDCO are happy. A TANGEDCO spokesperson comments: 'The shipping ministry has done a splendid job of improving performance of the ports by just changing the style of functioning and applying modern management systems. It's certainly a turnaround.'

As soon as Gadkari came, he started changing the rules of the game. The focus was on getting maximum results by exploiting the full potential of the twelve ports. In a dynamic move comparable to that of CEOs of corporate houses, he said that performers and laggards won't be treated in the same way. 'The performers have to be encouraged and the laggards penalized but what is happening is exactly the opposite,' he said. In keeping with his vision, his ministry introduced a new set of rules that fixed the time for the ports' clients for loading and evacuating the goods, depending on the nature of the cargo. Based on this measure, efficiency charges were fixed.

Those who finished before the deadline now got concessions and those who exceeded the deadline had to pay penal charges. The move was introduced after increasing the loading and unloading capacity at all the ports to send a message to the private sector that the government meant business. Rajgopal Sharma, OSD to Gadkari in the shipping ministry, says: 'The saving to the national exchequer due to decrease in the turnaround time of ships is in fact much bigger if the fuel saving of ships and the foreign exchange saved on that count is considered along with the decrease in carbon dioxide emission in the global warming context.'[10]

How the logistical costs were brought down by increasing efficiency makes for an interesting story. When the Modi government came to power, the turnaround time of a ship was two days (the time that a container ship takes on an average to load and unload) against the global standard of one day. Now the turnaround time has been reduced by 40 per cent. The changes at Paradip port are exemplary. Against a load-handling capacity of 4000 tonnes per hour, the port's ship loader was doing just 1300 tonnes, a third of its actual capacity. As a result of the tightening of screws through the spread of awareness, the continuous monitoring by Gadkari himself and the use of online apps, Paradip now handles 2700 tonnes per hour. At a daily capacity of 1300 tonnes, only fifteen ships were loaded at Paradip every day, as against the thirty ships being loaded now. The rate of coal loading at Paradip was 30,000 tonnes per day earlier. It is 60,000 tonnes now.

The rate of loading and unloading of oil at Kandla has also risen, from 6000 tonnes to 8500 tonnes per day. At the Ennore port, the coal unloading has gone up from 22,000 tonnes to 38,000 tonnes per day. Kandla is proving to be a great turnaround story. In 2014–15, its coal-handling capacity was just 4 million tonnes a year. In 2016–17, it came close to 16 million tonnes, taking in the process the market share of competing private ports.

Innovative and bold measures made all the difference. For example, very large ships couldn't be anchored at Kandla because of its comparatively low draught (water depth). So Gadkari decided to start trans-loading operations at Kandla for the first time. It meant anchoring large ships mid-sea, using floating cranes to unload them and taking the help of small ships to bring the cargo to the port for the final unloading. Gadkari says: 'India had so far failed to exploit the full potential of the ports. We aimed at bringing down the logistical costs of domestic goods through a port-led economy.'

Mitesh Dharamshi, who heads the Kandla Port Steam Ship Agents Association, remarks: 'The 40 per cent increase in efficiency that the Kandla port has witnessed in the past two years is due to the system of efficiency and penal charges introduced for the clients. This system is new in the port's history. Clients are making huge amounts in logistical cost saving because the laid-back culture has been replaced with a result-oriented one.'[11] The port is now in the process of getting its own mobile harbour crane for the first time to increase handling capacity by five times to 120 tonnes.

The ministry is not leaving any stone unturned when it comes to bringing down the logistical cost to the optimum level. In the process it is employing bold and innovative methods. By partnering with IIT Madras, the ministry has found a way out of the problem of high dredging costs at many ports. The Kolkata port used to spend ₹430 crore annually on dredging. IIT experts found a solution to the problem by conducting a precise hydrological study and discovering a new channel to the port that requires less dredging. This has brought the dredging cost down by ₹200 crore to ₹230 crore a year. A new, less costly dredging technique is also being tried out. It is expected to reduce the dredging cost at the Ennore port from ₹180 crore to ₹110 crore annually and at Cochin port from ₹130 to ₹90 crore.

Gadkari's plan for improving the ports took root when his ministry hired the Boston Consulting Group (BCG), a US-based management consulting firm with which Urjit Patel, now the governor of the RBI, was associated earlier. The minister asked the group to draw up a plan to increase the efficiency of the ports. After a careful study, the group came out with its findings and a list of suggestions to enhance performance. Its main conclusion was that the ports were performing far below their potential capacity as their equipment was underutilized due to ignorance or lethargy. As many as 104 initiatives for the twelve major ports were identified under Project Unnati (Progress), which are benchmarking studies aimed at enhancing their performance in terms of time and cost while avoiding capital expenditure.

These have to be implemented by 2019. But over fifty of these have already been executed. Due to these initiatives, the performance monitoring system has undergone a radical change. Gadkari and Shipping Secretary Rajive Kumar get a day-to-day report on each port's performance in terms of the time taken in the loading and unloading of goods, among other indicators. The ministry has invested ₹30,000 crore for the upgrading of the port infrastructure by involving private players. In this drive, the emphasis is on mechanization to meet the best international standards. There had been a huge gap among ports when it came to mechanization. It varied from just 30 per cent at the Kolkata port to 90 per cent at the Ennore port.

Ports have largely been seen in India in terms of exports and imports and not as a platform for inland trade. The core vision of Modi and Gadkari is to use and expand the port infrastructure to bring down the logistical costs of domestic inland trade. In China, the logistical cost of goods is one-third of India's because it has an extensive port network. Modi and Gadkari believe that manufacturing competitiveness can come only through port-based industrialization. For example, 30 per cent of the Indian garment exports today is done by air—which result in a transportation cost that is four times the money spent on transportation by sea. Interestingly, the average distance between ports and the major industrial centres is 700 km in India, while it is 300 km in China and less than 100 km in South Korea.

Arun Narendranath, adviser to the shipping ministry, observes: 'The vision of the entire ministry has undergone a change. Under the new vision of the prime minister and shipping minister, ports are as important for the domestic trade as the Exim trade. The improvement in performance is due to the change in vision.'[12] Significantly, no major port has come up in the country in the past two decades. So Modi and Gadkari plan to add six new ports as part of their newly mooted Sagarmala programme, which is aimed at port-led development. The Sagarmala project, which is now ready for implementation, aims to cut down logistical costs by ₹40,000 crore per annum—₹30,000 crore in domestic cost savings and ₹10,000 crore in exports and imports.

Not a single Indian port is located on a major international shipping route. China has taken advantage of this by investing in the Colombo and Hambantota ports in Sri Lanka that are on a major international shipping route. Modi and Gadkari plan to make a large transhipment hub in the southern tip of India to counter the Chinese presence in the two Sri Lankan ports. As part of this plan, the Kerala government is developing the Vizhinjam port by roping in the Adani Group. The Modi government has sanctioned another port at Enayam in Tamil Nadu. The two ports will be located on a major international shipping route. Right now, all Indian goods bound for the West have to go via Sri Lanka, Singapore or Dubai before reaching their final destinations.

A new plan for inland waterways is also being developed to bring down the logistical costs of the inland transfer of goods. As a first step, work has begun on the 1600-km-long Varanasi–Haldia Ganga waterway with a view to converting the Ganga into an economic lifeline for poorer states like Bihar, Uttar Pradesh, Jharkhand and West Bengal. The project is based on the way China converted the Yellow River into a cheap transport medium, thereby offsetting the disadvantage of non-maritime regions. With an investment of ₹4000 crore, the work is on to construct four multimode terminals on the Ganga at Varanasi, Ghazipur, Sahibganj and Haldia. The Ganga has on an average a depth of 3 metres, which is enough to carry barges of 3000-tonne capacity—which is equivalent to 100 large trucks or one goods train. Looking at the port and inland waterways sector as one of logistics solution providers constitutes the new vision of the shipping sector. But experts believe that converting the ideas related to inland waterways into action will turn out to be a stupendous task for the simple reason that the concept is new to the country.

One of the factors behind the greatness attributed to the Maratha warrior-statesman Chhatrapati Shivaji is his foresightedness in seeing the sea and inland waterways as corridors for commerce and security. Similarly, Narendra Modi demonstrated a special vision for Gujarat while showcasing Gujarat's coastal strength. Now, in Delhi, he has found the right man in Nitin Gadkari for the conversion of that vision into reality. A former mariner now working for an MNC in the port sector says: 'In just close to three years there has been a 180-degree turn in the port sector. The sector will soon be seen as an end-to-end provider of logistical solutions.'

The change is not cosmetic or restricted to a few areas. Satinder, a mariner attached to a foreign-bound commercial ship, didn't get the receipt for a particular fee he had to pay online in 2016. That seemed to delay his vessel's departure as the payment of that fee was mandatory. Satinder took the help of a new system started by Gadkari. He filed a complaint on a dedicated Twitter account of Rajgopal Sharma, Gadkari's OSD, to have a look. Sharma forwarded the tweet to a dedicated WhatsApp account handled by the director general of shipping. Satinder immediately got the confirmation and the commercial vessel started moving.

A couple of years earlier, this process might have taken a lot of time, resulting in a delay in the vessel's schedule. But now all the processes for the mariners have been standardized. As an indication of a truly hands-on approach, Sharma himself invites complaints so that these are immediately addressed. The application and approval process for various tests have been made online. For the first time in the history of India's ports, every survey that the surveyor under the director general of shipping is doing is an actual physical survey of the ship. Till 2014, the survey of a ship by a surveyor was just a matter of signing a paper for the purpose of keeping a record. Now, the inspection report of the ship has to be filed online with proof in the form of actual photographs. Geotagging ensures that the photographs can't be tampered with by the inspecting officials.

But the vision is not without holes. Investors' confidence in the Indian shipping sector remains comparatively low because of the disputes going on between leading investors and the shipping ministry on account of the retrospective regulations slapped by the A.B. Vajpayee government fifteen years ago. The companies involved in these disputes are leading international players like the Maritime and Port Authority of Singapore, DP World and APM Terminals, which is associated with the Danish firm Maersk Group. A solution to these disputes is yet to be found by the ministry.

Soon after it took over, the Modi government had promised to turn the shipping ministry's ports from trusts to corporations in order to bring professionalism. But the promise remains unfulfilled. It is not surprising then that foreign investors are more inclined towards investing in the ports of a small country like Sri Lanka rather than in those of India.

Piyush Goyal—Man on a Mission

Six months after Piyush Goyal, the Union minister of state for power, coal and new and renewable energy, had launched a grand project to sell LED bulbs to people and institutions at low prices as part of his green energy initiative in January 2015, he happened to meet Prime Minister Narendra Modi at a meeting. When the two were coming out of the meeting, Modi asked Goyal about the total number of LED bulbs sold till that date. Goyal was nonplussed. He was frank though. He told the prime minister that he didn't know the exact figure. Modi then sat him down and gave him a small lesson on the importance of day-to-day monitoring of projects for getting the best results. The upshot of this dialogue was the National Ujala Dashboard, an app made at Goyal's behest that shows the real-time sale of LED bulbs in the country.

This gives a glimpse into two things: Modi's vision and style of functioning in carrying forward his ideas of development and the sincerity of Goyal in taking Modi's vision to its logical end. Goyal is a man possessed. Call him during the day on his personal mobile phone and you will invariably get a return call the same night if your topic of discussion is his work in replicating the Gujarat model in the power sector all over India. If asked questions on this subject, a tired Goyal is suddenly on his feet and eager to share his 'exploits'. Goyal is a living example of a '24x7 minister', geared towards the 'Mission of 24x7 Power for All'. His hands-on and meticulous approach has taken the power sector to new heights in less than three years. India is now poised to become a power-surplus nation for the first time since Independence. Goyal follows a multipronged approach, laying equal emphasis on all aspects, from coal, mining and renewable energy generation to improving the power transmission and distribution network. His approach and attitude is best summarized by the high praise he elicits from power officials and even ministers of non-NDA states.

A policy paralysis had affected the power and energy sector because of corruption and mismanagement under the UPA. The results produced by Goyal's hard work are there for all to see now. The level of transparency he has managed to introduce is unprecedented. India registered its highest-ever growth in coal production in the first two years of his tenure, with Coal India Limited (CIL) producing 538 million tonnes in 2015–16. A comparison of the conditions prevailing between 2014 and 2016 in the three major power-related portfolios Goyal holds, gives a sharp picture of the difference he has made. The day Goyal took over as the power minister, as much as two-thirds of the major power plants had critical coal stocks, meaning stocks for less than seven days, and plants with an aggregate capacity of 24,000 MW were lying unutilized. Now there is none. Most of them have stocks for around fifty-one days now. For the first time in history, Goyal opened up the mines for auction (e-auctions) and introduced the system of reverse bidding to encourage stiffer competition in order to get as many offers as possible from the private sector, thus bringing down the cost of thermal power, the benefits of which are being passed on to the consumers.

Prakash Goel, a research analyst on utilities and fertilizers and vice president of ICICI Securities Ltd, observes: 'Under the new dispensation Coal India has seen a complete transformation from a monopoly coal producer to an energy solution provider, thanks to the change in its vision. It is moving away from being an indispensable partner to a preferred partner. It is because of a sharp improvement in employees' communication which is visible in employees' focus and performance.'[13] For example, the PSU has opened an online portal for contract labourers in coal fields who have come via private contractors to ensure that they get wages and benefits as per industry standards. The wages of the labourers are deposited directly in their bank accounts and the labourers can see their names registered on the portal. 'My trust in Coal India has gone up by many times because of its attitude towards the daily wager,' says Ranjit Kumar Chaudhary, a worker in a CIL mine.[14] Justice is also being done for the first time by CIL to small and medium enterprises (SMEs).

Under a new system, the SMEs are provided with coal through an SME portal in a transparent manner. This has made a huge difference for this lot, which had been marginalized earlier by bigger players and had to buy coal from the black market at exorbitant rates for survival. They had to bear this in spite of being better job creators, in a way, than the big companies. Aqueel Anjum of Maharaja Processors, a small enterprise in Burhanpur, Madhya Pradesh, agrees: 'The high level of transparency is indeed laudable. The SMEs have a voice now.'[15]

Towards the end of 2016, India's power deficit stood at its lowest ever, at 14 million units, down from 110 million units in 2014. The country is fast moving towards a power-surplus scenario—a result of multiple measures, including the laying of 50,215 ckm (circuit kilometres) of transmission lines over 2014–16. This is the most undertaken in any two straight years and the rate is 1.5 times higher than in the preceding two years, i.e. 2012–14. As a series of firsts gets recorded in the history of India's coal, power and renewable energy sectors under Goyal's stewardship and Modi's watchful eyes, the ambitious targets set by them seem to be within reach. But the targets are quite formidable—doubling coal production to 1 billion tonnes per year by 2020, and a fourfold increase in power consumption by 2030, along with a fivefold increase in renewable energy capacity to 1.75 lakh MW by 2022, in addition to energy saving of 10 per cent (of current energy consumption) by 2020.

A confident Goyal says: 'Surplus, cheap and environment-friendly power with transparency is our governing mantra.'[16] Goyal's secretary, Anuj Gupta, an IIT Madras graduate, tracks the progress of 100 major power plants on a day-to-day basis. Gupta collects data through SMS and collates them prior to placing it before his minister every morning. If a plant is underperforming then Goyal moves in with a whip. All this sounds like sweet music when one recalls that horrible day in July 2012 when 62 crore people were thrown into darkness as a result of a national power breakdown. A major step that has made a huge difference is the selection of the right officials. Distribution companies (discoms) are handled by A.K. Verma, a joint secretary from Gujarat who had done a good job at Gujarat's discoms. Similarly, Vivek Bhardwaj, joint secretary, coal, has a clean record.

One index of success is the money saved as a result of the increased transparency in dealings in the coal sector. While the CAG calculated a loss of ₹1.86 lakh crore to the exchequer due to corruption and irregularities in the allotment of mines under the UPA tenure, auctions of the same mines under the NDA, acting on directions from the Supreme Court, will result in a potential revenue of ₹3.44 lakh crore to coal-bearing states during the lifetime of the mines. Additionally, the transparent auctions to meet the coal demand have saved more than ₹24,000 crore for the country by reducing coal imports. The figure could touch ₹40,000 crore annually in the future. Ashok Jhunjhunwala, a power expert who teaches at IIT Madras, says: 'The turnaround in the power sector is for real. And it touches almost every sphere of the sector. But there is still a way to go when one talks of electricity without breakdown for the entire country.'[17]

Goyal knows what Jhunjhunwala is referring to here. Hence, the power ministry's work to electrify the 18,452 non-electrified villages in the country is going on at a breakneck speed. Over 70 per cent of villages have already been electrified in more than two and a half years (the original plan was to cover all villages in 1000 days) and the initiative appears well ahead of schedule. That a change is coming is reflected in the way the Union power ministry has taken up the domestic efficient lighting programme by selling LED bulbs through Energy Efficiency Services Limited (EESL), a PSU. When the NDA took over, the sale of LED bulbs was about 6 lakh units annually. In a little over two and a half years, the government sold a whopping 20 crore bulbs, which is over 300 times more than the previous figure. The reasons behind this transformation: standardization of specifications, increased volume and complete transparency. These brought down the price of an average bulb by almost six times as compared to 2014—from ₹330, an LED bulb is now available for just around ₹60. The price is expected to come down further. The Modi government's renewable energy initiative has impressed global experts.

One of the best compliments to the Union government for its efforts in the solar energy sector was given by Michael T. Eckhart, MD and global head of environmental finance and sustainability at Citibank, who has paid over twenty-two visits to India in the past two decades. He says: 'The Modi government is one of the best examples of a government understanding the issue in minimum possible time and addressing it effectively from a public policy point of view. Some countries have taken up to three decades to evolve in this sector because of their step-by-step approach. I must compliment Prime Minister Modi for his vision.'[18] What has impressed professionals like Eckhart are the government's attempts to bring down the per-unit cost of solar power and, as a result, reduce tariffs. Goyal has achieved this with the help of multiple measures like reverse bidding and the decision to make strong entities like NTPC Limited sign projects with big solar companies so that investors and promoters are assured of their future safety in terms of returns. When the NDA came to power, the ongoing per unit cost of solar power was around ₹7. In 2016, in one particular project in Rajasthan, it came down to ₹4.34 per unit, and in 2017, to ₹3.30. This is a big development considering the fact that the Central Electricity Regulatory Commission still allows up to ₹7 per unit.

Dawn of discoms and the road to recovery

One of the biggest challenges before Goyal was how to improve the power scenario when power is on the concurrent list. It

was believed that many states ruled by opposition parties would
not follow the NDA government's directives to take strong
apolitical measures in improving the power distribution systems
in those states. The politics of giving free or subsidized power at
the cost of the exchequer has made a mockery of the country's
power distribution system. But Goyal acted with guile and
transparency while dealing with the states on their discoms.
Instead of behaving like a big brother, he went to them with
an attractive discom-revival package called Ujwal Discom
Assurance Yojana (Uday), which has impressive incentives for
the states. The combined debt of the discoms in September
2015 was ₹4.3 lakh crore—a reflection of the political use of the
power sector by previous governments to seek votes.

Uday provides relief on the interest being paid by discoms
on 75 per cent of their loans by moving the loans from the
discoms to their state governments and also by sharing a part
of the interest burden. The reason is that under the prevalent
norms, discoms have to pay 12–13 per cent interest on loans,
while the states pay 8 per cent on their loans—a huge difference
of 4 to 5 percentage points. Earlier too, the discoms' loans were
being paid by the state government, although they had been
taken directly by the discoms. The shift makes all the difference
to the discoms. But while helping the states to overcome their
discom debt, Uday also binds them to take efficiency-oriented
measures like upgrading transformers, deploying smart meters
and launching campaigns against power theft. Twenty-four
states and union territories have already given their consent to
join Uday, of which 22 states and union territories have already
signed memoranda of understanding (MoUs) with the Centre.

To create an atmosphere of cooperative federalism, Goyal
holds regular monthly meetings with state power secretaries to
sort out matters in person. The meetings are also attended by
the MDs of discoms. Additionally, he organizes a state power
ministers' conference every six months. Goyal observes: 'Politics

is all about power but I am taking power out of politics.' Uday certainly creates hope of a big revival in discoms. Rajasthan, which has seized the Uday initiative and restructured its discoms accordingly, is a good example. Its discoms will be earning profits from next year. The discoms of Haryana and Andhra Pradesh governments too are on the path of improvement. According to P.K. Pujari, the Union power secretary, Uday has already started bringing down the losses of some of the discoms, which are poised to make a turnaround by 2017-end.

Vinayak Chatterjee, a strategic adviser to many companies and government institutions, sums up the performance succinctly. Chatterjee says: 'We have to just compare the state of the power sector in the summer of 2014 with the summer of 2016 to appreciate the transformation. The recovery staged is simply phenomenal in a span that is very small in a nation's economic history. I would call it the single largest burst of creative energy ever. Uday has prevented a tsunami of NPAs hitting the banking sector.'[19] Like Chatterjee, most observers believe that the ministry is moving quite confidently in the direction of One Nation, One Grid and One Price, which, in effect, means a uniform rate of power across India and uniform transmission through a common grid.

It sounds like a dream, but there are enough indications that the day this will start happening on a regular basis is not very far off in a country where rates have varied abnormally from state to state and region to region, based on various factors. For example, on one particular day in 2016 a unit of power was selling for as low as ₹2.26 per unit in south India, where it used to cost over ₹4 per unit not long time ago. Goyal says: 'The possibility of power flowing seamlessly across India at the same price looks like a reality because the interstate transmission line laying work is going on at high speed and there is the prospect of greater availability of much cheaper renewable energy and surplus power.'[20]

The Modi government's power push with its emphasis on the latest technology is also helping the growth of the power-related market. If the LED lights sector is growing fast, ancillary industries in the power sector are marching ahead in a phase of relatively low manufacturing. A good example is Goyal's drive to induct dry transformer bushings made with resin-impregnated paper technology to reduce fire accidents in electric transformers. The oil-pregnated paper bushings, which are now being discouraged, caused these accidents. The moment the power ministry took the decision, a small Baroda-based manufacturer of transformer bushings, Keyur Shah, tied up with a Swiss company to make these new type of bushing in Baroda. In more than one year, the turnover of his company, Yash High Voltage Insulators, has increased by 100 per cent to ₹25 crore. Says Shah: 'The PM's Make in India campaign and the drive for latest technology in the power ministry has really helped many like me. There is an atmosphere of growth.'[21]

The renewable energy vision

What EESL, the power ministry's vehicle for selling LED lights, is bringing about at the micro level in terms of energy savings is a coup of sorts. Virtually the new pivot of energy efficiency in the country, it has multiple aims, chief among which is replacing 3.5 crore ordinary streetlights with LEDs under the Ujwal Bharat scheme by 2019. The target seems tough as there has not been much to show till now in terms of achievement, thanks to the resistance on the part of municipal bodies. Since palm-greasing is a part of the work culture in many of these municipal bodies and the EESL programme doesn't offer anything in that direction, progress has been slow. Saurabh Kumar, the MD of EESL and the man behind the imminent reform, says: 'We are trying innovative ways to increase our sales in not just the street lighting sector but also across sectors.'[22]

One look and the efforts indeed appear innovative. EESL has suggested a tripartite agreement between the state discoms, municipalities and EESL, under which the latter replaces streetlights with LED lights in the town concerned and recovers the cost from the energy savings of the municipal body. A hundred and thirty of the 300 bodies that have signed the agreement so far have already been covered. But the total number of lights replaced has not reached even 10 per cent of the target. An insider says that EESL and Goyal will have to put pressure on the municipal bodies to cut red tape.

EESL also has a plan to replace the pumps of farmers with energy-saving machines. According to a study by the power ministry, as many as 20 crore agro pumps in the country—which help farmers draw groundwater for irrigation purposes—are inefficient and demand repair every three to six months. Every time, the repair work costs ₹5000 to ₹10,000. So EESL has undertaken an agro pump replacement plan similar to its tripartite scheme to replace streetlights. After a tripartite agreement among EESL, the discom and the farmer, EESL will replace the pump costing ₹30,000 for a five-horsepower device in the farm at just the installation cost. The farmer won't have to pay anything extra as the energy saving will take care of the pump's cost.

EESL has emerged as one of India's best start-up companies despite being a government subsidiary. A credible international study has put the potential of India's energy-efficient sector (different from new and renewable energy) at ₹1.6 lakh crore. EESL's task is to tap this potential by identifying and then harnessing opportunities. By February 2017, EESL had sold over 21 crore LED bulbs across the country under the Ujwal scheme. The money this exercise is saving for the country is simply stunning—₹1100 crore annually and over 2.45 crore MW-hour in terms of energy.

Goyal has added over 26,000 MW in renewable-energy generation capacity in less than three years. If the rate of growth is maintained over the next four years, the target of achieving 1.75 lakh MW by 2022 doesn't seem to be a very challenging one. The progress is particularly good in the area of solar energy generation when compared with the figures of 2014, when the Modi government took over. The solar capacity stands at over 10,000 MW in the NDA tenure, up from 3000 MW earlier. The wind energy production too has seen a significant increase.

The country's total renewable-energy generation capacity was around 31,000 MW in May 2014 when the Modi government took over. It stood at 57,250 MW in March 2017. So the NDA government's performance is much better than the UPA's since the latter had taken several years to create that capacity which the NDA has done in just over two and a half years.

There are signs that solar energy generation might grow faster in the coming days, with the per-unit solar energy cost in 2017 having come down to ₹3.30, which is even cheaper than thermal energy. But even before the cost decreased, the implementation of projects of 30,000 MW, valued at ₹1.50 lakh crore, had already started. Projects with a capacity of 6500 MW are functional, in addition to the 2700 MW projects commissioned before the Modi government came to power. Santosh Vaidya, joint secretary, new and renewable energy, says: 'The coming down of the solar generation cost to around ₹3 per unit is a great development. It could end up spurring phenomenal growth at the national level.'[23] The sooner it happens the better it will be.

Prime Minister Narendra Modi has assumed international leadership in the renewable energy sector by putting together with his wise diplomacy the ISA (International Solar Alliance) of 121 countries. So India has to meet its tall renewable energy target set for 2022, come what may. However, as a writer, it is my duty to share here a very important episode involving me and Modi. The episode is directly connected to India's march in the new and renewable energy sector and gives an idea of the prime minister's vision.

Modi has to be called the father of India's solar energy revolution if we take into account the risks he took in coming up with the most attractive solar energy policy in India's history when he was Gujarat's chief minister in 2009. Modi had centred the policy on a high rate of return to solar entrepreneurs against the warning of many doubting Thomases that the rate he offered would plunge Gujarat into a financial crisis in the future. When I raised the question to him in 2009 as the associate editor of *India Today* in charge of Gujarat, Modi's reply was: 'It is foolhardy not to tap the abundant solar energy in this country because of the fear of paying a high price in the initial period. Let Gujarat take the lead in it. So what if the cost is high today, let Gujarat bear the high cost if the entire country is going to benefit from it in the future.' When the solar generation cost came down to around ₹3 per unit in February 2017, Modi's words turned out to be true.

New and renewable energy is one area in which Goyal will have to remain proactive, given the fact that it is on Modi's international agenda as part of his world strategy on climate change. Goyal's aide, Bhoovan Soral, exudes confidence: 'We have a plan to achieve our targets. In that plan, takeoff is steady, but once it gathers speed, capacity addition will be very fast.'[24] But an area in the sector that invites a critical look is the in-house manufacturing of solar panels. The country's solar generation capacity is largely dependent on panels imported from China. Adequate efforts to produce the panels in India have not been made despite the Make in India initiative. The renewable energy target will continue to face some execution risks as long as it relies on imported raw materials and components.

Progress reports on palms

Taking technology to a new level, the power ministry has developed an app (Garv-II) that shows the real-time electrification of villages on your handset. Similarly, one can track in real time the number of LED bulbs sold every minute, on the Ujala Dashboard. An SMS on the status report of the coal scenario comes to Goyal every day from CIL. It shows the target for the day against the coal produced and also the figure for coal production on the day against the annual target. The number of railway rakes loaded for coal transportation is displayed too. But the great change brought about by Goyal involves the Vidyut Pravah app, which he has connected to the India Electricity Exchange, which records the supply and demand of power in the country every fifteen minutes and sells surplus power at a price based on a well-structured demand–supply mechanism. Anybody, whether a private company or a state government's power subsidiary, can buy power from the exchange if it finds the rates attractive or affordable. Goyal himself tweets the rate and the time slots coming up on Vidyut Pravah when these are striking. For example, on a particular day during the monsoons in 2016, power was available for as low as ₹2.15 per unit in one time slot. Goyal was quick to tweet the price. The challenger seems clearly capable of meeting the challenge.

Suresh Prabhu—Leaving Nothing to Chance

Railways: Fast forward

Suresh Prabhu, the Union minister for railways, has an unusual way of functioning that is indicative of his style. A few months ago, while leaving for the Delhi airport from Rail Bhavan on his way to Jaipur, he hurriedly asked his OSD, Anant Swarup, to hop into his car. Prabhu started giving Swarup a list of tasks that needed a follow-up. By the time they reached the airport, the list had grown to six items. Dropping Prabhu at the airport, Swarup headed back to the office. There was a severe traffic jam, which delayed him. When he was about to reach his destination, his phone started ringing. It was Prabhu on the other side asking for an update on the follow-up list. Prabhu had landed at Jaipur, which is a twenty-five-minute journey by air from Delhi, before Swarup could reach Rail Bhavan. An astonished Swarup told Prabhu, 'Sir, let me at least reach the office before I start clearing up the list.'[25]

That's Suresh Prabhu, a man in fast-forward mode. This quality of his is getting reflected in the pace of his work in the railway ministry, which had initially given the impression of being slow in decision-making. There have been drastic improvements not only in the day-to-day working of the world's fourth-largest railway network, but also in the pace at which railway expansion is taking place. This is having a deep impact on the lowering of the logistical costs of transporting goods in the country. There is a visible shift from costly crude oil import-consuming road transport to the much cheaper railways. Lower crude imports are a major requirement for India if it wants the economy to touch 10 per cent growth in the coming years since it will save valuable foreign exchange.

So the targets that Prabhu has set for himself are stiff. When unfolded, they create an exciting scenario for the common train traveller. It is for real, not frivolous. With the dedicated freight corridors on the Delhi–Kolkata and Delhi–Mumbai lines expected to be operational in 2020, passenger traffic will ease unimaginably. Prabhu expects about 80 per cent of passengers will get on-the-spot reservations in a majority of the trains on these two routes by 2020. In another move, the average speed of passenger trains on the Delhi–Mumbai and Delhi–Kolkata routes is sought to be increased from 135 km per hour to 200 km per hour by resorting to advanced technology.

The transformation that is taking place in the daily workings of the railways is commendable in many ways. When Prabhu took over in November 2014, there was nothing by way of grievance redressal for passengers except the complaint book and the dedicated helpline. Within months of taking over, the minister officially sanctioned Twitter and Facebook as mediums of complaint registration and redressal. Today, as many as 5000 tweets are received on a dedicated Twitter handle every day from passengers and about 1000 actionable tweets are handled by a team from a control room in Delhi's Rail Bhavan. The tweets are forwarded to the railway divisions concerned for immediate action. The average response time on every Twitter complaint is thirty minutes. Anjaan Sharma's is a good example. In August 2016, Sharma lodged a Twitter complaint that the air-conditioning system of his second-class AC two-tier coach was not working properly. He tweeted as soon as he boarded the Haridwar–Jammu–Tawi Express from Haridwar. In another thirty minutes, Sharma tweeted 'thanks' as the AC was set right.

Taking a leaf out of the book of his boss, Narendra Modi, who has made it a rule for all ministers to tweet compulsorily to share their initiatives and successes with the people, Prabhu has directed all the key railway officers, right from general managers to divisional railway managers and below, to have official Twitter handles. As the next step towards speedier complaint redressal, an integrated redressal system is being planned with updated technology, whereby complaints, whether they land via Twitter, Facebook, phone or letter, will get automatically directed to the officer concerned for action and the action-taken report will be put on record.

Passengers admit that railway stations are cleaner now than before. One of the reasons behind this is that now 400 select stations across India are subjected to a cleanliness audit every six months by a third party. This ensures the station staff are alert at all times. Changes in the system have also improved the cleanliness of railway stations. Earlier, cleaning work on platforms, tracks and inside stations was handled by different railway departments. Now a separate housekeeping department headed by a senior-level officer has been created, with personnel drawn from different departments. The department oversees all types of cleaning in a station.

True to his chartered-accountant traits, Prabhu spent weeks in identifying the main problems of the railways after he took charge. These were: declining modal share of the railways (as compared to roads), poor infrastructure, lack of modernization, sub-optimal service delivery resulting in poor food, lack of hygiene and improper mechanism for grievance redressal, besides lack of punctuality, time-consuming processes and systems and, of course, corruption. After a careful study of the problems, Prabhu, who had offered innovative ideas to the power ministry during his earlier tenure in the A.B. Vajpayee government over a decade ago, gave two pieces of advice to the railway officials: 1. These are not problems but symptoms of the problems and if you continue treating the symptoms, the problem won't get solved. The problem, he said, was underinvestment, which needed to be dealt with in order to achieve success. 2. The IR has always seen commuters as passengers, whereas they should be treated as customers if passenger service is to improve. These two explanations cleared the confused minds of the railway officials.

The problem of acquiring funds to address underinvestment was solved by Prabhu himself. First, he called for offers from foreign companies for investment in the railways. This exposed him to the possibilities of loan-servicing and its cost. Next, in the Team India spirit, he opened negotiations with Life Insurance Corporation (LIC) of India, requesting it to give long-term soft loans to the IR out of its unused funds. The move clicked and created a win-win situation for both the LIC and the railways. LIC sanctioned a loan of ₹1.50 lakh crore, the highest amount ever borrowed by the railways, covering a thirty-year period.

With money in his hands, Prabhu started cleaning up the system by carefully choosing honest officers who could be

counted on to be effective and would prevent the pilferage of
funds. He posted them in vantage positions, thus dismantling
one of the biggest transfer-posting industries in the Indian
government. The extent of corruption in the railway ministry
can be gauged from the fact that during some corrupt regimes
in the past, bribes worth up to ₹5 crore had been taken by
political bosses for lucrative postings. In one case some years
ago, a ₹25-crore bribe had allegedly been taken by a political
boss from a very senior official with the promise of getting the
latter a top post. As part of the ugly deal, the officer, since he
didn't have ready money, paid the amount in instalments after
getting the posting. That showed the uncontrolled corruption
prevalent in the railways.

Once Prabhu had posted the right people in the right places,
the infrastructure expansion began in earnest. The figures tell
the whole story. During 2009–14, the railways' capital expense
was ₹45,000 crore, which rose to ₹59,000 crore in 2014–15
and a whopping ₹95,000 crore in 2015–16. In 2016–17, the
capital expenditure was ₹1.21 lakh crore while the allocation for
2017–18 is ₹1.31 lakh crore. So, in just three years, the NDA has
spent over six times the amount that the UPA had spent in five
years in capital expenditure. In the next five years, Prabhu will
spend ₹8.5 lakh crore, increasing the cargo-carrying capacity
of the railways many times and saving a huge amount for the
country in terms of logistical costs, besides spurring the per-
day railway-line-laying speed to 19 km in 2019 from 4.3 km
during 2009–14 and 7.6 km during 2015–16. His efforts are
showing results in the IR's financial health, which continues to
improve. In 2016–17, it posted its highest-ever total revenue of
₹1.68 lakh crore, up from ₹1.62 lakh crore in the previous year.
In March 2017, he floated a Railway Development Authority,
an independent regulator with advisory powers, to determine
passenger and freight tariffs. The move is significant in the light
of the fact that tariffs have so far been determined more by

the political needs of the ruling parties than by any intent to improve railway infrastructure.

To set an example, Prabhu has delegated all powers regarding tenders at a functional level. Since good officers have now been posted, this is having a great impact. The set-up being transparent and driven by a new, accountable system, the former irregularities in the tendering process stand curbed. And the minister has enough time for policymaking while supervising the implementation of tasks. The performance appraisal system was defective when Prabhu took the reins. The biggest proof was the fact that 95 per cent of officers ended up getting outstanding appraisal reports from their seniors. Now a new system is being introduced based on key performance indicators (KPIs) comprising eighteen points in a tough but innovative bid to introduce accountability.

The Railway Board has now signed MoUs with all the seventeen general managers based on these eighteen points, giving them specific targets to achieve. The general managers will, in turn, sign similar MoUs with sixty-eight divisional railway managers. The eighteen points include targets for revenue collection, passenger traffic, infrastructure creation, bringing down the accident rate and human-resource training of officers. The performance appraisal reports of officers will now be cleared by the railway minister on the basis of the KPIs. Posting norms have been revised to curb the room for nepotism. The earlier norms left discretionary power in the hands of the minister, who could arrange for the posting of his favourites to top positions.

The result of the increased pressure to deliver is best reflected in the speedy redressal of passengers' grievances using the social media platform, now that passengers are being seen as customers. For example, two incidents of quick redressal of complaints on trains took place on 31 March 2016 and 26 November 2015. In the first episode, a passenger, Bibhuti Srivastava, travelling on a Mumbai–Delhi train, tweeted that her child had fallen from the upper berth and was bleeding in the head. She sought quick medical help. She mentioned the passenger name record (PNR) number on her railway ticket. She got a reply saying 'help reaching quickly'. Within minutes, a railway staff member was at her berth with first aid. A grateful Srivastava tweeted, 'Help reached in quickest possible time. Awesome support.'

In the other incident, a woman, Namrata Mahajan, who was travelling on a Mumbai–Kolkata train, tweeted that a passenger was harassing her by not vacating her authorized berth and that she was feeling terrorized. She tweeted when the train was at Shevgaon station. At Bhusawal station, jawans of the Railway Protection Force (RPF) were there to help her. The passenger accused of troubling her was moved to another coach as he was holding an authorized but unreserved ticket. 'Thanks, sir,' tweeted Mahajan to Prabhu.

Prabhu's mandate to the railway ministry that only when the Indian Railways perceives passengers as customers would it be able to provide better services is clearly paying off in the form of improved food quality and cleanliness. A new policy is being chalked out for making quality food available to passengers by putting food-making and distribution under two different departments. This is based on a study that revealed that the problems of poor-quality food and overcharging were rampant because food-making and distribution were handled by the same contractor. Sizeable, well-equipped kitchens are being created in selected stations on major routes. Food will be prepared there and served on trains. The names being considered for the administration of these mega kitchens are well-known ones such as Haldiram, Sky Chefs and even Taj. Passengers will have the option of placing the order for food while booking the ticket, as is the case with air travel.

The railway station modernization programme that has been launched is equally attractive. It aims at developing 400 stations with all the modern amenities across India in the public-private partnership (PPP) model. Private parties are being given contracts to develop the stations, with the right to use the station space for commercial purposes within certain parameters to recover the cost in a given time and earn profits. Habibganj, near Bhopal, requiring an investment of ₹100 crore for modernization, is the first railway station to come under this scheme. But in forty-nine other stations, the investments have been scaled down in the first phase to make it look more affordable—around ₹30 crore for each station. Under the new design, the stations will have control. To reduce congestion at stations, the entry and exit points will be different. Solar panels will provide green energy. Escalators, digital signage and green spaces will be part of the modernization package, along with executive lounges. But the plan will take three to four years to become operational.

But one area in which the thrust is missing is in the induction of new technology to match Modi's vision of taking India to the level of developed countries at least in the area of infrastructure. Nothing proved it better than the four accidents in the railways between November 2016 and January 2017 that claimed nearly 200 lives and left over 370 injured. Of course, one of these accidents was allegedly the result of sabotage by anti-national elements, but the accidents did underline the need for advanced technology in making train journeys safe. Although the Ahmedabad–Mumbai bullet train project has been sanctioned, there is a host of areas like operating systems and inspection where the Indian Railways needs the latest technology but isn't ready to take up the challenge. The coaches are from the 1980s while the world market is now flooded with new designs. The latest sensor-based technology for coaches and wagons is also missing.

Even the signalling technology is not the latest. The most modern technology in signal operations is fitted within the engine and allows the driver to see the signal in the engine itself. Funds are no longer as big a problem as they had been before 2014. The improvements in the management systems and services have to be matched with the use of the latest technology. That the government is aware of the problem was more than proved when the 2017–18 budget allocated ₹1 lakh crore for ensuring safety in the railways by introducing the latest technology. This would involve automated inspection of railway tracks, a collision-avoiding system and sensor-based signals for drivers in the engine. A great change in the mindset and culture is also needed for faster decision-making. Hamish Yadav, OSD to Prabhu, explains: 'The minister is going ahead in a meticulous and phased manner. Modernization of operations with the latest technology, with a focus on safety, is a top priority, now that we have funds. Earlier IR didn't have the funds.'

Prabhu's challenge is huge, given the size of the Indian Railways and the burden it carries in a country where the aviation sector is neither well spread nor easily affordable. In 2015–16, the railways carried 8.107 billion passengers annually—or more than 22 million passengers a day—and 1.101 billion tonnes of freight. It boasts of 119,630 km of total track and 92,081 km of running track over a total route length of 66,687 km, with 7216 stations, and is one of the world's largest employers. But undeterred, Prabhu says: 'We are determined to change the face of the railways.'[26] The will is evident in the face of the challenge.

Dharmendra Pradhan—The Quick Learner

Petroleum and gas—A new energy vision

When the simple and straightforward Dharmendra Pradhan, a BJP national general secretary, was appointed the Union minister of state for petroleum and natural gas on 26 May 2014 directly under Prime Minister Narendra Modi, there were whispers in the then fusty corridors of power in Delhi as to

138 Marching with a Billion

how a postgraduate in anthropology could handle a ministry where the stakes of big corporate houses seldom allowed a nation-centric vision to develop. Some others rejected his selection as a downright mistake on Modi's part.

Less than three years later, the sceptics have been left thinking. They had failed to comprehend the fact that behind that simple exterior is a hard-working man willing to learn and learn fast, with the openness, enthusiasm and willingness to follow his prime minister like an honest learner. Normally, joint secretaries of departments are supposed to have the deepest knowledge about projects and about what is going on in the ministry. Pradhan is perhaps more knowledgeable about every aspect of his ministry than the joint secretaries. Says the minister's personal secretary, Binay Pradhan, an officer from the Indian Foreign Service: 'The minister has an eye even for the smallest little thing, which results in the perfection that we see in his work.'

It's visible on the surface. In keeping with the prime minister's goals, Pradhan has nearly freed the ministry from the clutches of corporate houses, which have not only run the show in the ministry almost ever since the petroleum and natural gas sector was opened to private investment in the late 1990s, but have also often dictated the government's policies to suit their business interests. When Pradhan took over, Modi had issued clear-cut directions to all the ministers to bring transparency and end the role of businessmen in policymaking, more so in the infrastructure ministries, where the stakes in terms of government revenue were high.

Pradhan's ministry is not just free of the stranglehold of business houses but is also charting out a new course for the country by creating a level playing field and removing unnecessary government control. It has facilitated the ease of doing business. Plus, the ministry has made some wise diplomatic moves at the international level to further India's energy interests, of course, with help from the prime minister himself. Under the UPA I and II governments, level-two reforms, which were so necessary after opening up the sector to private investment, were just not carried out. If a few steps were taken in that direction at all, they were clumsy, to say the least. The Modi government, with Pradhan as pilot, has brought about significant reforms in less than three years. Vipul Tuly, CEO of Singapore-based utility services provider Sembcorp Industries, which deals with many Union ministries, including petroleum and power, says: 'The minister owes his success to a very high degree of sincerity and diligence and an eye for details besides transparency. Plus, due to his purposefulness he is also a quick learner.'[27]

One of the biggest reforms involves changing the pattern of sharing the returns from explored oil and gas blocks between the private oil companies and the government. Under the New Exploration Licensing Policy (NELP) floated in the late 1990s, the exploring company—whether a private-sector firm or a PSU—had to share the profit with the government. However, under that policy, the company could recover the cost of exploration from the government without waiting for the final outcome. This pattern, on the one hand, led to a lot of litigation between the exploring company and the government—the Reliance Industries' dispute with the government in the Krishna–Godavari basin is one of the dozen-odd litigations triggered off by this policy. On the other hand, it left room for private companies to manipulate, if elements in the government were willing to collude with them or look the other way.

So the Modi government has put together a new policy called Hydrocarbon Exploration and Licensing Policy (HELP), under which the exploring company will share revenue—and not profit—with the government, and the cost of exploration will be borne by the company. In a huge step towards ease of doing business in oil and gas exploration under HELP, the government will issue only one licence for all products, whether oil or coal-based gas. Under NELP, if the exploring company got a licence for oil but instead discovered gas in the allotted block, it had to apply for a new licence for gas.

Moreover, the companies have been given the freedom to set prices and market the explored product. Under NELP, this was subject to certain regulations that left the government room for manipulation. Then, in a major step, all the four public-sector oil companies—Indian Oil Corporation Limited (IOC), Hindustan Petroleum Corporation Limited (HPCL), Bharat Petroleum Corporation Limited (BPCL), Mangalore Refinery and Petrochemicals Limited (MRPL)—have been given the liberty to devise their oil import policy in coordination with one another and get better bargains through smart deals.

Earlier, there were restrictions from the government that allowed them to buy oil only from ten designated international oil companies, two of which, surprisingly, were closed when the NDA came to power 2014. Since the oil PSUs worked in silos, they often ended up being competitors while buying oil from international companies. For example, IOC and MRPL used to buy oil from Iran under different terms and conditions. Now they purchase oil in close coordination.

The impact of the changed atmosphere was apparent when the directorate general of hydrocarbons auctioned thirty-one smaller oilfields in 2016 under the new formula for revenue sharing, with the rates at an impressive 30 to 50 per cent. According to a rough estimate, the figure would have been much less in the former set-up, which was dominated by big players and marked by political interference. The biggest indication of transparency in operation was the fact that thirty-seven new players came forward to place bids—which wouldn't have happened under the earlier regime. One big player was Sun Pharmaceutical Industries Ltd, headed by Dilip Shanghvi. Atanu Chakraborty, the director general of hydrocarbons, says: 'Our aim is to instil more transparency in the bidding process. Now we are opening the entire subsurface data for the private and public sectors to give them full chance to understand the subsurface reality.'[28]

But it is on the turf of energy diplomacy that India has charted out a new course under the Modi government. Two shining examples are the Russian oil exploration deal and the renegotiation of the Qatar gas deal. The Russian deal showcases the Modi government's commitment to protecting national interest by going the extra mile using diplomatic pressure. Against reported Chinese competition, India made a bid for and bagged a 49 per cent stake in the Vankorneft field, Russia's second-biggest field. It also grabbed a 29.9 per cent stake in Russia's smaller Taas-Yuriah oilfield.

Against an investment of $5.46 billion, the two fields are expected to yield 15 million tonnes of oil and gas per annum. In sharp contrast, during UPA II, the government had invested $2.116 in 2009 in Imperial field in Russia when it was publicly known that the field's value was almost a third of that price. It was a loss-making deal from day one. Its final yield was just 0.3 million tonnes. The Modi government's Vankorneft deal stands out even when compared with India's overall performance in the field of oil exploration abroad.

The Modi government's energy diplomacy and strategic planning with transparency seem remarkable when weighed against India's accomplishments in exploration in the past five decades. India has spent about $28.5 billion in exploration and production of oil and gas in about thirty countries abroad since the 1960s. Surprisingly, the average annual yield in these has been 10 million tonnes, which is five million tonnes less than what is expected as a certainty from just two oilfields of Russia acquired in Modi's tenure. Of course, the final verdict will come only when the fields actually yield the volume. A private player in the petroleum sector who doesn't want to be named says: 'The private player can feel the transparency that has been injected under the present government. Plus, there is zeal to take the sector forward through innovative strategy.'

The renegotiation of the Qatar deal is another success. The 1999 deal struck between India and Qatar aimed at securing India's interests by fulfilling the latter's LPG need was based on a rationalized price structure which guarded India from spiralling crude oil prices. But it did not take into account the fact that the crude oil price could fall to as low as $6 per barrel in the future. And that's what exactly happened after the Modi government appeared on the scene in 2014, when the oil price dropped to $6 per barrel. The downward spiral created a dilemma for the newly elected government because, under the deal, India was supposed to buy at $12 per barrel.

The argument that when oil prices had hit the roof in the past, the same deal had helped India because of its rationalized price structure, could have been used to keep the old deal going. But Modi and Pradhan rose to the occasion and started negotiating. Modi once called the emir of Qatar on the phone. He explained to the emir that savings from a renegotiated deal meant a lot for India and that the previous deal had unfortunately failed to take into account the fact that oil prices could drop to such a low level in the future. Pradhan went to Qatar to take the case forward. After protracted negotiations, Qatar agreed to bring the price to the current level on condition that India would buy 1 million tonnes of extra LPG from that country. The renegotiated deal means an annual saving of ₹10,000 crore.

Modi and Pradhan have clearly outlined the role energy will play in fuelling India's economic growth. Their energy vision rests on four pillars: access and affordability for all citizens, improved energy efficiency, transition to a low-carbon world driving energy sustainability and, above all, energy security. Interestingly, the experience of providing Gujarat with innumerable energy options, be it in the space of gas, power or renewable energy, has given Modi first-hand knowledge and experience on a holistic energy model of sustainability, sufficiency and efficiency. So, what is visible is the juxtaposing of those successful policies on a national scale.

Sashi Mukundan, India head of the BP Group and chairman of the national committee on hydrocarbons of the Confederation of Indian Industry (CII), observes, 'Today, we see a collaborative engagement between global energy leaders, think tanks and analysts. Through such interactive discussions, the prime minister is revisiting the energy roadmap for India, taking geopolitical and economic considerations into account. With a clear vision, he is focused on both the direction and pace of energy reforms. The transparency that one sees in the ministry today is another spurring factor.'[29]

The vision is admirable but it is also a challenge to give it a proper shape. Modi and Pradhan want to bring down India's crude oil imports from 76 per cent at present to 66 per cent of the country's total annual oil requirement by 2022. This has to be done by increasing local production from 24 to 34 per cent. Modi has made big green energy commitments at the Paris convention. To meet these commitments, the use of gas has to be increased.

But it's a Herculean task. India's gas usage from the energy basket is just 6.5 per cent, against a world average of 24 per cent. Only Gujarat has an impressive 26 per cent of gas use, which is a result of Modi's own efforts as Gujarat's chief minister. One way out is to mix costly imported gas with the less costly local gas to create a pool to bring down the average gas price, enabling more consumption. Such a pool has been attempted on a small scale in the fertilizer and power sectors but needs to be replicated across the board. Pradhan appears equal to the task.

Harsimrat Kaur Badal—Towards a New Era

Food processing: No more a mirage

Harsimrat Kaur Badal has typical traits. Focused, she likes to talk to the point. In the process, she looks tough, if not stern. Officials or businessmen facing Badal have to be attentive. For, the Union minister of food processing has a peculiar habit.

Like a teacher, or more precisely, like a student, she sometimes takes down notes on what is being discussed. In the notes she even records dates of important discussions. There have been occasions on which she has reminded an officer or an investor when he has forgotten his former promise or appeared confused. She does this by going through the dated entries in her diary or by recalling the incidents from memory. Not surprisingly, because of these traits, she is always up to date on minute information. Few can take her for granted.

In many ways, this precision is also due to the high stakes that Prime Minister Narendra Modi has in her ministry when it comes to fulfilling his promise of doubling farmers' income in the country by 2022. CEO Modi has a great vision of value addition in agriculture. He knows the importance of food processing, having used it as one of the springboards for promoting agriculture during his tenure as Gujarat's chief minister. A huge private food-processing unit in his home town of Vadnagar in north Gujarat—which has created several jobs for the locals, besides increasing farmers' incomes—is a testimony to his vision. However, he couldn't exploit the full potential of the food-processing sector in Gujarat because of various factors.

In Delhi, the prime minister, who is wiser now, is determined to implement his vision fully, leaving little to the imagination. His directive: no stone should be left unturned while tapping the possibilities in the food-processing sector. In January 2016, Modi announced 100 per cent FDI in food-processing retail, sending a thrill through the sector. The step was taken in response to figures revealing farm wastage that surfaced in March 2015 following a survey ordered by Badal.

The survey clearly showed how food processing could change the fortunes of Indian farmers. Carried out by the Central Institute of Post-Harvest Engineering & Technology, Ludhiana, a unit of the Indian Council of Agricultural Research (ICAR), the survey revealed that the value of untapped agro waste in

India came to an astounding ₹92,600 crore annually at 2014 price levels. Farm produce in India has to be thrown away when it is not sold because of a lack of cold-chain and food-processing facilities. And 60 per cent of this waste consisted of fruits and vegetables. Badal ordered the survey because a similar study conducted in 2010 under the UPA government had not been accurate.

Opening up food-processing retail to FDI won accolades for the Modi government. Rightly so, when the facts are considered. India is the second-largest producer of fruits and vegetables and also the second-largest waster of the two produces in the absence of an adequate food-processing infrastructure. As Piruz Khambatta, co-chairman of the Confederation of Indian Industry's National Committee on Food Processing Industry, puts it, 'The opening up of FDI in the food-processing retail sector, accompanied by some sharp initiatives, will make all the difference to India's food-processing scene. Things have at last begun to look up on an important front of the Indian economy.'[30]

Khambatta's hope doesn't seem to be misplaced. If the performance of the Ministry of Food Processing Industries over the past two and a half years or so is any indication, then it is on the right track after a topsy-turvy ride between 2008, when it was floated, and 2014, when the NDA took over. Out of the 133 cold-chain projects sanctioned during the UPA tenure, only thirty-five were operational in 2014. Today the figure is ninety-seven—an addition of sixty-two in close to three years. And half a dozen more will be operational soon. The ambitious Mega Food Park (MFP) scheme, announced in 2008–09, which was supposed to be a great deliverer in terms of job creation and farmers' benefits, had seen little work. Of the forty-two MFPs sanctioned between 2008 and 2012, only two were operational in 2014. Now the figure stands at eight. And four more will be operational sometime in 2017—including the ones in Satara in

Maharashtra, Raigada in Odisha and Agartala in Tripura. Each MFP, costing between ₹200 crore and ₹250 crore, provides employment to around 6000 people and benefits around 30,000 farmers.

But a lot more needs to be done in this area and a mere comparison with the dismal performance of the UPA government won't be enough to claim a really good record. But it is true that after the NDA came to power, about 1 lakh farmers have been benefited and over 30,000 people have got jobs just through the revival of old MFPs at a cost of ₹1000 crore. Khambatta, who is also the chairman and CMD of Rasna Private Limited, which produces the soft drink Rasna, observes: 'Under Badal, things are indeed moving now and moving at a good speed. Clearances are much faster now and potential investors are not just welcomed but also chased. The disbursement of subsidy is also quicker now.'[31]

Badal went about her task in a planned manner. She did a careful study of the food-processing scene in the first six months of her tenure. Being from India's agro hub, Punjab, she already had some idea of the job Modi had given her. As the daughter-in-law of Parkash Singh Badal, one of the longest-serving chief ministers of Punjab, her administrative ability is also good. Her plan became clearer in March 2015 when she got the ICAR study, which pointed out that farm produce worth ₹92,600 crore went to waste annually. She started cracking the whip, both on the ministry officials and on the promoters of agro-processing units, in order to push the delayed projects that had been sanctioned by the UPA government.

The idea was to make the projects take off without delay. In meeting after meeting, the promoters were told either to fix a deadline for completing their projects or to exit. Six of the forty-two old MFPs in which there was inordinate delay either because of the promoters or because of reasons beyond the promoters' control were dropped. This sent the right signals to the officials and the promoters and had the desired effect. The officialdom and the private players got to know what to expect from Badal. Four more MFPs cleared during the UPA tenure will be operative soon. As Badal's OSD, Hardeep Singh, says, 'She is a very quick learner and truly businesslike.'[32]

However, there are people in the industry who feel that she needs to wield the whip more firmly, especially on the bureaucracy and the states. The plans of Modi and Badal in the food-processing sector can succeed only when the states keep pace. A proper follow-up mechanism is lacking in the case of the states, some of which are proactive, some average performers and some laggards. There is an inter-ministerial committee of officers headed by Badal comprising the agriculture secretary, a nominee of the NITI Aayog and other officials, for the approval and review of projects. However, the follow-up with the states, among the main drivers on the ground, is done in a manner which isn't structured. A food-processing player says: 'A structured approach with the right use of carrot and stick can produce better results in spurring the projects.'

These were Badal's priorities after she crossed the halfway mark of her ministerial tenure—making old projects operative by the time her terms ends in 2019; in the same time frame, completing work on 100 new cold chains and 250 new small food-processing units with a total investment of ₹4500 crore, while sticking to the PPP model involving private entrepreneurs, self-help groups or non-governmental organizations. She has kept a deadline of two years for the new projects—a tall order but not impossible to achieve, considering the fact that 100 food-processing units are of a smaller size, requiring an investment of just ₹10 crore each. They would take twenty-four months to become operational.

Although the food-processing ministry has been in place for more than eight years now, India's processing level is quite low. Only 10 per cent of the total farm produce is processed in the country, of which a large part is covered by milk products which come under agro produce. In comparison, the food-processing levels in Western countries are very high—70 to 80 per cent of the total farm produce gets processed in countries like France, Germany, the UK and Italy. A great performer is Poland, which is seen as one of the leaders in food processing. Badal's target is to more than double India's food-processing capacity, from 10 per cent to over 20 per cent, by the time she completes her term in 2019.

She is offering innovative ideas along with hard work. Under Badal's guidance, her ministry has prepared a food map of India which points to specific produce-deficient and produce-surplus areas for investors in every state. This gives investors an idea of the national food-processing scene and allows them to invest accordingly. The map shows in which regions certain farm items are in surplus and where food-processing units connected with those items would work, and also points out regions where a processing unit would not be feasible because certain types of farm produce are in short supply there.

Food processing is an interesting area that requires research. The term 'food processing' includes the processing of milk, cereals, pulses, fruits and vegetables as also meat, fish and chicken. The cold-chain concept includes five major components:

1. Simple cold storage
2. Distribution hub, which is supposed to be near the market
3. Minimal processing centre, where washing, quality grading, sorting and packaging takes place
4. Reefer transport (refrigeration transport) vehicles
5. Irradiation facility with nuclear technology, where radiation is used to prolong the shelf life of certain farm products; nuclear technology is mostly used in masalas and onions to remove pests and boost the products' shelf life

For a cold-chain project to get a government subsidy, it has to have at least two of these five features. Significantly, the wastage of fruits and vegetables is a major area of worry since it constitutes 60 per cent of the total farm produce going to waste in the country, amounting to over ₹55,000 crore annually. As much as 60 per cent of 100 new cold chains and 250 small food-processing units are planned to handle fruits and vegetables.

Even tough measures can only have limited effect while dealing with states whose cooperation is necessary for the Modi government if it wants the country to grow in the food-processing sector. States like Rajasthan, Gujarat, Telangana, Punjab and Haryana have strong policies and structures to boost growth. This is not the case with big states like Uttar Pradesh and Bihar, and some southern states like Karnataka and Tamil Nadu. Incidentally, all four of these states are blessed with the availability of surface and underground water. Badal plans to reduce the Centre's 50 per cent capital subsidy to food processing (minus land cost) to 35 per cent, in a bid to push the industry towards self-reliance. The step is in keeping with the Modi government's overall vision of self-sufficiency and the belief that the saved amount could be spent on attracting more units in the food-processing sector. No wonder then that the food-processing plans of the Modi government are on the upswing.

6

India and the World

Foreign Affairs Strategy

The arrival of protectionist Donald Trump as the new US President poses a challenge to Prime Minister Narendra Modi's much-talked-about negotiation skills on the international arena. An important question comes up here: can he save Indian jobs in the US, and, if yes, how much can he protect, given Trump's intent to live up to his promises on American jobs, come what may? There are other questions: what will be the impact of Trump's rabid pro-American stance on Indians' chances of getting the H-1B visa? It remains to be seen how Modi steers the Indian ship, playing on Trump's openly expressed anti-China stance in almost all areas—from jobs to the geopolitical and geostrategic turfs—and wins concessions for India. Observers are eagerly waiting to see how Modi makes use of Trump's supporters in the US's Indian business community to bring the new President round.

While maturing his Trump strategy, Modi also has to factor in the US President's unpredictability. Given his strong anti-China stance, inviting President Xi Jinping to the US shouldn't have been his first priority. Jinping was the second leader to visit the US, following the visit of Japanese Prime Minister Shinzo Abe, and hold parleys with the President. Raj Chengappa, group editorial director of *India Today* who has analysed Trump closely, says: 'Modi will have to play his cards very deftly. The arch negotiator will have to give his best in this case, given the hard work he has done to strengthen India–US relations.'[1] Shalabh Kumar, a known Trump supporter in the US and a Republican businessman who worked hard for Trump's victory, is, however, more than hopeful: 'India hasn't much to fear from Trump. His moves on the H-1B visa are only aimed at stopping the abusers of the law—not genuine people. With Trump's emphasis on trade cooperation, the trade between India and the US will treble by 2010, creating one million jobs in the US and seven million in India. The arrest of the terrorist Hafiz Saeed in Pakistan was due to Trump's pressure. Those who are promoting terror will have to pay a price. Trump doesn't have a dual face.'[2]

Given the paradigm shift Modi has brought about in India–US relations on multiple fronts, the prime minister is expected to display the necessary skill to surpass this challenge too. The signs of Modi's efforts in this direction following Foreign Secretary S. Jaishankar's US visit in March 2017 might be visible. On 19 April, Trump chose to ignore the legislative route for the stricter H1-B regime visa he had promised under his 'Buy American, Hire American' poll campaign slogan and instead passed only an executive order to the bureaucracy to scrutinize visa applications effectively and come up with policy suggestions to ensure that only the true professionals that the US needs get the visa and the visa laws are not misused. This brought relief to many Indian IT companies which could have been greatly affected by a stronger step. In one sense, Shalabh Kumar's prediction was coming true. However, the last is yet to be heard on this front. Even otherwise, Modi's task looks somewhat easy given the fact that the friction with Trump is assumed to be mainly on the job front and that too not beyond a point, in view of the business scenario between the two countries and the technically qualified Indian hands that the US would always need to sustain its economy. The shadow of uncertainty in no way extends in the area of the unprecedented geostrategic defence partnership forged between India and the US by Modi and the previous US President Barack Obama. This is certainly the belief among most Modi observers, given his highly successful forays into foreign lands so far.

The sixty-six-year-old Dana Rohrabacher is no ordinary Congressman. A former speech writer of late President Ronald Reagan, this Republican of German–English origin representing California is well known for his strict stand on issues related to his nation's security. Seen as a gadfly by some, he is a known figure in the diplomatic circles of South Asia, starting from India and Pakistan to Afghanistan. In October 2016, he, along with another Congressman, Ted Poe, moved a bill in the US Congress to declare Pakistan a terror state following the attack on the Uri army base in Kashmir Valley and evidence that an accused in a terror attack in the US had Pakistani links. They withdrew the bill but reintroduced it recently after the arrival of Donald Trump. In the late 1980s, much before he entered the Congress, Rohrabacher had fought in his private capacity with the Pakistan-backed Afghan Mujahideens against the Soviets near Jalalabad. After getting to know the true nature of the Pakistan state and the role of the Inter-Services Intelligence in promoting terror, he started turning against Pakistan. In 2003, he backed Afghanistan's new Constitution and in 2013, he not only supported the Baloch freedom movement but also called for trying Pakistan for war crimes against the Balochis, thus upping the ante against Pakistan.

Rohrabacher is one of the many US Congressmen who have been charmed by Modi, especially after the Indian prime minister's masterly speech to the US Congress on 8 June 2016, for which he got ten standing ovations and sixty-nine rounds of spontaneous applause from the US lawmakers. Speaking in English, a language he was not comfortable with till a few years ago, Modi was eloquence personified as he delivered his speech with remarkable authority, knowledge and candour on the significance of the India–US partnership for the new world order plagued by terrorism and economic challenges, and the depth of India's gratitude to the US for its support. In the same vein, he virtually warned the US against rewarding India's neighbour and alleged terror sponsor before stressing the importance of renewable energy for India–US partnership while eulogizing India's environment-friendly ancient traditions.

Congressmen were spellbound by the address, which was touted as the best possible in terms of content and response among the speeches delivered to the US Congress by six Indian prime ministers so far. The canvas of Modi's speech was vast. It didn't leave any significant issue between the two nations untouched. He pointed to the possibility of the US and India coming together to set the world agenda based on human values to meet emerging challenges. But what seemed to have moved the hardened US lawmakers the most was the depth of Modi's climate change vision, when he spoke about development with less and less carbon footprint, and about the importance of technological cooperation between the US and India, and the need for simpler lifestyle to reduce the pressure on nature.

Modi's repeated emphasis on saving the world from a climate change disaster had a remarkable impact on the lawmakers of a country which has seen the most devastating effects of global warming in the form of tornadoes and hurricanes that have uprooted entire townships. These disasters have, in fact, instilled the ultimate fear into a country which otherwise fears few because of its technological and military prowess. One of the reasons why Modi was seen as a man with conviction on climate change was the lead he took in 2015 in floating the ISA, headquartered at Gurgaon, to spur solar power usage by tapping into the solar energy of 121 sunshine countries.

No wonder then that Modi got the maximum number of standing ovations when he spoke of the need to lessen the nations' carbon footprints. Subsequent statements by the US, during the Obama administration, on joint cooperation with India had climate change on the top of the list. The statements clearly carried the imprint of Modi's US Congress speech. A statement by Peter Lavoy, a White House spokesperson then, issued after India's surgical strikes inside Pakistan-held territory to destroy terror launch pads across the line of control (LoC) in Kashmir, recognized India's right to react in self-defence. It described the Uri attack as an act of cross-border terrorism and went to great lengths to describe the new India–US relationship: 'The US welcomes the more prominent and effective role that India is playing on a wide range of world problems from climate change and global health to peacekeeping, maritime security and cyber governance. There is no country in the world that we are supporting in this manner as an emerging global defence leader. This is unique. Never in our history have we supported an indigenous aircraft programme in any other country.'[3] The increasing India–US engagement, particularly against the threat of China, is best illustrated by the fact that President Obama visited India twice in one year during Modi's tenure, something no US President had done in the past.

Defence cooperation, apart from, of course, economic cooperation, is the greatest factor in India-US relations. India is buying surveillance equipment and Apache helicopters, and there is a proposal for cooperation even in India's aircraft technology programme. American defence exports to India today stand at $15 billion, up from just a million a decade ago. Ashton Carter, who was defence secretary in the Obama administration, and former Indian defence minister Manohar Parrikar met five times in a year during 2015–16. Carter paid three visits to India, indicating the value of the emerging India–US defence cooperation. With Donald Trump as President,

India–US ties, particularly in the defence sector, are only going to get deeper by all indications, notwithstanding the President's different approach on some other issues.

India's new relationship with the US is over and above India's growing influence at in the UN, where India's voice echoes more loudly than ever before, as symbolized by the UN's acceptance of Modi's suggestion to declare 21 June as the annual International Day of Yoga. This is a singular achievement of Modi's many-sided diplomacy. Rohrabacher has twice tried to seek an appointment with Modi but without success, because of the Indian prime minister's busy schedule. A source close to the Congressman revealed: 'Egyptian President A.F. El-Sisi met Rohrabacher for three hours. The Indian prime minister should find time for individual Congressmen too, especially those who have a strong stand against terror-sponsoring countries.'

Relations with the US: The Historic Shift

If one analyses India's diplomatic journey since Modi paid his first visit to Bhutan after taking over as prime minister—and more than that, the purport of his fifty-odd foreign visits in close to three years—one can't help but recognize the fact that India's foreign policy has undergone a paradigm shift after Modi's arrival. A great reform of the Indian diplomacy, on a scale not seen since Independence, is under way. The trajectory from the days of the Nehruvian order was first sought to be changed by former Prime Minister P.V. Narasimha Rao in the 1990s. Later, A.B. Vajpayee sought to take the reforms further. As thirty-four Union ministers visit sixty-eight countries under an elaborate plan devised by Modi and Sushma Swaraj, the Union minister for external affairs, in an effort to reach out to almost all the major countries, Modi's diplomatic initiative emerges as one of the biggest-ever undertaken by an Indian prime minister. The main idea behind the ministerial visits is to forge stronger economic and strategic relationships mostly with countries that Modi and Swaraj hadn't visited.

The direction to the visiting ministers was clear: they should establish a rapport with at least one important leader of the nation they are visiting or, at least, with their ministerial counterparts, and identify a common ground between the two countries. The list of ministers and the countries they were given was strategically finalized after gathering inputs from the ministries concerned, apart from the external affairs ministry, and the ministries of commerce, finance, defence and culture. It was aimed at extracting maximum advantage for Indian interests in keeping with Modi's global vision. Nuanced cultural and economic diplomacy with strategic planning is, in fact, a new thrust area under the Modi dispensation. The giant initiative is rooted in Modi's belief in the destiny of the Indian nation as expressed by him on various public platforms in the past: 'One day India will re-establish its position as a *Vishwa Guru*, a teacher of cultural and human values and traditions in a conflict-ridden world on the strength of the ancient Indian belief *vasudaiva kutumbakam* (the world is one large family).'

The impact of his high-pressure global initiative is there for all to see. The isolation of Pakistan in the world community after the Uri attack is felt more than ever before, though Pakistan continues to needle India and remains a military and security challenge. But it is not that Pakistan is not facing pressure. More significantly, even China is feeling the pressure of India's aggressive and strategic diplomacy.

One of India's biggest successes is its entry into the thirty-four-member Missile Technology Control Regime (MTCR), a development that gives India a huge boost in space technology because MTCR allows the passage of high-level space technology to India. This had been denied earlier on the pretext that India will use the technology to produce unmanned missiles—the same technology works for both. India's entry into MTCR with active help from the US in what is the most strategic relationship emerging between two nations is no small feat, considering the fact that China has been trying unsuccessfully to enter MTCR for a decade now.

The importance of the development can be estimated only when one goes into the history of India's space technology. Russia's denial of cryogenic engines to India under US pressure in the 1990s, when an economically unstable Russia was dependent on the US for financial help after the break-up of the Soviet Union, delayed India's satellite launch programme by more than two decades. India was forced to indigenously develop its own cryogenic engine, which took time. In that post–Cold War era, the US and other Western nations wanted to deny India space launch technology because of the fear that India would use it to develop missiles and get more powerful vis-à-vis their ally, Pakistan. They were also wary of India's potential to grow and match their overall prowess in future with the help of such a powerful technology.

This was the reason why Modi, in his forty-seven-minute US Congress speech on emerging India–US relations, emphasized the necessity of leaving behind 'hesitations of history'. The phrase was symptomatic of the India–US relationship as it developed in phases over a period of a decade and a half with hiccups in between. The US–India engagement started taking shape during the tenure of P.V. Narasimha Rao, but it was under duress, against the backdrop of the collapse of the Soviet Union, India's biggest ally since Independence, in addition to the severe political and economic pressures at home.

It was during A.B. Vajpayee's tenure that Jaswant Singh, the external affairs minister, and Strobe Talbott, the US deputy secretary of state, gave India–US relations a positive turn in a free atmosphere. Even after the nuclear deal was signed by India and the US during the tenure of the former prime minister Manmohan Singh, the hesitations of history remained and prevented the two nations from ratifying the defence logistics pact, which India signed with the US in 2016. This was a token of Modi's dynamic approach towards the US based on his 'move forward without hesitation' policy.

What perhaps impressed the US was the fact that Modi himself left behind a murky relationship with that nation—US lawmakers had tried to block Modi's political rise in many ways, citing the episode of the 2002 Gujarat riots—for the sake of a better future for his country. According to Talbott, an expert on India–US relations and the president of Brookings Institution, Modi's instincts, approaches and policies on some of the big issues of present times are appreciated in Washington as well as by people outside the government who have studied India for a long time. Talbott thinks Modi is handling the China policy well and that his strong relationship with Japanese Prime Minister Shinzo Abe is welcome. 'It's good to see India consolidating its efforts to advance not just its regional interests but also its role in the world,' Talbott said in an interview.[4]

The purport of the defence logistics agreement that India signed with the US in September 2016 is yet to dawn on many. Short of setting up military bases and lending troops, it allows cooperation between the two nations on a grand scale when it comes to defence logistics. For example, if reasons of political stability force US warships to intervene in the South China Sea, they can avail themselves of help from India in terms food, oil, spare parts and so on. On the flip side, if India has to intervene in the Middle East or in Balochistan by sending special forces, the US warships in the Middle East can provide logistical support to India. Similarly, MTCR, of which India became a member in 2016 within just one year of applying for membership through a unanimous resolution, puts India ahead of China in space technology.

China is, of course, blocking India's entry into the Nuclear Suppliers Group (NSG) by using its veto (in the thirty-four-member body, the entry is through a unanimous resolution by the member nations). The chances of India getting into the NSG in the near future appear weak despite the fact that the US has publicly committed to make India a member. As a result of India's strident stand against China on many issues, the communist nation is sullen with India and not going to yield easily on India's NSG bid. But many observers believe that despite China's hard position against India, Modi is building up enough pressure on China to get a good bargaining position with it in the times to come. But this view is severely contested by another set of observers who think China is too commanding in every way to allow India any bargaining power.

According to Daniel Twining, a foreign policy expert and director for Asia at the German Marshall Fund of the US, Modi is making all the right moves in the diplomatic arena, including in developing the India–US relationship vis-à-vis China. As he puts it: 'Modi is demonstrating the right vision against the backdrop of the emerging Chinese hegemony, the Russian stance and the growing terror threat. India and the US together can be great pace-setters. But to realize India's full potential in the international arena and against China, Modi has to raise India's woefully low defence spending of around 1.62 per cent of its GDP and take it at least beyond 2 per cent at a time when countries like the US spend 4 per cent on defence.'[5]

Walter Anderson, an expert on India at Johns Hopkins University who has studied the growth of the RSS, observes: 'The most important factor in Modi's diplomacy is the recognition he has given to trade, which is reflected in the highest-ever FDI he has secured for India. He has made the right approach to the US, but he has to realize that getting closer to the US and signing the communication agreement could distance him from China beyond redemption.'[6]

Paradigm Shift in Attitude towards China: India No More the Underdog

But few would contest the observation that Modi's China diplomacy signals a great change in India's attitude towards that nation—from a defensive posture maintained over several decades to that of equal, controlled aggression. India's approach to China has so far been marked by a meek kind of diplomacy where the big brother could take undue liberties with the younger brother who found himself powerless to act. The Indian approach to China was based on platitudes like 'good brotherly relations'—denoting a soft diplomacy, which, in the parlance of foreign affairs, rarely succeeds when not backed by hard power, particularly against a ruthless China.

The effort so far has been to engage China on a moral high ground at the cost of hard deal-making, which involves deterrents and checkmating moves. That soft diplomacy never pays is best displayed by the India–China story on the issue of a permanent seat in the UN Security Council. In early 1950s, when the US wanted India to be a permanent member of the council, India backed the Chinese claim to the seat despite severe opposition from many Western democratic powers and in spite of the fact that the Chinese had already intruded in Tibet. Today, one of the main factors in the way of India becoming a permanent member in the UN Security Council is China's hostility.

But Modi is slowly changing the rules of the game not just by appearing as a hard negotiator, but also by bringing in the powerful angle of cultural diplomacy by engaging in a skilful manner with the people of the Buddhist nations that affect China. India is no longer China's underdog. India's new confidence in tackling the dragon was evident in Modi's visit to Vietnam, China's rival in the South China Sea, and the signing of the defence cooperation pacts with Hanoi when he was on his way to China for attending the 2016 Group of Twenty (G20) summit in Hangzhou.

It was perhaps the strongest signal to China that India won't take its bullying lying down any more. Modi gave another sign of India's new stance soon after the G20 summit in the way he chose to react to the China–Philippines dispute in the South China Sea at the summit of the Association of Southeast Asian Nations at Laos. On the topic of the award given by the International Court of Justice at the Hague to the Philippines, Modi unambiguously called for accepting and respecting the decision in the letter and spirit of the UN Convention on the Law of the Sea. It is a different matter that the Philippines has, of late, moved closer to China.

All these years, China has practised an encircling policy against India—what is called China's 'string of pearls' strategy— to surround India with strategic bases by befriending its neighbouring nations and countries in the Indian Ocean and the Pacific regions to check Indian interests on multiple fronts. Modi is now using his own disentangling strategy to counter China's scheme that has on its radar strategic spots in Pakistan, Sri Lanka and Myanmar, and coastal points in Thailand and Indonesia. It can be labelled as Modi's China doctrine.

In following this policy, Modi has used multiple means, like a true Chanakya—friendly gestures, economic cooperation, military and strategic partnerships and backdoor moves like the one in Sri Lanka. The China-friendly President Mahinda Rajapaksa, who had allowed Chinese military ships to anchor on the Sri Lankan coast, lost the elections to the India-friendly Maithripala Sirisena, reportedly with a good degree of Indian intervention. India, however, strongly denied the charge. However, Modi's Sri Lanka challenge for tackling China hasn't ended, with China trying to woo the island nation with redoubled vigour.

Modi is intelligently using cultural diplomacy to connect with the people of South-East Asian nations, who are mostly Buddhists. In 2016, his government organized the World Buddhist Conference which was attended by religious heads of Buddhist nations from East and South-East Asia, in addition to Sri Lanka and Bhutan. The move was a part of India's China strategy in the cultural domain, aimed at engaging with the people of these Buddhist nations to build a pro-India pressure on their governments in the long run. The HRD ministry has also started a contest called Shodh Yatri that as a reward aims to send the winners to Cambodia, Vietnam (where the second-biggest religious group are the Buddhists), Thailand, Sri Lanka, Myanmar and other Buddhist nations, in an attempt to increase people-to-people contact.

Modi hasn't ignored the importance of even a small country like Seychelles in the China game plan. He visited the island nation to guard against Chinese penetration in the Indian Ocean. In 2015, he became the first prime minister to visit it in two decades. India gifted a high-capacity radar to Seychelles on the occasion. Myanmar, a nation seen as being in the Chinese sphere of influence, is also being wooed with skilful diplomacy, which is giving good results. With Japan, India is on the strongest wicket in the economic and technology arenas, thanks to the personal relationship Modi has established with Prime Minister Shinzo Abe since his days as the chief minister of Gujarat. It is being termed as a dynamic partnership between the world's largest democracy and the Land of the Rising Sun. The close cooperation between the two countries is helping India counter China, with which Japan has major differences in the East China Sea.

Such is the level of cooperation with Japan that China has openly said that India is trying to encircle it with the help of Japan and the US. But the China road is still rocky for Modi, as recent developments show. A fresh challenge has emerged in the form of a new relationship between China and India's key ally, Bangladesh. Xi Jinping, in his 2016 visit to Dhaka, the first by a Chinese president to Bangladesh in three decades, pledged aid of $10 billion, which is ten times what India had given Bangladesh during Modi's 2015 visit. Next, Bangladesh took the delivery of a submarine from China, causing flutters in the Indian camp and indicating the monumental challenge Modi faces while tackling Xi Jinping. Modi has tried to handle this with some warm diplomacy. When Bangladeshi Prime Minister Sheikh Hasina Wazed visited India in March 2017, Modi broke protocol by going to receive her at the airport and then took a special initiative for solving the Teesta river-water-sharing problem with Bangladesh, a bone of contention between the two nations. China's moves vis-à-vis the Maldives pose a challenge to Modi, who also has to find ways to contain the spread of Wahhabism in the Maldives by Saudi Arabia, which is increasing its influence on the tiny nation by pumping in huge amounts of funding.

Getting China to support the UN resolution declaring Pakistan's Masood Azhar as a terrorist and to approve India's entry into the NSG is turning out to be the ultimate test of Modi's brand of multifaceted diplomacy. It is proving to be difficult to get China to deviate from the path of backing Pakistan on Azhar. This was proved during the 2016 BRICS summit hosted by India in Goa, where China put its foot down when it came to naming Jaish-e-Mohammed and Lashkar-e-Taiba as terrorist organizations in the joint declaration that had otherwise named Al-Qaeda and the Islamic State. Jinping went a step further and unabashedly advised India to solve the Kashmir problem through dialogue. He used the term 'regional hotspots' and hinted that India should tackle the root causes of such issues before taking a hard line.

Other than this, the BRICS summit and the subsequent BRICS-BIMSTEC (Bay of Bengal Initiative for Multi-Sectoral

Technical and Economic Cooperation—a group of seven countries, including India) outreach summit proved to be another master stroke by Modi, securing India's interests and achieving two objectives at one go—isolating Pakistan, which isn't a member of BIMSTEC, and tackling China's encircling policy towards India because BIMSTEC nations include Myanmar, Sri Lanka, Thailand and Bangladesh, the very nations China is eyeing as part of its strategy.

Modi, who described Pakistan as the 'mothership' of terrorism without naming it, managed to get all the four member countries of BRICS except China and the seven BIMSTEC nations to take a strong stand against terrorism. Modi's plan of hosting the first-ever BRICS–BIMSTEC outreach summit also pre-empted Pakistan's efforts to have a larger summit of the South Asian Association for Regional Cooperation (SAARC) by roping in Central Asian nations and Iran with the help of China to counter the cancellation of the 2016 SAARC summit in Pakistan. That cancellation had been brought about with the application of pressure by India, which used diplomatic strong-arm tactics after the Uri attack.

Using the occasion, India managed to bring around Brazil, which too had been opposing India's entry into the NSG, under pressure from China. India's suggestion to the BRICS nations to have their own rating agency was accepted, thus strengthening the institutional foundation of the five-nation body. That 115 meetings involving ministers and officials of five countries during the BRICS summit discussed a wide range of issues did credit to India as a host nation for the 2016 edition of BRICS. The twelve member countries of BRICS and BIMSTEC together represent two-thirds of the world population and Modi's success in getting recognition for his vision by all but one nation at the outreach summit was no small achievement. Representatives of the BIMSTEC nations included two of the world's most well-known figures—Myanmar's new state counsellor, de facto prime minister and Noble laureate, Aung San Suu Kyi, who is known for waging one of the greatest battles for democratic freedom, and Bangladeshi Prime Minister Sheikh Hasina Wazed, one of the bravest fighters in the world against ultra-Wahhabi terrorism.

Modi hosted Suu Kyi in Delhi and signed a series of pacts with her government after the BRICS-BIMSTEC outreach summit. This event, coming just six months after Suu Kyi's party came to power in Myanmar, gave yet another indication of Modi's strategic diplomacy, marked by his expertise in striking a personal rapport with world leaders. Modi's overtures were significant because Myanmar had moved very close to China some years ago. Modi's gesture promised rich diplomatic dividends. Although Suu Kyi heads a small nation, she has a unique standing in the world because of her fight for democracy. R.S.N. Singh, an averred strategic affairs expert and former officer of the Research and Analysis Wing (RAW), says: 'On the whole, it was brilliant diplomacy by Modi.'[7]

Analysed clinically, Modi's imaginative forays in diplomacy and strategic planning have been bearing fruit. Take, for example, his diplomatic strike in relation to Balochistan. It was taken after careful thought and a lot of groundwork and planning by his national security adviser (NSA), Ajit Doval. As it turned out, the move not only left Pakistan dumbstruck but has also baffled China. The reason: it is directed as much against Pakistan as against China in the context of the 3000-km-long economic corridor that China is building from the Gwadar port on the Makran coast in Balochistan to the Xinjiang province in China and the mining activities (including gold mining) of the communist nation in Balochistan. Gwadar is virtually developing into a Chinese base that can be used to monitor the activities of India, as well as the US's movements in the Middle East. Any military build-up at Gwadar affects India because of its closeness to India's land as well as sea borders. By the land route, Gwadar is less than 900 km from Jaisalmer. By the sea route, it is equally close to Jamnagar, which has crucial Indian oil refinery installations and one of its foremost air force bases.

Gwadar's importance for China's economic interests can be figured out by considering the trading distance it will lessen for China in purely logistical terms. The distance from Gwadar to Beijing is 12,000 km via the South-East Asia corridor and also involves travel by sea. The distance between the same two destinations via Xinjiang is less than 6000 km and that too by only road and rail. Moreover, the distance from Gwadar to the China border is just 1800 km by road. According to Baloch freedom activists, China has been mining over 15 kg of gold a day in Balochistan for three decades and that China is as responsible as Pakistan for the helpless situation of the Balochis. China sees Gwadar as an answer to its 'Malacca riddle'—which represents fear on its part that the US or any other rival power could hold the Chinese economy hostage by blocking the narrow straits of Malacca, through which its major goods traffic passes right now.

To counter China's Gwadar move, Modi has signed a deal with Iran to develop the Chabahar port there, which is just 100 km from Gwadar on the same coastline. It is aimed at ensuring easier Indian trade with Afghanistan and the nations of Central Asia by road, apart from countering China and Pakistan. The Chabahar port proposal was developed when the A.B. Vajpayee government was in power. Due to American sanctions against Iran and other factors, the proposal was on the verge of dying before Modi revived it. The Afghan border from Chabahar is about 1300 km. With India's rivalry with Pakistan and China assuming a sharp edge and Modi emerging as the new saviour of the Balochi people, the Chabahar port proposal has assumed a greater significance than ever before. However, it has limited use against China and Pakistan considering the fact that it is a smaller port than Gwadar in terms of draught, and unlike Gwadar, where China will also anchor its warships, Chabahar holds the prospect of purely commercial use for India.

The punch in Modi's moves to counteract China comes from a deep understanding of the Chinese situation and an unstinted belief in the destiny of India based on the loftiness of its aims. Modi understands that China's rise was due to both military and economic growth made possible by an autocratic one-party rule. But its economy, though still strong, is beginning to wane. He also sees a flaw in the Chinese belief that its military and economic superiority will force everyone to accept it as a great power, overriding the fact that it lacks a culture of accepting and managing contradictions in a spirit of give-and-take, and is prone to bulldozing others in a fast-changing world where freedom has a new meaning.

Cracks have started appearing in the Chinese economy. Though India stands nowhere near China in terms of exports and GDP, it outpaced China in FDI in 2016—the first country to do so in several years. India got $63 billion in FDI while China got $56 billion in 2016. China's exports have also started dropping and its currency was at a six-year low at the end of 2016. China's GDP growth was also slower than that of India during this period. On the employment front, China has started losing its workforce superiority.

China's population-control measures in the form of the one-child norm have had multiple effects. The rule helped China check its population, but has also led to its workforce becoming costlier and not easily available. The labour problems have even led to some Chinese companies moving out of the country. So the demographic advantage is shifting towards India. Yes, the trade deficit between China and India remains huge due to China's advantage, but Modi knows that if India needs Chinese investments, China also needs markets to sell its goods and sustain itself at a time when its economy is shrinking. There is no bigger market than India.

What is more, blessed with sound traits of detached observation, precise analysis and interpretation, Modi comprehends that China has aligned with forces that are on the wrong side of history. These forces are dangerous and irresponsible nations like Pakistan and North Korea, which use terror and strong-arm tactics to make their presence felt. Despite its tough exterior, China might be getting itself into a swamp, from which it might it find hard to emerge without losing face. This situation might seem hypothetical at the moment given China's fearful might, but can't be ruled out as a future possibility.

Besides, how far can China manage the contradictions wherein it supports Pakistan's ultra-Wahhabi terrorists for its strategic objectives but cracks down ruthlessly not just on its own Wahhabi terrorists but also on common Muslims in the province of Xinjiang located on the border of Pakistan-occupied Kashmir (PoK)? History shows that the fortunes of mighty empires and superpowers have often changed dramatically in a short span of time. The Mughal empire seemed to be at the height of its glory when Aurangzeb ascended the throne in 1659, but had lost all its power within just ten years of Aurangzeb's death in 1707.[8]

In south India, the Vijaynagar empire seemed to be at its zenith for a long time, having withstood Muslim invasions from the north for over two centuries. But it was all gone in 1565 in the battle of Talikota. This happened within just thirty-five years of the departure of Krishnadevaraya, Vijaynagar's most powerful emperor. Krishnadevaraya had never lost a battle against his powerful Muslim rivals and expanded the empire in all directions with his prowess. In China's case, the one-party rule has started to elicit hush-hush reactions from the Chinese in a world that yearns for more and more freedom. Some of these reactions are in the open, like when some groups in Hong Kong openly called for freedom in October–November 2016.

Both China and Pakistan failed to read the shrewd Modi correctly. Modi tried to begin his innings as prime minister on a positive note with both China and Pakistan, perhaps due to his respect for India's image as an honourable, straightforward nation and his own strategic prerogatives. He invited all SAARC nation heads, including Pakistan's Nawaz Sharif, for his swearing-in ceremony in 2014, and held a small summit with Sharif on the next day. Later, in 2015, Modi made an unscheduled stop in Lahore to attend a function in Nawaz Sharif's family. He had also invited Xi Jinping to India and hosted him in his home state, Gujarat.

Both Pakistan and China didn't get Modi's welcome signal right. Perhaps they saw it as a sign of India's weakness, looking at it through the prism of the Nehruvian era. When the Modi-Jinping engagement was on in India, China practised its old policy of letting Chinese troops enter India's north-eastern border. China was doing what it has done many times in the past at the time of any high-level Indo-Chinese dialogue—planning an incursion into Indian borders to create pressure on India during negotiations. Pakistan also continued with its old policy of stabbing India in the back when its troops attacked the Pathankot airbase within a week of Modi's unscheduled and extremely warm Pakistan visit. But both the nations had calculated wrongly. Modi is no Jawaharlal Nehru, who allowed China to get a seat in the UN Security Council in the 1950s despite China's aggression in Tibet. Modi is a hardened politician with a strategic view on geopolitics.

Jinping got a dose of Modi's medicine inside the very tent where he was being hosted on the banks of the Sabarmati river in Ahmedabad. Modi reportedly told him, looking deep into his eyes: 'This was not expected of your country. Can you tell me when the troops are withdrawing?' Jinping gave a deadline of a week and the troops had withdrawn after a few days. China got more doses of the same pill when, immediately after this episode, Modi and US President Obama issued a joint statement expressing their concern over the rising tensions due to maritime territorial disputes in the South China Sea while affirming the importance of maritime security and freedom of navigation in the region. The South China Sea is crucial issue for China, which wants to maintain its military hegemony in the region. Nations like Vietnam and Japan are objecting to this.

The roadmap for Modi's global initiatives was prepared by Foreign Secretary S. Jaishankar, with the national security focus coming from Ajit Doval in the case of countries in India's immediate neighbourhood, particularly Pakistan. Jaishankar's worth lay in quickly grasping Modi's global vision while dealing with different nations and then preparing the roadmap accordingly—not an easy job considering the fact that Modi thinks ahead of most others and very deep. Jaishankar has boosted the policy planning and research division of the Ministry of External Affairs in such a way that crucial inputs while planning a Modi foreign trip are a click away. Obviously, inputs based on deep research have played a big role in Modi's successful foreign visits. One of the greatest achievements of these carefully crafted visits is securing FDI for India with inputs from the commerce and finance ministries. In the countries that matter, Modi has gone the extra mile to woo local business groups to invest in India, his accompanying officers providing them useful inputs on how they could go about investing in India, with information on specific industries. No wonder that India has emerged as the world's number one destination for FDI.

Ambassador to the US and China before becoming the foreign secretary in 2015, Jaishankar was already well versed in cutting-edge diplomacy. He was a favourite of even the previous government, which used his services as Indian ambassador to the US in laying the groundwork for the India–US nuclear deal under Manmohan Singh. But with the arrival of Modi, Jaishankar's talent found a new and much better outlet capable of harnessing his capacity to the optimum level.

Man of Diplomatic Sagacity

Holding out and reaching out are two very important dimensions of world diplomacy, or, for that matter, any level of diplomacy. The second trait of good diplomacy is a precise sense of timing embedded in the saying 'every time has its moment'. Precise moves at the precise time with apt words make all the difference when they are backed by economic exchange offers, which often work as bait. Yielding ground to a diplomatic friend at some loss to oneself to strengthen the friend in his community with an eye on long-term gains is another trait of a consummate player. Modi has exhibited these traits in his diplomatic career of nearly three years. His way of functioning stands out for his skilful manoeuvres, mature understanding and stealthy moves. Before Modi, only two leaders had shown such diplomatic traits— Indira Gandhi and P.V. Narasimha Rao. Gandhi displayed it in the age of the Cold War and during the period of international engagements preceding the 1971 India-Pakistan war.

In 1974, Gandhi is reported to have aided the native freedom fighters of Tanzania who were fighting for independence from Portugal, thus displaying rare foresight when it came to boosting Indian interests among the African nations that were coming out of the stranglehold of the European powers. Gandhi's moves helped create a relationship of camaraderie with these nations. However, in her golden moment, which came in the form of the 1971 victory over Pakistan and the creation of Bangladesh out of East Pakistan, she also committed a historical blunder. She failed to force Pakistani Premier Zulfikar Ali Bhutto to hand over PoK in spite of the fact that India was holding 93,000 Pakistan soldiers as prisoners of war. How big a blunder it was is more than evident today. The price: the killing of thousands of our soldiers and civilians in Kashmir in Pakistan's proxy war through terrorism and the increasing shadow of Wahhabism in an essentially Sufi Kashmir Valley.

P.V. Narasimha Rao's steering of the Indian ship through the troubled post–Cold War diplomatic waters was not an easy job either. His diplomacy shone during a time when India had not only become a near basket case but was also facing severe international pressure from the Comprehensive Nuclear-Test-Ban Treaty, the General Agreement on Tariffs and Trade, the World Bank and the International Monetary Fund. It was also evident in the phase following the dismantling of the Soviet Union. Rao can be credited with opening the doors to the US, which should have been India's natural ally from day one.

Modi's diplomacy comes in a different age and has a different agenda—an agenda that necessitates sharp manoeuvres. Modi took over when the UPA government had lost sight of the great Indian goal at the world level, thanks to its poor and corrupt governance at home coupled with its mishandling of the economy that sullied India's international image at a time when the country should have been on the top position on the economic front. Modi, on one hand, took up the task of setting the economy right and cleaning up the Augean stables with the aim of ushering in policy-driven governance, and, on the other hand, undertook the mission of engaging nations at different levels with different objectives—all aimed at securing India's interests to make the country a world leader in the twenty-first century.

A cursory glance at Modi's diplomatic journey would reveal that most of his diplomatic initiatives have seen India's interests being secured in one way or another, whether on the geostrategic, geopolitical or economic front. For example, with Mauritius, India signed a treaty that closed the flow of black money through that nation. This route had become convenient because of certain loopholes in Mauritius's laws that allowed Indian businessmen to convert black money into white and channel it back to India. Similar treaties to curb black money were also initiated with twenty-one other countries.

What sets the prime minister apart is that he has displayed a great ability to convince other nations of the loftiness of the Indian aim. This trait of Modi helped India in its efforts to isolate Pakistan after the Uri attack. Had Modi not given up everything, including his macho reputation in his own anti-Pakistan, Indian nationalist (read RSS-BJP) constituency, to woo Pakistan in an attempt to bring it on board in the first two years of his tenure, the world would not have been convinced about India's sincerity in solving the Pakistan problem and, in turn, would not have backed India's surgical strikes in response to Uri.

His diplomatic sagacity stands out when one considers his success in bringing Russia back on the main track, at least partially, after its initial confusion following the Uri attack, the signing of the border accord with Bangladesh against the wishes of his own party, and turning the new Nepali Prime Minister, Pushpa Kamal Dahal, alias Prachanda, a die-hard communist, into a Modi admirer at the cost of displeasing his ideological ally, China. Russia had been veering towards Pakistan and China of late—of course, it was more in the spirit of securing its strategic and economic interests than in an anti-India tone. Russia also held a military exercise with Pakistan for the first time ever, a clear sign of the alteration in Russia's India policy. But by the time the BRICS summit was hosted by India in Goa, within less than a month of the Uri attack, Modi had brought Russia around to a significant extent with his skilful diplomacy.

Even as India signed a slew of defence, infrastructure and economic deals with Russia before the BRICS summit, Modi met with Russian President Vladimir Putin, underlining the fact that 'an old friend is better than two new friends' in a bid to set at rest questions about India-Russia relations. Knowing well that the Western economies are all in bad shape, Modi is intelligently using his defence shopping list as leverage by giving it a strategic spread when it comes to buying from different countries. R.S.N. Singh believes that Modi is a doing an excellent job of leveraging

India's strength as the largest importer of arms to secure its strategic interests. To be fair to Modi, Russian diplomacy with India is also dictated by extraneous factors like the deterioration of Russia-US relations based on their conflicting stances in the Middle East. When the apparently Putin-friendly Donald Trump was in the saddle in the US, the Russian stance towards Pakistan, and by extension, with India, was expected to alter again. But US-Russia relations took a nosedive once again when Trump ordered military strikes against Syria in April 2017, in reaction to that country's use of chemical weapons against rebels.

The prime minister has shown the same diplomatic wisdom while signing the border accord with Bangladesh, which involved the exchange of villages and was being opposed by the BJP unit of Assam. But Modi knew the worth of the move for Bangladesh, India's close ally in the war against terror, and also for the personal image of the exceptionally brave Prime Minister Sheikh Hasina Wazed, who has persistently faced the allegation of being too pro-India and has taken on radical Islamists head-on like few other Muslim leaders in the world. The border accord has strengthened Wazed in her home constituency at a time when she has backed India's moves on ultra-Wahhabi terror.

Inducting as minister of state for external affairs M.J. Akbar, the renowned journalist with a preference for Jawaharlal Nehru over Sardar Vallabhbhai Patel, is also an example of Modi's diplomatic sagacity. There was opposition to Akbar's appointment from within the BJP because of his known Nehruvian views, but Modi found him useful for setting India's relations with the Middle East in order. True to Modi's expectation, Akbar is performing well in the role assigned to him.

Even as the struggle between India and Pakistan continues, with an increase in Pakistan-sponsored terror attacks on India, the recognition of Modi's diplomacy in relation to Pakistan comes from within that country itself. In a 2016 interview to a Pakistan channel, Zaid Hamid, a writer from Pakistan close to the ISI wing of the Pakistan Army, extolled the virtues of Modi while pointing out the danger posed to Pakistan's interests by the Indian prime minister's strategies. Hamid said: 'Pakistan was never in such a helpless situation before, which indicates the failure of Pakistan's diplomacy against Modi's. We are totally isolated today and left with only one ally, China. Even Saudi Arabia and other Muslims countries in the Middle East have veered towards India due to Modi's clever diplomacy. When Modi's steps out of India he does so to secure his country's interest. While our prime minister [Nawaz Sharif] goes out to secure his business interest.'[9] Being close to the ISI, Hamid would be naturally severe towards Sharif. Yet Hamid's overall analysis adds a lot to Modi's image and indicates how people in Pakistan see him as a threat.

Understanding the Potential of the Indian Diaspora and Turning It into India's Soft Power

What has set Modi's diplomacy apart from that of most of his predecessors is his vision aimed at utilizing the strength of the powerful Indian diaspora. Modi is turning NRIs into India's ambassadors in their respective countries by injecting them with a sense of pride about the country's onward march. He is achieving this by having large public meetings with the diaspora during his foreign visits, where he shares with them the stories of the economic strides India is making and the new standards his government is setting at home. He is turning the diaspora into India's soft power by holding NRI shows like the ones at Wembley Stadium in London and Madison Square in New York in almost every country he visits where NRIs matter. Lieutenant General Syed Ata Hasnain, a defence and foreign policy expert who had held military command in Kashmir before his retirement, says: 'The prime minister's understanding of India's soft power and its role in India's forward march on the international turf is simply outstanding.'[10]

Modi appears convinced that engaging nations having NRIs pays rich dividends. India has so far failed to tap the full potential of its soft power and use it as a powerful supplementing force. Modi also understands that in the big immigration debate that has started in the Western countries after the Iraq crisis and the terror threat raised by migrants from Islamic countries, Indian immigrants, who are known all over for their positive and peaceful attitude as well as for their brilliance, are much more welcome and acceptable, notwithstanding their image of a job-grabbing lot in some nations. Modi knows that this diaspora soft power, if used properly, will give India a distinct edge in foreign relations over the likes of China and Russia.

Modi's wooing of the diaspora is not limited to holding meetings with them. To empower NRIs and bring them closer to India, he has adopted many positive measures. In the first place, he has ended the hassle NRIs had to face in getting multiple eligibility cards when they came to India. He has designated the Person of Indian Origin (PIO) card as the only official document. Modi and Swaraj have removed many other small logistical hurdles and made Indian embassies accessible to NRIs in their countries 24x7.

What is commendable is that Modi has not ignored the less powerful diaspora of Indian workers and skilled artisans in the Middle East who have been sending back huge amounts money, but have felt neglected because of the way they have been treated by the Indian government in the past. Modi has invariably met them and heard their problems while visiting the Middle East. Kanchan Banerjee, an NRI based in Boston who has known Modi since the 1990s, when Modi used to visit the US at regular intervals, says: 'The best part is that Modiji is changing the mentality of the NRIs settled in developed countries that nothing can change in India. By talking about innovative concepts and schemes like Swachh Bharat, Jan-Dhan, Mudra loan he has been changing India's image in the eyes of the diaspora. For the NRIs this is such a new, vibrant connect with India. They now really feel the change that is happening in India.'[11]

Apt Beginning: Global Vision with Regional Emphasis

From the day Modi undertook his first visit to Bhutan soon after becoming the prime minister, his vision in terms of foreign policy has been crystal clear. It is divided into two parts—global and regional. The global vision includes the US, Russia, China and the European powers. The regional vision has Asian countries. There is a bifurcation in the regional vision. It includes the eastern part, which has the Buddhist nations of the east and south-east across the Bay of Bengal that have civilizational and cultural ties with India, and the western part, which comprises the Islamic nations beyond the Arabian Sea right up to the Gulf of Aden. The latter have had economic ties with India since ancient times. In the first year, Modi visited the eastern countries in a planned manner, and then in the second year engaged with the Islamic countries to the west.

On the western front, he struck an unprecedented chord with the United Arab Emirates and Saudi Arabia, with the latter going to the extent of conferring on him its highest civilian honour, the King Abdulaziz Sash. In dealing with the Islamic countries, including the Wahhabi nations that are now riven by ultra-Wahhabi terror and threatened by the shadow of the Islamic State, he has capitalized on India's ability to maintain peace at home in spite of having a large Muslim population. This has created a new place for India in the Middle East. In Abu Dhabi, the rulers have donated land for a Hindu temple in an unprecedented gesture. What is remarkable is that while strengthening India's relations with Israel, he has not overplayed them, thus striking a diplomatic balance. In fact, Modi's first-ever visit to Israel was tipped only after the completion of his three years in office.

Further west, Modi has effectively engaged with Kenya, Tanzania, Mozambique and South Africa. Here he has shown the boldness to look beyond the Indian Ocean and tried to take India's strategic border up to the South China Sea and the Pacific, through which over 50 per cent of our trade passes. G. Parthasarathy, a former Indian ambassador to Pakistan who has observed Modi's foreign policy initiatives closely, says: 'Modi deserves high marking on his diplomatic strategy. He has displayed a rare global vision with strong regional emphasis. No other leader has developed such close relations with nations in India's immediate west. Plus, he has demonstrated cutting-edge cultural and economic diplomacy. He aims at restoring India to its position of a major trading power in the world, which it lost after the onset of the British rule.'[12] No wonder that after the departure of US President Barack Obama, Modi is perhaps not just the most watched leader but also perhaps the most popular one. His Twitter following of 28 million is one indication of his popularity.

The Challenge

Modi has raised the bar through his dealings with China and Pakistan. Now the challenges facing him are as huge as his grand diplomatic designs. Having confronted China, he can't look back now. He has virtually invited the wrath of a nation that always saw India as inferior. China issued a statement after the BRICS summit in which it described Pakistan as a nation which is itself affected by terrorism. Then it asked the world not to forget Pakistan's 'great sacrifices'. Such a statement almost amounted to the antics of a rogue nation, coming as it did when Pakistan-backed terrorists were attacking Indian security forces in the Kashmir Valley after India had conducted the surgical strikes in response to the Uri attack.

In a way, China was virtually behaving a like jealous elder brother who bullies his younger sibling. The younger brother has finally chosen to hit back after putting up with the big brother's high-handedness for years. At this stage, Modi has to take a call on whether he must have a second look at business relations with China, which has been allowed to double its trade surplus with India. Powerful sections of the public in India are already calling for a boycott of Chinese goods. If this trend is backed by Modi then it could dissuade Chinese investments in India, bringing bad consequences.

According to Brahma Chellaney, a security affairs expert and a specialist on China and Pakistan, Modi has to be stricter with both Pakistan and China to get results. Without imposing direct costs on Pakistan's military and the Pakistani state, India can't hope to deter Pakistan's terror tactics, Chellaney feels. He believes that China is culpable for the death of Indian soldiers in the hands of the Jaish-e-Mohammed when it shields Masood Azhar. Chellaney thinks that this is an indication of the extent to which China can go to shield Pakistan's patronage of terrorism against India. He asks whether China should be allowed to double its trade surplus with India in this situation.

Chellaney also questions whether India can apply pressure on China till it itself seeks Pakistan's complete international isolation by taking a series of steps—such as downgrading Pakistan's diplomatic status, withdrawing the one-sided, 'most favoured nation' status in trade that it granted to Pakistan two decades ago on a non-reciprocal basis and designating Pakistan as a sponsor of terrorism or declaring bounties on the head of UN-designated terrorists operating openly from Pakistan.[13]

But no argument on this issue is valid unless one considers that Modi has been in office for just three years and is still grappling with the fractured legacy of India's previous governments. He is going step by step. He will raise the bar as the $2 trillion-plus Indian economy goes further up and India improves its military might by ending a tradition of soft diplomacy and poor strategic calculations. Modi has added new contours of cultural diplomacy to India's foreign policy. He might be waiting for the day when India becomes a $3 trillion, and then a $5 trillion, economy and sufficiently adds to its economic might. So he is putting emphasis on economic growth even at the cost of some other important things. Economic development is also important to his plans to increase India's defence spending. Significantly, China is an $11 trillion economy today, and the US's GDP is $18 trillion.

Modi's foreign affairs map is precisely designed. But it is dotted with a series of challenges that are usual in a truly democratic nation—a factor about which China, even Pakistan, have little or no worries. Modi can at least take solace in the fact that Indian foreign policy has started coming out of the Nehruvian 'cocoon'—a process started by Indira Gandhi and advanced further by P.V. Narasimha Rao and A.B. Vajpayee. Now with Modi in charge, it is realizing its full potential, commensurate with India's inherent strengths in a fast-changing world. Of course, the results of his next test—Donald Trump—are yet to come.

7

Balancing the Balance Sheet

Fiscal Manager with a Difference

Prime Minister Narendra Modi took oath on 26 May 2014 with the heady promise of 'achhe din'. But within just a few days of moving into South Block, Modi found himself in a dilemma. His predicament was surprising given the massive mandate he had got. The normally stress-free Modi had been in such a predicament only twice in his political career, which began in 2001. The first time was when the Gujarat riots appeared uncontrollable after the Godhra episode in 2002 which claimed over 1200 lives in a communal conflagration. The second time was in 2010, when the UPA government seemed bent upon winding up his political career in the wake of Gujarat police's encounter cases, after having already sent behind bars his man Friday, Amit Shah.

This time the cause was very different. It had to do with the account books of the administration he had taken over. The issue was a major decision he was being called upon to take as the new pilot of the nation. It was to have a lasting impact not just on the fragile financial health of India but also on the country's international image. It was connected to his own promise of good governance that had fashioned his historic 282-seat win.

The outgoing UPA government had left behind very stiff fiscal deficit targets for the new government. They seemed stiffer to Modi when he saw the financial jugglery on the account sheets. Some of the spending splurges of the UPA had been window dressed and pushed on to the next government's account books. The UPA's outgoing act was perhaps the short-term and long-term ripple effect of its political decisions similar to the ₹60,000 loan waiver it had given to farmers.

BJP insiders allege that it was deliberately done by the UPA in the interim budget, which had been presented a few months before the 2014 Lok Sabha polls, knowing well that it was not coming back to power in the 2014 polls. Congress leaders deny the charge. But this was not the only issue. In a desperate bid to woo poorer sections of voters on the eve of the elections, the UPA had also passed the controversial National Food Security Act (NFSA) which made it mandatory for the government to spend around ₹1.25 lakh crore annually. Many Modi supporters thought the UPA had practised a scorched earth policy, leaving a burdened treasury before withdrawing.

The fiscal deficit issue demanded a bold decision on Modi's part amid conflicting advice. A section of senior BJP leaders and bureaucrats wanted the NDA government to begin its new innings by disowning the unreal fiscal deficit target set by the UPA. The advice to Modi was to reject the target and allow himself the room to spend and create a positive impact on the new voters who had chosen him. The first impression you make on the people, they said, can often turn out to be the last one. They wanted the Modi government to come out with a White Paper on the bad financial health of the country that had been allegedly caused by the reckless, non-productive spending of the UPA.

But for Modi, who had come to power on the promise of restoring national pride at the international level, that would have meant washing dirty linen in public. It would have given the world's largest democracy the image of a banana republic, severely compromising Indian interests among international rating agencies, world financial institutions and foreign investors. Moreover, the decision would have meant short-term gains for his government but trouble if it got re-elected in 2019. His fiscal indiscipline would have stared him in the face in 2019.

Yet the other course left before Modi if he was to honour the previous government's obligations was very difficult. It was almost like the balancing act of a trapeze artiste—reduced spending but piloting a carefully structured growth. It was a vicious circle in which private investments would be low while reduced government spending would mean taking the bad economy further down. But a prime minister geared by a long-term national vision and the support of his image-conscious Finance Minister Arun Jaitley decided to take the honourable course. They chose to stand by the difficult targets left behind by the UPA.

Historical Fiscal Recovery

A foolproof plan was soon drawn up to tackle the challenge. This required some bold decisions. In two brave strokes, the Modi government increased FDI from 26 to 49 per cent first in the insurance sector and then in the defence manufacturing sector. Increase in FDI in insurance was a landmark decision as it had been hanging fire for about ten years, with both the RSS and the Left parties opposing it tooth and nail. This sent a strong message that India was treading a positive path on FDI that was so necessary for the nation in an economic era of slow manufacturing. It also sent the signal that the government was moving in the right direction while tackling long-pending and complex issues. Simultaneously, the finance ministry took a series of motivative and strong measures to increase the income tax net. This led to an unprecedented surge in the number of new taxpayers in a span of just one year, from 4.88 crore in 2013–14 to 5.43 crore in 2014–15. The figure touched around 6 crore in 2016–17. Within three years of the NDA coming to power, nearly 1.10 crore new taxpayers have been added.

As the NDA government came close to the halfway point of its term, Jaitley's efforts to increase the tax net with transparent, tough measures and effective use of technology and social media tools showed impressive results. A four-month, time-bound income disclosure scheme (IDS) netted over ₹65,000 crore from just 65,000 people at an average of ₹1 crore a person, the highest ever in India. Another whopping ₹76,000 crore came by way of seizures and detection of undisclosed income. The IDS disclosures, of course, had some names whose disclosure figures turned out to be false. This brought down the figure to ₹52,000 crore—still impressive.

A Herculean effort had, however, gone into making the IDS a success. The finance ministry dispatched letters to 7 lakh people who had carried out high-value transactions without revealing their Permanent Account Number (PAN). They were asked to share their PAN and their accounts were scrutinized for further action. That the government didn't extend the deadline of the scheme despite pressure was a clear sign that the rules of the game had changed after the arrival of the NDA and that the former lethargy in tax administration was gone. The Union financial services secretary, Hasmukh Adhia, tweeted a week before the announcement of the scheme that there will be no extension of the deadline. As a result, people made a beeline for disclosures in the final phase.

It is true that under the NDA, manufacturing was slow in the first two years, due to the global slowdown and two consecutive droughts and high interest rate. More needs to be done in this area. But thanks to Modi's high international pitch on investment, India's FDI inflows backed by his Make in India campaign touched around ₹9 lakh crore (close to $150 billion) in over two and a half years, leaving behind China, the world's FDI giant. India's foreign exchange reserves stood at around an impressive ₹22 lakh-plus crore during this period. The food inflation, which was almost 19 per cent during the last years of the UPA tenure, is now less than 6 per cent—a recovery of 70 per cent. Retail inflation, based on the consumer price index (CPI), has halved to 5.5 per cent from 11 per cent in 2013–14. That this was achieved despite two consecutive drought years and amid extremely tight fiscal conditions is a result of the Modi regime's skilful financial management.

Little known but crucial steps also played a role in the economic recovery. In a first in independent India's history, the Modi government gave the RBI an inflation target and the freedom to act in achieving that target. This is exactly the way it is done in developed countries like the US, the UK and Germany, where the government gives inflation targets to the central bank. In the past, the RBI has often been directed by governments to keep the inflation under control but has never been given a specific target.

The target that the government gave to the RBI for 2015–16 and for the year after that was 4 per cent with 2 per cent tolerance. And as the government was close to its third anniversary, the fiscal deficit stood at 3.2 per cent—within earshot of the world standard of 3 per cent. This enabled India's central bank to keep the interest rate at a level which squeezed out easy money from the market to the benefit of the economy, although there are people who believe that the interest rate maintained by the RBI during this period affected manufacturing and the sector under the Ministry of Micro, Small and Medium Enterprises (MSMEs). Moreover, there was unanimity between the RBI and the finance ministry during this difficult period on interest rates despite differences. For the first time, the finance ministry was not playing the 'dada', or the big brother, to the RBI. This was in contrast to its attitude in previous years.

Even when the Modi government came up with the new arrangement of having a Monetary Policy Committee (MPC) in September 2016 to fix interest rates after the departure of Raghuram Rajan and the arrival of Urjit Patel, the finance ministry continued to follow the golden rule of giving significant freedom to the RBI, unlike in previous regimes. It left the task of guiding the RBI to economic experts in the MPC and that too in a very structured way. Hasmukh Adhia, the revenue secretary, observes: 'On the one hand, the government has set one of the best examples of healthy fiscal management, and on the other hand, implemented reforms in an innovative and effective manner.'[1]

In due course, the FDI reforms got more resonance. The FDI limit was increased to 100 per cent in civil aviation and the food-processing industry's greenfield projects. In a big move, 100 per cent FDI was allowed to the railways when it hadn't been there at all before. In fact, 100 per cent FDI is allowed in almost all sectors now except space (74 per cent), defence (49 per cent) and news media (26 per cent). Diesel was deregulated for the first time, the low international crude oil prices coming in handy for the government in this.

Alongside this, there have been several bank reforms under the label 'Indradhanush'. With an eye on controlling NPAs, the BBB was formed under Vinod Rai, the former CAG of India. Private hands were brought from outside to head and professionally manage important banks like the Bank of Baroda and Canara Bank. Under a new plan to bring the banks on track and streamline their working, the government is going for the merger of nationalized banks. However, even economists who admire the Modi government's courage believe that not enough has been dome to reform the banking sector, which is weighed down with gigantic NPAs. Rai too has expressed concerns about the bank bureaucracy. But none can contest the fact there has not been creation of any new NPA under the Modi regime, though they continue to rise because of the interest factor.

Before demonetization, there was another significant development that had gone unnoticed in 2016. This concerned the law that the NDA had brought about to curb the generation of black money with stringent punishment to the guilty. It dealt an instant blow to the black-money-creation industry, particularly in the retail sector. So on the eve of demonetization, the flight of black money to safe havens stood significantly curbed. The same applies to the real estate sector, where a new law protecting the interests of consumers has helped control the menace. This has been a bitter pill for the real estate sector in the initial phase, affecting its growth, because of the fact that the sector has been a repository of black money in India. But this is being seen as a natural but passing phase. It is also important to note here that the prices of homes have come down for the consumer, more so after demonetization.

Interestingly, before 8 November 2016, the government had attracted flak for not doing enough to bring back the black money stashed abroad. But those who criticized it failed to appreciate the fact that the NDA had struck at the roots of black-money generation through a series of measures. NITI Aayog CEO Amitabh Kant, who oversaw Modi's Make in India campaign, observes: 'No government in independent India's history has carried out such wide-scale structural changes in the functioning of the government as the Modi government. The prime minister is indeed laying the foundation of a new India.'[2]

If one leaves aside strongly Left-leaning economists, most of the others in the profession are appreciative of the Modi government's handling of the economy. According to veteran economist Surjit Bhalla, who has worked with the Brookings Institution and the World Bank, India's growth during the ten-year UPA tenure was due to extraneous factors because the UPA didn't implement a single policy to accelerate growth.

However, in almost three years of the NDA government, there has been a slew of measures to push growth despite strong handicaps in the form of a global slowdown and two consecutive drought years. Bhalla says: 'There have been more reforms in three years of Modi rule than in the past twenty years or since Manmohan Singh left office in 1996 after carrying out the 1991 reforms. Moreover, Modi's is the first government since Independence that is trying to set right the wrong direction of the agro economy by removing mindless controls.'[3]

The shape that the Modi government is giving to agricultural growth is one of its biggest economic reforms when compared to India's poor agro policies and growth in the past seven decades. The slow pace of India's growth in the previous decades has largely been a result of government controls that allowed middlemen to flourish and take away a substantial part of farmers' legitimate income. Not many are aware that India's aggregate growth rate in agriculture has been just 3 per cent since 1950, when India began its economic march. This poor growth rate was understandable till the late 1970s, when the agriculture infrastructure, including the irrigation network, was still being laid out. But even after that was completed, aggregate growth has remained at the same low level.

The reasons, according to competent economists, were embedded in the faulty support pricing system as well as in wrong government interventions like the ban on interstate transfer of some commodities in states like Punjab and making farmers sell their products at mandis dotted with middlemen. The selling structure, for example, prevented an MNC from buying directly from a farmer till some years ago.

What the Modi government has done is that it has replaced negative interventions with positive ones. For instance, it has introduced an innovative and easy-to-avail crop insurance scheme that makes the accrual of crop insurance to an honest farmer more likely than ever before and much faster in case of loss due to crop failure. The government is also well on its way to delinking production from distribution in agriculture, allowing market forces to step in. Agro scientists and economists believe that the Indian farmer is in for a good period after the arrival of the NDA government, which has introduced NAM, thus digitally linking farmers with the highest bidder for their produce through e-auction.

The irrigation sector has received a major push in the form of the prime minister's irrigation scheme, which is marked by innovation and an integrated approach. Bhalla says: 'In two to three more years, the scene in the agro sector will be very different. From an aggregate of 3 per cent growth, India could be moving to a growth between 4 and 6 per cent or even more, a few years from now.' Economists are also impressed with some of the growth-oriented labour reforms introduced by the Centre and by some of the BJP-ruled states, particularly Rajasthan, where the hassle of getting major permissions from the labour department has been removed for industrial units employing up to 300 workers.

However, some economists, like the NITI Aayog member Ramesh Chand, who has played a major role in the Modi government's agro reforms, believe that the reforms, particularly in the agro market, need acceptance and penetration at the state level, without which they can't realize their full potential. 'There has to be a mechanism to make the states implement these reforms in Team India spirit,' he says.[4]

The Centre's crop insurance scheme for farmers, for example, was not properly implemented by the previous Uttar Pradesh government under the Samajwadi Party. There are also problems with states in the implementation of NAM. In fact, the NITI Aayog has made some great suggestions for agricultural growth, like turning tractors into Uber or Ola taxis so that small farmers, who are unable to buy tractors, can hire them online when needed and plough their farms. The NITI Aayog has also developed a model land lease law for the states to help them enhance their performance in agriculture and make optimum use of land for farming.

The 2017–18 Budget Is Proof of Skilful Fiscal Management

The jugglery of figures in public accounts can seldom go undetected, particularly in a democracy. The benefits of good fiscal management, if the exercise is truly skilful, have to show on the surface. The 2017–18 budget of the NDA government is one such exercise. The ₹21.50 lakh crore budget shows a surprising rise of almost 30 per cent over the budget of 2013–14, when the NDA took over. This is an achievement in fiscal management. The increase in the size of the budget every year under the NDA government is indeed a story of fiscal recovery, with some wise accounting based on transparent governance. Right from the day the government assumed power, it started plugging the holes of corruption and wasteful expenditure, chiefly by using the DBT route for the disbursement of subsidy. It began to divert the saved money into plans for increasing the budget size and into other productive schemes. Increasing the tax base by resorting to some shrewd financial planning and stopping the role of corporate houses in policymaking also played a role.

The impressive increase in budget size has meant a rise in allocation for infrastructure by almost two times in three years, from ₹2010 lakh crore to ₹3098 lakh crore, and a threefold rise in the allocation for agriculture from ₹17,000 crore to ₹55,000 crore. The allocation for the Mudra loan scheme, which has emerged as a major source of self-employment in the context of a drop in manufacturing and direct job creation, has almost been doubled to ₹2.50 lakh crore. The budget aims at productivity enhancement through infrastructure creation and the doubling of agriculture income of farmers by 2022 through a sharp agro push. Nripendra Misra, principal secretary to the prime minister, says: 'It is significant that the marked increase in India's budget size in an environment of global headwinds is unlike the last big growth India saw a decade ago in an atmosphere of global economic boom, when all the major nations were seeing high economic growth and BRICS was mooted.'[5]

Direct and indirect taxes grew by an impressive 17 per cent in 2015–16 and by a still more impressive 35 per cent in the first two quarters of 2016–17, before dropping somewhat in the last two quarters due to demonetization. That there is a growth of around 20 per cent in direct and indirect taxes year after year clearly shows that the saved money is being used productively. The focus area in the budget is the digital economy, which is perceived to be the next revolution under India's leadership, like the West-driven Industrial Revolution was in the eighteenth century. In the transformation being brought about in this area, the UPI will be a major tool because it represents the easiest way of making digital payments—with just a few taps on a smartphone. India is now expected to make and sell digital products all over the world, just as Western countries made and sold machines to the East in the decades following the Industrial Revolution.

The other push of the budget is in the governing vision in the form of efficient and foolproof delivery of services like LPG, passport, land record, Aadhaar card, transport, metro and rail systems. But one of the main features of this annual budget is the preponing of its presentation in Parliament by one month, from March to February, which will be its presentation schedule from now on. It is a big step in finance management. The one-month push is expected to improve budgetary spending drastically and curb meaningless expenditure. Economist Vivek Dehejia says: 'This is indeed a revolutionary move with direct impact on governance and spending.'[6]

Earlier, with board examinations in school, vacations and the monsoon following the March presentation of the budget in quick succession, there used to be a delay in spending the budgetary allocations initially. And when it became too late, there would be a rush to spend the allocated money through haphazard means by various departments in the fear that if not used, the grant would lapse and lead to lesser allocation by the government next year on the basis of the assumption that the department concerned was unable to spend the allotted money or simply didn't need it.

But going several steps ahead, the government is now mulling over the idea of a January-to-December financial year instead of the current April-to-March one. Modi is the mover of this idea as he believes that, in a country where agriculture income matters, it is important that the budget is prepared immediately after the receipts of the year. Modi has impressed even the states with this idea. If this happens, then the budget utilization would further improve substantially across the board.

Budget-making under the NDA government has undergone a fundamental change in many other ways. The annual national budget is no longer based on the expectations of financial experts operating from London and Hong Kong or on the needs of those who are only concerned with the rise and drop of the Sensex. It is now based on the needs of the people. So the Sensex is becoming irrelevant to the budget—it no longer goes up and down on the budget day, as it did before. Getting more into the tax net through prudent tax structuring has been one of the main objectives of the NDA government. This is indicated by an addition of 1.10 crore taxpayers in three years.

Still, it is an area where the government has a long way to go. But it can expect better results in the coming days with the formalization of the economy following demonetization and a series of other measures. India compares very poorly with developed countries in tax compliance—in Sweden, 100 out of 100 people pay tax, in the US, sixty-five, and in Canada, ninety-five. In India, only seven out of every 100 people pay tax, indicating the size of the informal economy and the extent of tax evasion. Only one Western country comes somewhat close to India in this dismal record—the UK, where only twenty out of every 100 people pay tax.

Passing of the GST Gives EU-like Muscle to India and Impacts Social Cohesion

In a phase largely marked by a global slowdown, back-to-back rain-scarce years till 2016–17, low manufacturing and relatively low exports, the great achievement of the government has been the passage of the GST bill. With the GST rollout becoming a reality the Indian economy is on the way to becoming as strong as that of the European Union (EU), which is the second-largest economy in the world after the US, if considered as one unit. It is, in fact, as big an economic development on the national political turf as the formation of the EU in the 1950s and next only to the political integration of India in 1950 under Sardar Vallabhbhai Patel. Although India is a political and constitutional union, it has never been a fully integrated economic union. The GST has the potential to achieve for India what the EU project did for Europe in terms of raising the standard of living of the people after the slowdown that Europe saw after World War II. The GST could end up demonstrating more transformational potential for India than even the EU because the EU has never been a political union.

GST and the huge jump in digital transactions that the country is seeing following demonetization opens a new chapter on the economy of India, a country that has been notorious for the lack of tax compliance due to a variety of factors, including the very nature of certain local trades. The cost of many goods is now expected to come down as a result of a single taxation structure which in other terms means greater tax compliance based on the principle of 'low tax, greater compliance'. The transparency as structured in the GST law makes tax evasion very difficult. The benefits are simply innumerable—all pointing towards a great tax kitty and money saving. Manufacturing is also set to benefit. All in all, GST heralds a significant increase in India's GDP and the starting of India's march towards becoming an economic tiger.

The GST with its slogan of 'one nation, one tax and one market' opens unlimited opportunities not only for India's economic growth and integration but also for solving other problems. When the states and the Centre sit together and jointly decide the tax rates, it may encourage the Team India spirit, which in the normal course of events soars only when an Uri or a Pathankot happens, or when a natural calamity hits the nation. When the states and the Centre continue to work year after year on a crucial thing like the setting of tax rates, it could bring about social and political cohesion to solve state-vs-state and Centre-vs-state problems. With a powerful institutional mechanism in place to bring Team India together on a regular basis to decide on one of the most important aspects of governance—revenue collection—disputes like the one over river-water sharing between states like Karnataka and Tamil Nadu, for example, could find faster solutions.

Clearly, if there is one development that establishes Narendra Modi as a leader of great sagacity and long-term vision, it is the passing of the GST. Facing stiff opposition from major political parties, he has done a great job of bringing the states on board the administrative platform, of course, with the resourcefulness of Jaitley and a set of bureaucrats who worked with missionary zeal behind the scenes to make GST a reality.

However, under the NDA government, manufacturing, a major driver of the economy, continued to be low in the first two years before picking up impressively following a good monsoon in 2016. Demonetization affected it for a brief while. Manufacturing growth was minus 3 per cent in 2012 and was expected to reach about 5 per cent (or more) at the end of the two years of the NDA government. But it either hovered around 1 per cent or remained in the negative at the end of the first two years. This has had a direct impact on job creation in the NDA's first two years before stabilizing. As a rule of thumb, every new direct job creates four indirect jobs in the manufacturing sector. So, one job in the manufacturing sector means sustenance for five families. However, during this period, the government tried to tackle the unemployment problem by offering a series of opportunities for self-employment by changing the Nehruvian norms that considered the job creation scenario only from the point of view of direct employment.

The government has come up with innovative schemes like Mudra, Stand-Up India and Startup India. That over 6 crore common people like ironsmiths, carpenters, flower sellers, owners of cycle repair shops and general stores have been given over ₹2.24 lakh crore in loans without collateral under the Mudra scheme is proof of the government's sincerity in tackling the problem of job creation. What is more, these loans are not a 'gift' to secure vote banks, as they have been in the past. The result: under the Mudra loan scheme, the percentage of return on loans taken in the form of instalments is over 98 per cent.

Merchant Modi Makes India the FDI Capital by Hard-Selling Make in India During His Foreign Trips

But all these efforts of the NDA are dwarfed in the face of India emerging as an FDI giant by attracting the highest FDI in the world in just two years, outpacing China, which had held the number one spot for over two decades. From the fifteenth spot in 2013, India moved to the top position in just two years and continued to lead even in the beginning of 2017. Two strokes by Modi fixed the FDI path. First, he floated the Make in India scheme in September 2015, announcing incentives and a simplification of rules for twenty-five different sectors, including automobiles, defence manufacturing, aviation, food processing, electronics, construction, pharmaceuticals and railways. Significantly, 100 per cent FDI was permitted in almost all the sectors except defence, space and news media. Secondly, Modi started selling Make in India in each of his foreign trips by holding meetings with business of the countries concerned, his officers providing them specific industry-based inputs on how to go about investing in India. In his meetings with the businessmen during these foreign trips, Modi drew an encouraging picture of India's economic march and the distinct advantages that India presented, like the demographic dividend—India has the largest population of youth in the world.

The minister of state for industry and commerce, Nirmala Sitharaman, who has worked hard to make Make in India happen, says: 'One of the main focuses of the PM's foreign trips has been attracting FDI. We have worked to a plan. Through the Make in India policy, the PM gave a platform to entrepreneurs, both new and old, to show their potential in an atmosphere of freedom from mindless control. And then we started selling it at national and international levels to potential investors. It worked. Make in India has played major role in getting FDI for India. Modiji's hard sell made all the difference.'[7]

The high-powered growth of China all these years was based on its FDI muscle. That India has left China behind is a precise measure of India's future potential as an economic power. The increased FDI is also an answer to those who question Modi's visits to around fifty countries in a period of about three years. His visits have clearly played a role in attracting FDI. The FDI phenomenon has to be seen in a particular context to realize its true potential for India and to understand what Modi means when he says that India will lead the world in the coming years.

India overtaking China in FDI is an interesting story. China being overpowered by India in FDI isn't a victory over a weakling.

It is no big deal to outpace a rival at your normal speed when the rival is weak. But China still stands strong on FDI. According to the *Financial Times*, London, in 2016 India netted $63 billion in FDI while China managed around $56 billion. But it was for the first time in more than two decades that a country had overtaken China in the FDI race. The importance of the development can be understood only against the backdrop of past FDI figures. China has continued to attract around $50 billion in FDI annually, while India crossed $20 billion only in 2010. Before that, India's annual FDI figure used to hover around $10 billion. Importantly, the spread of the incoming FDI is more balanced in India than in China. This points to India's efforts at ensuring uniform growth. For example, among the world's six top FDI destinations, four are in India (Gujarat, Maharashtra, Karnataka and Andhra Pradesh) and only two in China (Shanghai and Jiangsu). In the last year of the UPA government, India got $24 billion in FDI. So, within less than three years of assuming power, the NDA obtained two and a half times more FDI than in the last year under the UPA.

The *Financial Times* is not the only international publication that has taken note of India's arrival as an economic force. A survey by *The Economist* in its September 2016 issue gave a big thumbs up to India on its management of the economy and fiscal discipline covering several parameters. In the same article, it predicted growth figures for the world's major economies for the next financial year. For India, the predicted growth was 7.8 to 8 per cent (revised to around 7 per cent after demonetization), 6.3 per cent for China and 2.8 per cent for Australia. All other major countries, including the US, the UK, Germany and Canada are expected to grow at less than 2 per cent. For the UK, *The Economist* has predicted a growth of as low as minus 1.1 per cent.

Moreover, the government has managed well its current account balance (CAB), a major parameter for assessing the health of an economy, along with inflation. For a good economy, inflation has to be moderate, growth has to be high and the CAB either marginally negative or marginally positive. In 2012–13, India's CAB was in 5 per cent deficit, one of the highest in the world and an indication of its poor economic health. It reflected the atmosphere of despair in the Indian economy.

The deficit figure for the US during the same year was 2.6 per cent, for Japan 3.4 per cent and for France 5 per cent. As soon as the NDA took over, the CAB started improving due to the new government's strong fiscal measures, marked by transparency and prudent fiscal planning. In 2015–16, India's CAB improved to minus 0.8 per cent. But in the first quarter of 2016–17, there was a small surprise in store for India as its CAB came in surplus for the first time in thirteen years and stood at 0.7 per cent before touching zero per cent in the last quarter. So, on all the three major parameters of the economy—growth, inflation and CAB—India is in a sweet spot perhaps for the first time in two decades.

The stiff fiscal target and unwarranted financial burden of schemes like the NFSA were not the only financial challenges that the NDA inherited from the UPA. Political decisions like the splitting of Andhra Pradesh into two states also had deep financial consequences for the NDA because of the promises that the UPA had made to the newly formed Telangana state. The state has to be given special category status for five years. This means that the Centre will ultimately have to squeeze out over ₹40,000 crore from its treasury, out of which over 20 per cent has already been released by the NDA. The NDA government also has to shoulder the economic burden of certain unproductive schemes of the past.

For example, the problem of sinking funds in unproductive wages under the MGNREGA couldn't be controlled because of one big defect left behind by the UPA. The defect was the stipulation in the MGNREGA that says wages are to be given only to unskilled labour under the scheme. Had this provision not been there, the scheme could have been put to good use by getting jobs done by unemployed but skilled persons. However, the NDA has found innovative ways to infuse productivity into the MGNREGA by linking it with asset creation in the agriculture sector, including watershed management.

Some dark spots of the economy under the NDA rule are also turning bright now, thus giving further proof of good fiscal management. After two years of low growth, India's exports registered an impressive increase in 2016–17, growing by 4.71 per cent over the previous year and touching $272.65 billion. It has also indicated an increase in manufacturing, following the growth in FDI. One reason, according to a top businessman, why manufacturing didn't pick up as much as it should have during the first two years of the NDA rule was the failure of the RBI to lower the interest rate on loans from 9.5 per cent to 8 or 7.5 per cent—which was possible and didn't involve any risk.

Reforms, Innovations and Transparency

The Modi government's reforms story began with the disbanding of the Planning Commission and its replacement with NITI Aayog in 2014. It constitutes the most powerful change that Narendra Modi has effected to break the Nehruvian order ever since he took over as the prime minister in 2014. Initially, the decision drew admiration as well as flak. It attracted praise because it was a bold step in keeping with the spirit of cooperative federalism wherein states become equal partners in the nation's development. It allowed states to shape their progress according to their needs instead of having to come to the Centre with a begging bowl every year for fund allocation. It also permitted the Centre to shape its developmental strategies.

It invited flak because many thought that an adequate framework for replacing the sixty-five-year-old model was not in place and that it will create confusion. Most, however, were unaware of the purpose behind NITI Aayog. According to its vision document, NITI Aayog is supposed to be a think tank that will help bring about structural changes to the governing system while helping the states and the nation with new ideas of development and ensuring the replication of successful models of development across India. It has collected examples of good governance practices from the states and put them in the form of a book so that these can be implemented across the country. So, after more than two and a half years since it was floated, much of the confusion over its objectives and role has been cleared.

By the third quarter of 2016, NITI Aayog had started advising the PMO on a series of matters that needed expert opinion, particularly in the area of structural changes in government policies and institutions. It covered a vast area, from reforms in various sectors to employment generation and new benchmarks in education, including medical education. The most important reform it has recommended is the replacement of the allegedly corrupt structure of the Medical Council of India with a high-powered panel led by the Union cabinet secretary.

If implemented in the form that NITI Aayog has suggested, it will bring about a revolution in India's medical education, which is marked by manipulation and lack of merit. Now, even important private colleges charging high fees will be able to admit a student only after a test. NITI Aayog has recommended an exit examination for every medical student wanting to practise as a doctor to address the problem of the poor quality of medical education. Then, NITI Aayog has suggested the closure of seventeen PSUs and the privatization of twenty-two others. Reform of the University Grants Commission is also under way under NITI Aayog's guidance, and so are efforts to elevate standards in ten public and ten private universities.

It has also drawn up a plan for the government to set up two coastal employments zones of 500 sq. km each on the western and eastern coasts of India to create employment through port-related development. The move is also aimed at wooing some companies in China—especially in the electrical, electronics and clothing sectors—that want to move out of that country because of increased wages. It is also helping the states bring about reforms and implement a series of good governance measures. One reform that NITI Aayog is helping the states with involves a reduction in the number of unnecessary departments and obsolete laws.

NITI Aayog has selected six parameters to map results in the implementation of schemes and areas of governance and to identify problem zones in states. They are spread across diverse sectors, from the district level upwards. They cover areas like education, health, roads, water, electricity and mobile penetration, among other things. And this will include both state- and Centre-funded schemes. In areas where the government is unequal to the task, NITI Aayog will recommend the involvement of the private sector. Such an approach at the district level is unprecedented in independent India's history. Economist Arvind Panagariya, the vice chairman of NITI Aayog, who studied as a free market economist in the US under the legendary Jagdish Bhagwati, says: 'By effecting this tectonic shift to federalism prime minister Modi has made the states equal partners with the Centre in planning and policy evolution, thus making the states and their chief ministers rise over narrower interest in favour of national interest. This is unprecedented in the history of the Centre–state relationship.'

Economist Bibek Debroy, a member of NITI Aayog who plays a key role in giving direction to the states, says: 'It is perhaps for the first time, in contrast to the earlier top-to-bottom Planning Commission model, that CMs cutting across party lines are sitting together and jointly thinking about the nation and giving policy inputs. It constitutes a major shift to federalism. Its results will show in the time to come in the form of grounded, realistic policies suiting the growth of the nation on an organic platform.' The institution is also playing a key role in shaping some of the revolutionary agriculture policies of the Modi government, based on the studies and recommendations of NITI Aayog's member on agriculture, Ramesh Chand.

By April 2017, when the prime minister chaired NITI Aayog's annual chief ministerial meeting as its chairman, the institution seemed to be finding its grooves as a replacement to the Planning Commission in a Team India spirit. The meeting under the prime minister saw the presentation of 300 ideas for good governance that had come from a cross section of sectors—state governments, the private sector and media. Even some chief minsters made presentations of their successes for other chief ministers to know. Though the Modi government is at loggerheads with the AAP government, the latter's suggestion that the real estate sector too be brought under the ambit of GST was appreciated by many including Modi—a good example of the Team India spirit. Moreover, NITI Aayog is now hiring professionals and experts from the private domain to upgrade itself into a top-class think tank of good-governance ideas. Plus, it is working on a fifteen-year long-term vision, seven-year midterm strategy and a three-year action agenda. Interestingly, Modi is also using the NITI Aayog platform to convince the rival ruling party leaders to support his revolutionary idea of conducting simultaneous Lok Sabha and Vidhan Sabha (state assembly) polls to save time and money and supplement good governance. Clearly, the NITI Aayog vision of the PM is now on track after what some perceived as a slow beginning.

The government's innovative approach is no less visible in some of the budget reforms it has implemented. For example, the government has done away completely with non-planned expenditure in the budget. This is a great reform that will save money for the exchequer by removing an artificial division in budgeting that many believed was either mindless or purposely made for the window dressing of unjustifiable expenses. The move guarantees cleaner account books in the future. Another big budget reform involves merging the railway budget with the main budget, which will also result in savings for the exchequer.

But there have been natural factors beyond the government's control that have impacted its management of the economy. The drop in crude oil prices came as a blessing in disguise as it saved precious foreign exchange. But for the drop, the government might have been struggling while tackling the economy. It may have been forced to take shortcuts. At the same time, the government's failure to push the amendments to the Land Acquisition Act in Parliament came as a big setback. Had those amendments been passed, the nation's economic recovery would have been faster. The challenge for the government now is to encourage the growth of the manufacturing sector through a planned emphasis on MSMEs.

One of the major steps that Modi and Jaitley have taken is the simplification of the tax filing and assessment processes by using technology, thus countering the fear of Inspector Raj. In the income tax department, this has been taken to a significant level where the common man is feeling the difference. Says Ahmedabad-based young chartered accountant Abhishek Patel: 'The changes I am seeing when it comes to reducing manual interventions to the bare minimum point to a golden era in tax compliance in the time to come.'[8] In this, the GST is going to make all the difference, thanks to its structure which is so transparent being largely based on self-verification.

Could the Government Have Done Better?

But one big criticism of the government on reforms is what many people call its failure to disinvest big PSUs like Air India, SAIL and CIL, in keeping with Modi's promise of 'maximum governance, minimum government', and instead resorting to incremental reforms in that sphere. But Modi has had his reasons for not doing so. One of the reasons is his reported belief that the time to disinvest is not right as the global economy is still down and disinvestment at this stage won't fetch a good price for the government. On the other hand, he has sincerely tried to ensure that these PSU don't bleed any more like before due to poor management and corruption. CIL has, in fact, achieved a turnaround and Air India has started improving due to these efforts.

The downsizing of ministries, as recommended by NITI Aayog member Bibek Debroy, and the cutting out of bureaucratic flab have been on the list of expectations of Modi's admirers, who seem disappointed on these counts. Plans to boost the economy by using underutilized government resources like land worth ₹22 lakh crore that the IR owns or the similarly huge holdings that the army possesses have also not materialized.

There is also the view that taxation and banking reforms could have been faster. For example, before introducing the legislation to curb black money, the government didn't implement the necessary tax reforms such as simplifying laws and lowering the net effective tax rate to make the law more efficient. A senior BJP leader with sound knowledge of the Indian economy says: 'What was needed was a transformational approach on reforms, but many steps indicate the government's approach has been selectively incremental.'

Then many in Indian industry, notably jewellers, are unhappy at what they feel are burdensome taxes slapped on them. According to those in the jewellery sector, these taxes have affected the industry, particularly the small artisans. Jaitley increased the import duty on gold from 8 to 10 per cent, besides introducing 1 per cent excise duty. So on 10 grams of gold, the buyer has to pay around ₹900 more. To top it all, it has been mandatory to submit one's PAN for buying jewellery worth more than ₹5 lakh and gold biscuits over ₹2 lakh. This is unhealthy considering the fact that gold is an unavoidable item in any Indian marriage, whether in a middle-income family or a rich family. Large sections of the farming class at the lower level still don't have PAN cards. So underhand dealings in gold have increased—this goes against the vision of a low-tax, efficient economy that people expected from the NDA. Incidentally, when Modi was in the Opposition, he had himself protested against the imposition of 1 per cent excise duty by the UPA. It was withdrawn at that time.

Ashok Zaveri, the owner of a jewellery showroom in Rajkot, says: 'Thousands of workers from far-flung corners of India, particularly from Bengal, who earned a good living in Gujarat as artisans in the jewellery industry left for their home states because of the slowdown caused by high taxes. The tax hike affected the common artisans more than the jeweller. But the jewellers have a different problem. They are forced to sell gold without bills as there is demand from both common and high-end customers to buy gold under the table to save themselves the burden of high tax. However, by April 2017, there were signs of recovery with the return of 50 per cent of the artisans, but the recovery is slow.'[9] The jewellery sector is not part of the thrust areas of the Make in India campaign, despite being one of the highest generators of revenue. In strong economies like China and Japan, the rulers have encouraged people to buy gold, recognizing it as a sign of economic prosperity of the common people according to ancient Eastern traditions. But in the wake of demonetization, the government's moves concerning gold are being seen as part of the preparation for demonetization, to curb black money by preventing people from investing their unaccounted for wealth in gold.

Although slow manufacturing has, till recently, been a thorn in the side of the NDA government's Make in India plan, there has been no lack of enthusiasm among new entrepreneurs, who are emerging via start-ups. The participation of young entrepreneurs in the 2016 Make in India award function organized by the *India Today* group in Delhi amply demonstrated the promise that the campaign holds out in spite of the problems. The enthusiasm measures up to Modi's plan in which he sees Make in India as an opportunity for the country's young population to become entrepreneurs by starting small businesses. Clearly, the success of the Modi government on the economic front ultimately has been its skilful piloting of the economy through one of India's more difficult times since 1991. The long-term challenge, however, for the Modi government is to take India's growth to around 10 per cent, which is possible only by encouraging not just manufacturing but design, innovation and engineering and making India a great nation of innovators. Plus, it must become an integral part of the global supply chain by working on innovation. The difference between around 7 per cent at which India is growing at present and 10 per cent is huge. According to NITI Aayog CEO Amitabh Kant, at 7 per cent, India's per capita income by 2032 would be $4000, while at 10 per cent it would be $6800, enough to enable India to find a solution to its biggest problem—poverty.

To the Modi government's credit, it is working hard towards this goal. Rules, regulations and procedures have been eased and even new laws have been enacted to add to the ease of doing business which have pulled India twelve positions up in the world ease of doing business index. Over 1000 archaic laws have been done away with. Full FDI has been allowed in most sectors. Procedures for floating small industrial units have been eased beyond expectation and a national company law tribunal has been floated. Plus, it is encouraging a healthy competition between the state governments on ease of doing business and development indexes. Says Kant, who thinks India is now one of the most open regimes in the world to do business: 'For 10 per cent growth, we have to think big and concentrate on exports and not just domestic market, because it is only exports based on innovation which would bring big growth.' Clearly, the government seems committed to that path and has put the nation in a commanding position on the international economic map.

8

Demonetization

A Bitter Pill for a Better Future

Forty-four-year-old Kuldeep Ratnoo, a PhD in clinical psychology, was a teacher at Mayo College, Ajmer, before he joined the RSS's economic wing, the Swadeshi Jagran Manch. Some years ago, Ratnoo returned to teaching and decided to move back to his home town Jodhpur from Delhi. Coming from a typically middle-class background, Ratnoo was in need of money last year. So he decided to sell the flat he had bought in Greater Noida in the National Capital Region. While hunting for a buyer, he got a very good offer. But the offer got stuck since Ratnoo wanted all the money in cheque while the buyer wanted to pay half the amount in cash. After a lot of argument, Ratnoo brought down the cash amount to 20 per cent. The payment was to take place on 9 November 2016.

On the evening of 8 November, Prime Minister Narendra Modi fired the salvo called demonetization. The same night Ratnoo called up the buyer and authoritatively told him that he will have to pay the entire amount in cheque. He agreed and Ratnoo collected the cheque the next day with glee. Ratnoo says: 'India's real estate was one sector where even the most honest had to fall in line and give or take a certain percentage in black. Demonetization and the new laws on housing and *benami* [false] transactions have dealt a body blow to the circulation of unaccounted for money in the real estate sector, notwithstanding the initial disruption and distress that many had to suffer because of the drastic move.'[1]

The dust from 8 November 2016 is finally settling down. People like Ratnoo who think charitably about the decision rather than the other way around despite the hardships they went through are a huge majority. After three months of medium- to full-scale turmoil and trauma, a vast majority of Indians accepted the Indian prime minister's earth-shattering step to invalidate 86 per cent of the Indian currency—all high-denomination, i.e. ₹500 and ₹1000, currency notes—at one stroke as a positive long-term move aimed at turning the black-money economy of the country into white. The BJP's landslide win in the Uttar Pradesh elections in March 2017—following victories at multiple levels in several elections across the country—in the wake of demonetization has given the measure the stamp of the people's approval.

This is notwithstanding the clever moves of many holders of unaccounted for wealth in successfully converting their existing black money into white. That, however, came to them at a huge price in terms of the amount wasted in greasing the palms of the bureaucracy, particularly the bank bureaucracy, and left an indelible impression that the exercise was not properly implemented. That after demonetization the finance ministry had to make nearly four dozen amendments to the norms of withdrawal of cash from banks in just over two months was proof of the confusion that followed the move in the absence of adequate deliberation and forethought. A glaring example was the jump in the figure of savings in the Jan-Dhan accounts. It went up from ₹47,000 crore to ₹87,000 crore in just two months after demonetization. It indicated that the holders of black money had used the Jan-Dhan accounts of poor people to launder their funds.

Obviously, the prime minister's obsession with maintaining secrecy about the move, as in many other administrative matters, prevented him from taking opinions on the decision's implementation in advance. He did not make adequate arrangements for keeping enough ₹500 and ₹100 notes ready along with the new ₹2000 notes before taking the step. Had adequate consultation and planning been done, the pain would have been much less and fewer black-money holders would have been able to manipulate the system.

But all that is past, and there is also a strong flip side to it. What is undeniable is the fact that the future impact of the decision appears to be positive, and positive only, for the Indian economy. The move is seen as historic and bold, driving India towards a less-cash economy by changing the economic behaviour of the people and curbing corruption and black-money generation to spur growth. The amassment of black money will be difficult from now onwards, with a set of new laws being put in place, including the one against benami (false) transactions that will hit behind-the-screen property deals involving unaccounted for money. The 7 per cent GDP growth figure for the third quarter of 2016–17 showed that even the short-term negative impact on the economy has been much less than expected, though the figure became a matter of debate in some quarters.

Undoubtedly, a new era of digital economy has begun for a country of 1.3 billion people, of whom less than 3 per cent paid income tax, not more than 2 per cent were part of the digital economy and only 24 per cent had declared annual income worth more than ₹10 lakh before 8 November 2016. Demonetization exposed for the first time the dark underbelly of unaccounted for money in the country and the reasons behind the high levels of economic disparity. Modi's move therefore was like a strong antidote to the anaesthesia that had for decades kept the country in a deep slumber while the menace of black money and corruption raged and prevented the creation of a level playing field for the people at large. The extent of the cash economy can be gauged from the fact that individuals, small firms and NGOs together, amounting to six million units, deposited banned notes worth a whopping ₹7 lakh crore in banks for replacement. It comes to an average of ₹11 lakh (or $15,000) per unit.

Despite marked growth after 1991, India has not been able to provide shelter, food and clothing to a large number of its citizens. The GDP growth as a result of demonetization was expected to dip marginally during 2017–18 and partially affect the job scenario in both the formal and informal sectors, besides impacting a part of the rural economy. But the initial trends in 2017–18 are proving the predictions only marginally correct, and even wrong in some areas. Interestingly, many experts, including economist Surjit Bhalla, see demonetization as a great exercise in behavioural change initiated by Modi to push people towards digital transactions, which is necessary if India is to realize its full economic potential. Bhalla goes many steps further: 'Make no mistake. It is an important first step towards what will be remembered as India's biggest reform. Those condemning the move are mostly those who have lost unaccounted for money or won't be able to generate black money in the future. Everyone else has welcomed the move. Their percentage would be about 90 per cent.'[2]

Even after the initial puzzlement was over, the debate over demonetization continued. Was the apparently draconian measure timed well? Was it implemented properly? Most agree that it could have been implemented in a better manner, limiting the inconvenience to the common man and plugging escape routes for black-money holders. But there is a large section of economists and experts who believe that the move was precisely timed and the pain inflicted was intended to encourage people to switch from cash to digital transactions.

Economist Vivek Dehejia, a professor at Carleton University, Canada, says: 'Invalidation of currency has failed in many countries in the past because the rulers took the step under pressure of a dwindling economy. Modi's timing was perfect as he did it when the economy was doing well, unlike Venezuela which went for demonetization on 11 December 2016 when that nation's economy was down and invited more trouble. The prime minister is in fact the first person in history to do so when the economy was on a positive track and growing at a healthy rate of over 7 per cent, with an overflowing FDI. Undoubtedly, it is the biggest policy change move in the monetary history of the modern world. I see it as a precise plumbing and fixing job to clean up the system on the way to increasing the size of the Indian economy.'[3]

On the timing of the move, Modi himself has said it was perfect as demonetization can be successfully done only when the economy is doing well and not when the economy is weak. It is not very difficult to comprehend Modi's vision. The prime minister wants India to be a $5 trillion economy in the coming years and a $10 trillion economy in the long run to realize his dream of ensuring food, shelter and clothing for every household, and turning India into a superpower. So he believes that India can ill afford to have a $2 trillion official economy on paper and a $3 trillion unofficial parallel economy in cash.

Modi's Step-by-Step Plan

According to Dehejia, most elected political leaders across the world keep the next election in mind while adopting crucial measures, whereas Modi, in taking this historic decision, has looked at India's future in the coming decades. Dehejia sees it as part of Modi's moral crusade to improve the economy. People with black money have criticized it, but the common man sees it as a move that is aimed at long-term benefit. Dehejia has another interesting take. He believes that the pain caused by the disruptive decision was also thoughtfully induced by Modi, who rightly gauged that a short-term cash crunch would only give a bigger push to the digital economy. 'All his policy measures taken on the economic plane before the demonetization decision fall into a pattern. One has to take a long view to understand his long-term vision,' Dehejia says.

True. Whether it was using Jan-Dhan bank accounts, raising excise duty on gold, linking the PAN card to the Aadhaar card or making the disclosure of bank accounts necessary while filing income tax returns, the steps were directed at the formalization of the economy by hitting at the cash economy on his way to demonetization. If one carefully analyses his moves starting with the announcement of the Jan-Dhan scheme for bringing the utterly poor within the bank ambit, one gets a feeling that demonetization was on his mind right from the day he became prime minister.

Modi acted like a panther on the prowl as he charted out his course leading to the 8 November move. The pattern of demonetization can now be clearly discerned. As soon as Modi took oath in May 2014, he set up the Special Investigation Team (SIT) on black money. The next important step was to launch the Jan-Dhan scheme, with an initial target of opening 1 crore bank accounts in 150 days, which was met in 100 days. By 8 November 2016, the day Modi struck, a minimum of 50 crore people had come into the banking system. Next in line was his government's decision to make the disclosure of bank account numbers mandatory while filing returns. This was aimed at making a database of income tax returnees. Linking the PAN card with the Aadhaar card, yet another government move in that pattern, further tightened the screws on evaders and made the task of turning black money into white very difficult.

Steps aimed at preventing evaders from investing in gold and jewellery—a hike in excise duty and tax on both gold and jewellery and making the PAN card mandatory for the purchase of jewellery over ₹2 lakh—followed soon after. Then during 2015–16, ₹80,000 crore of unaccounted for money was unearthed following a series of raids on evaders by the income tax authorities and the Enforcement Directorate (ED) and by way of people declaring unaccounted for money in foreign accounts. The last opportunity to tax evaders was given in mid-2016 when, under a new Income Declaration Scheme (IDS), tax evaders were given a chance to turn their black money into white on payment of 30 per cent tax and 15 per cent fine.

The scheme brought disclosures worth ₹65,000 crore by 65,000 people, but around 20 per cent of the amount turned out to be a part of false disclosures. Still, the final figure of over ₹52,000 crore was impressive. And along with the scheme came Modi's warnings on public platforms: 'I warn tax evaders to come on track or else they will have to pay a heavy price.' Just a fortnight after the last warning, demonetization was enforced, thus revealing a pattern aimed at attacking black money.

Just as 1947 was a political watershed year in modern India's history, so demonetization seems to be a turning point for the nation's economy in the context of formalization of an informal economy. A comparison of India's economy with China's shows one of the main reasons why the size of the Chinese economy is large on paper. According to a study, in China's textile sector, 90 per cent of the firms employ fifty or more workers on paper. In India, 90 per cent of textile firms employ 10 per cent workers or less, indicating that these Indian companies operate informally to keep themselves out of the tax net. When these firms start adopting the formal route fully, it will be a win–win situation for all three parties—the employer, the employees and the government.

Small wonder then that the official figure for taxpayers shows that India has been one of the biggest tax-evading countries in the world. Here, an unimaginably large part of the population that has had the capacity to pay has kept itself out of the tax net. According to a study, only 7 per cent pay taxes in India as against 100 per cent in Sweden and 65 per cent in the US. Before 8 November 2016, around 12 per cent of India's GDP was in the form of a cash economy. Another 15 per cent was black money stashed outside the system. So, close to 30 per cent came under official and unofficial cash economy. Many predict that if Modi is able to bring the cash economy figure to below 10 per cent in around two years, India's GDP growth rate could become a double-digit number in 2018–19 or 2019–20 for the first time in history.

S. Gurumurthy, an economic analyst and co-convener of the RSS's Swadeshi Jagran Manch who has been a key campaigner against black money, says: 'The increasing use of cash in our GDP had brought distortions in the economy. It reflected in many areas like real estate and gold prices. Demonetization was the need of the hour to correct the distortion. But the decision warranted courage and the prime minister demonstrated it, to the nation's good fortune.'[4]

In fact, barring exceptions like Nobel laureate Amartya Sen, most economists have lauded the move, although some may have expressed reservations about the way it was implemented. Former RBI governor D. Subbarao called it a 'creative destruction of destructive creation [black money] and the most disruptive policy innovation since the 1991 reforms'. He was, however, critical of the way it was executed.[5] Economist Surjit Bhalla not only welcomed demonetization but also found the subsequent 2017–18 budget to be the most brilliant document since the 1991 budget and one that was designed to reap the full advantage of demonetization in terms of India's future economic growth.

These pro-demonetization economists have reasons to justify the move. They perhaps feel that the transition to a white economy won't be as difficult as once thought. They may not be too wide off the mark. Following demonetization, the entire financial system is undergoing a sea change on a scale never seen before. Digital transactions have increased hundreds of times after 8 November through multiple mediums. The fear that a lack of broadband connectivity in rural areas will disrupt the rural economy for a long, long time is proving to be wrong as people, even those without smartphones, are taking to digital payments by using the government's payment system via Unstructured Supplementary Service Data (USSD) codes, which can be operated on a simple mobile phone. For using USSD, one simply has to link his bank account to his ordinary phone and make or receive payments by using the star-hash option. One can even check one's bank balance. With the smartphone, people, of course, have many options like the UPI and digital wallets such as Paytm and State Bank of India's Buddy app.

Floated by the Modi government in the middle of 2016, the UPI is turning out to be a clincher in the digital transition. It is revolutionizing digital payments with the help of another invention of the Modi government, the BHIM (Bharat Interface for Money) app. The entry of BHIM is making money transfer as simple as sending an email. It features bank interoperability, for transactions between two banks. Every bank has made its own UPI app and linked it to the BHIM app, which has become the common UPI platform for all banks. So there is no need to know things like one's bank account number, the Indian Financial System Code (IFSC) and bank branch number while transferring money. An Aadhaar card–enabled payment system based on biometrics is also being popularized. The credit card system is, of course, already there.

The BHIM app alone had seen over 2 crore downloads by the end of February 2017 within just two months of its launch. This gives an idea of the pace of the transition. In terms of the value of money transactions, the use of UPI saw a growth of 1744 per cent between November and February, while USSD-based payments saw a growth of 5000 per cent during the four months. The USSD figure indicates the rise in digital payments in rural areas and among the urban poor. Even Aadhaar card–based transactions saw a jump to 2.8 million, during the period when the sale of PoS (point of sale) machines for digital transactions saw an increase of 13 per cent. Incentives in the form of lottery-type prizes on digital transaction played a key role in this transition.

Modi's Meticulous Digital Gamble-cum-Ad Campaign to Change Mindsets

The prime minister's meticulous planning ahead of the currency-swap initiative was also visible in the post-demonetization period when he took a series of well-thought-out and innovative measures to veer the society towards a digital economy in what was one of biggest mindset-changing exercises ever seen. Cutting-edge ad films in twelve major languages were created and broadcast on television and social media. These films demonstrated the merits of demonetization and the intent behind the move. They showed the common people how easy it was to switch over to digital transactions, even those without smartphones.

In some of these films, Modi himself became the brand ambassador of his government's go-digital campaign, telling people how they would be helping the nation by joining the digital economy. A film titled *My Mobile, My Bank: Cashless Transaction Possible for All* was a good example. In the film, an actor first showed how easy it was to shift to various phone-based methods of making payments and it was followed by excerpts from one of Modi's radio talks under his *Mann Ki Baat* series on the merits of a digital economy: 'My countrymen, join this revolution to spur cashless transactions to fight black money and corruption and free yourselves from problems and tension.' Most of the films were designed by film-maker Manish Baradia, an old Modi hand, and with very specific inputs from Modi's office on the direction of each film.

In the second innovative move, on 25 December 2016, Modi took to offering prizes through a lottery to the public and to small merchants in a bid to woo them towards digitization. The move came a good forty-six days after demonetization and six days before the deadline by which the prime minister had announced the government would settle the economy following the currency swap. The government announced the Lucky Grahak Yojana and Digi-Dhan Vyapar Yojana, offering a chance to win ₹1000 to ₹1 crore to those who made digital transactions. In order to keep the people connected with the scheme, the names of the winners of small prizes were announced on a daily and weekly basis.

That this enterprising step, criticized by a section of the bureaucracy initially, played big role in pushing people towards digital transactions was proved in April 2017 when the National Payments Corporation of India (NPCI), which implemented the scheme visualized by the NITI Aayog, revealed the figures of the prizes that people had won. Between 25 December 2016 and 9 April 2017, as many as 17 lakh people had won the prizes worth ₹259 crore under the two schemes—16 lakh individuals and around 1 lakh merchants. Not a single geographical unit in India was left untouched by the scheme, with 1000 prizes going to people of the Andaman and Nicobar Islands, thus indicating the sweep of the digital drive. It saw 100 DigiDhan Melas (fairs) being organized in 100 cities, where government officials, through ad films and practical demonstrations, taught people how to make digital payments. The government set a short-term target of more than trebling the number of annual digital transactions from 800 crore to over 2500 crore.

The optimism of Amitabh Kant, CEO of NITI Aayog and one of the people tasked with accelerating the shift towards a digital economy, induces confidence. Kant believes that mobile-based payment systems will end the reign of the credit card payment system by 2020. According to him, the transition is happening very fast as over 43 crore of the 110 crore Aadhaar cards are already linked with bank accounts. His optimism extends further: 'India is ready for a digital push. But what we want to give is a digital thrust. And I find the push more in rural areas than in the urban areas. Your mobile is becoming your bank now. The digital economy will also create a vast number of jobs with a spurt in digital products and smartphones.'[6] But in the same breath, he says that an emphasis on Wi-Fi is needed in rural areas to push digital transactions. These words count as they come from a man who is seen as the brain behind some of India's successful innovations like the Incredible India campaign of the Union tourism department, as well as the Make in India campaign.

Things Are Coming Around but There Are Bottlenecks

The path to a digital economy has hurdles despite the fact that disruption has given way to order much faster than expected. Surat, the Indian hub of polyester textiles and diamond polishing, is a good example of how things are getting back on track after the initial turmoil, while some crucial problems still remain to be tackled. For almost two and a half months, the textile sector of Surat, which had made the highest disclosure under the IDS in 2016, reeled under the impact of demonetization. Almost half of the 10 lakh workers fled Surat's textile making, processing and sales industry, and the daily turnover of the city's textile sector fell to ₹75 crore from ₹150 crore.

In the last week of December 2016, when I spoke to Jitendra Vakharia, president of the South Gujarat Textile Processors

Association, and the owner of a unit with an annual turnover of ₹30 crore, he appeared totally perplexed. Only one shift, instead of three, was on at his factory located in Surat's suburb, Pandesara. 'God knows what will happen to the industry,' he told me then with pain in his voice. When I contacted him again in the beginning of March 2017, less than two months later, Vakharia seemed relieved.[7]

The reason: in that short period, the Surat textile industry had regained more than 90 per cent of the business it was doing in October 2016. As he put it: 'Recovering the losses we suffered during the initial two or two and a half months might take some time, but our day-to-day business was almost back to the previous level by February first week.' At the same time, he had a litany of complaints about how the switch from cash to digitized payments was fraught with problems in the absence of adequate government planning.

On the one hand, banks just don't have the capacity to handle thousands of workers, who were taking their payments in cash earlier, when they come to withdraw money following digital payments into their accounts. On the other hand, workers are quite opposed to having their salary cut in the name of provident fund and Employees State Insurance Scheme (ESIS). Vinod Agrawal, the owner of a textile unit with a turnover of ₹60 crore, who welcomed demonetization, says: 'The prime minister was right in taking the step but it was implemented with inadequate advance planning. The understaffed banks are finding it difficult to take the extra load in business centres like Surat where regular bank customers have grown by thousands and lakhs in a matter of weeks.'

In many cases, Surat employees were simply turned away by the understaffed banks when they land up there for withdrawing their salaries at the start of a new month. This points to an urgent need to augment the banking sector till the working class learns to do all transactions digitally. Viral

Desai of Zenitax Textile and Garments adds: 'The government should also have mentoring projects for workers to explain to them the benefits of digital transactions, provident fund and ESIS. The labour department could be asked to take up the task.'[8]

Fear of Inspector Raj

Many observers of the economy fear that the wider role that income tax and other inspectors are getting in the post-demonetization era might result in a raid raj led by corrupt inspectors and make a mockery of Modi's slogan of 'Minimum Government, Maximum Governance'. The impression stems from the fact that the corruption in inspecting departments, including income tax, is unusually high. With these departments getting more power, it is going to grow, some fear.

But when seen against the backdrop of certain facts, that could be a passing phase restricted only to questionable attempts by many to turn their black money into white immediately after demonetization. Once the scrutiny of these cases is over, there are not many reasons to have the fear of a raid raj. Surat, the business city that also held the dubious distinction of being the city with the highest level of black money in India before 8 November, is a good place to test the ground. Most businessmen in Surat feel that due to the pressure brought on by demonetization, their next income tax returns would be much cleaner, thus reducing the possibility of income tax scrutiny.

Even Surat's diamond sector, which has one of the highest cash turnovers, is toeing the line, with the pressure on it building up from the top. Viral Desai says: 'Once things come on paper there is very little left for the inspectors to do. The fact is that the inspectors who deal with things like ESIS are already perplexed that they will have very little role to play after the economy gets formalized.'

Stunning Political Gains

Clearly, no one had anticipated the kind of political impact that one is witnessing after Modi's unprecedented decision. The commotion one experienced soon after demonetization shook even the BJP workers. After 8 November 2016, many BJP and RSS workers took up the task of helping tired and angry people standing in queues for hours and days outside banks to get cash. But a large number of BJP leaders across India were also scared of crossing into areas where there were mad queues outside banks. They were afraid of being targeted or called to account by irate mobs.

But in the final tally, over 90 per cent of the people interviewed by the media across India who were standing in queues over a period of two months expressed faith in Modi despite the hardships. They were apparently driven by the sincerity of purpose. That made me recall a comment Modi had made several times to me when he was the chief minister of Gujarat and I was covering the state for *India Today*: 'When a ruler is sincere, people are prepared to put up with any level of hardship caused by his actions and even willing to forgive his bona fide mistakes.' Nothing proves this better than the response of the common people to demonetization.

In reality, no one could gauge the final political impact till the results of various by-elections following demonetization started coming in, beginning with Gujarat. The BJP gave an impressive show in most of these elections across India. The party's performance in the local polls in Maharashtra, where the BJP fought against the power–caste combination of the Nationalist Congress Party and against its erstwhile ally, the Shiv Sena, was stunning. Equally stunning were the results of the Odisha panchayat elections. But what clearly shows the people's approval of Modi's decisions was the BJP's massive victory in the assembly elections in India's largest state, Uttar Pradesh, which accounts for a sixth of the country's population. The NDA coalition led by the BJP won 325 out of 403 seats in the state legislature, leaving the opposition parties and the negative pundits of demonetization speechless.

The voting pattern revealed that Modi has managed to wrest from the Congress and other so-called secular parties their 'poor vote bank' with his deft move. The have-nots are seeing his momentous decision as a courageous move aimed at benefiting them in the long term. This is a new phenomenon in the Indian political arena, which had seen the role of caste increasing, particularly in the nation's northern regions, in the past two decades. The politics of some of the southern states got divided along caste lines several decades ago. The new trend indicates a tilt towards class-based politics in place of caste-based politics. This may dilute the role of castes and other petty factors that have been playing a significant part in Indian politics after the emergence of the regional parties in the mid-1990s.

Much of the public support on demonetization perhaps came from the realization that the step has instantly brought down prices in a number of sectors, particularly real estate, and has therefore benefited the common man. Prashant Bhimani, a leading psychologist based in Ahmedabad, analysed the unique response of the people to demonetization. He says: 'People want a positive change after years of corruption and poor governance and they see in Modi that agent of change. They have faith in his sincerity. Psychologically, they see him as an action-oriented leader and a symbol of their hope who is trying to create a level playing field in a society where the rich rule the roost with their amassment of unaccounted for money. So, they are willing to endure hardships caused by his actions.'

The International Impact

At the global level, the step bolstered Modi's already strong image as a leader of action and vision. The headline of the

Independent, Singapore's leading newspaper, screamed: 'A New Lee Kuan Yew Is Born.' The accompanying article compared Modi with Lee Kuan Yew, the maker of modern Singapore who transformed the South-East Asian country into a vibrant international hub of finance and logistics from a backward, malarial nation, after it broke off from Malaysia in 1965. Incidentally, Modi has regarded Lee, who passed away in 2015, as one of his development icons.

In the Western world too, Modi's step earned similar appreciation. While *Forbes* called it a 'rather well done, clever plan', the *New York Times* termed it 'a wise move' and the *Washington Post* described it as 'an ambitious move in keeping with Mr Modi's election promise to crack down on black money'. China's state-run *Global Times* called it 'startling and bold' but claimed that the Indian prime minister has been inspired by the way China has dealt with corruption. However, when the queues of money seekers outside banks didn't shorten over a period of time and reports about black-money holders successfully converting a part of their unaccounted for wealth into white came to the fore, the same newspaper turned extremely critical of Modi, and blamed him for poor execution, though never questioning his intent.

The foreign response to the main decision was understandable given India's image as an international hub of black money. Foreign businessmen dealing in diamond and textiles and visiting Surat for that purpose have been startled by the extent of black money in circulation in India. In Surat, for example, the unusually high spending by diamond and textile merchants on charities and religious gathering—which is so common in Gujarat—allegedly came largely from the money saved through tax evasion. In the income tax department of the Union government, a posting in Surat was once considered to be the most lucrative for the corrupt because it provided them with ample room to make money from tax-evading businessmen.

What is remarkable about the prime minister is that he has himself given a degree of sanctity to his decision by his actions. After the initial debate, when leaders including Modi exercised their lungs to the fullest to score points over the merits and demerits of demonetization, Modi refrained from indulging in populism. This was indicated by his government's 2016–17 annual budget, which was presented on 1 February 2017, on the eve of the crucial polls in five states, including Uttar Pradesh in February and March. Many expected Modi to announce freebies for the poor, with an eye on gaining votes in Uttar Pradesh and rewarding the common man for standing beside him while bearing the torment of demonetization.

The opposition parties ran a campaign to get the budget postponed till after the polls because of the fear that Modi would use it to gain political points with voters. However, his government didn't do any such thing and stuck to the path of prudent fiscal management by increasing the spending on infrastructure, including social infrastructure and agriculture. Demonetization has clearly turned out to be a bitter pill for a better future.

Acknowledgements

My first book on Narendra Modi's chief ministerial tenure in Gujarat happened in 2014 by way of an accident as I had never thought of writing a book except on the subject of history, which is my first love. The book was a success, and eventually landed me a second book offer.

My second book on Modi's governance, in Delhi this time, would not have been possible without the encouragement and inspiration from my Jyotish Guru and counsellor, Niranjanbhai Shukla, who convinced me to write a new book on the prime minister's reign, dropping my original plan to update my first book by adding a few chapters on his Delhi innings. I continue to be grateful to my vastu shastri friend and astrologer, Dr Ravi Rao, and Komal Rao for their help. It was Dr Rao who had predicted in 2007 that I would become a writer when I turn fifty. The prophecy came true when I wrote my first book. It was extremely gracious on the part of the editor-in-chief of India Today Group, Aroon Purie, and the group editorial director, Raj Chengappa, to allow me the much-needed time and flexibility at work to complete my book. My news coordinator at *India Today* and executive editor, Ranjit Sahay, was a source of encouragement.

In terms of research and sourcing the material for my book, I would like to thank Prime Minister Narendra Modi's

Information Technology adviser Dr Hiren Joshi and Akhilesh Mishra, director of MyGov, the Modi government's interactive digital platform, which has demonstrated a new model of people's participation in governance. I deeply appreciate Mishra for sparing his valuable time and spending hours and days with me answering my queries and helping me with data and research. Indeed this book wouldn't have been possible without his support. I must also thank my journalist friend Abhishek Kapoor for sharing his useful insights into the present government's initiatives and impact.

I am grateful to Milee Ashwarya, my publisher and editor at Penguin Random House, for giving me the opportunity to write the first-ever book on Prime Minister Narendra Modi's core governance.

To my revered parents who were extremely accommodating and kept me free from social obligations so that I could concentrate fully on the book. My wife, Smita, who stood behind me like a rock as I struggled to cope with the dual pressures of working at *India Today* and writing the book. My daughter, Rigvedita, son, Samarjit Singh, and daughter-in-law, Hiteshwari Kumari, who were a source of encouragement despite pressure at home. I owe you too! Last but not the least, I would like to thank all the people—officials, experts, analysts and common people—who spared their precious time to speak to me on various aspects of the book. Your inputs have made the book what it is today.

Sources

Introduction

1. Nripendra Misra, interviewed by the author, 4 April 2017.
2. Viral Desai, communication with the author, 5 April 2016.
3. Kanchan Banerjee, communication with the author, Ahmedabad, 12 January 2013.
4. Ram Madhav, communication with the author, 6 December 2013.
5. Bhupender Yadav, communication with the author, New Delhi, 18 October 2016.
6. Aroon Purie, editor-in-chief, *India Today*, speech at the India Ideas Conclave, Goa, 6 December 2016.
7. T.S.R. Subramanian, communication with the author, New Delhi, 15 October 2016.
8. Kaushik Deva, 'Modi Plays the Hero', *Daily Mail*, 5 March 2017.

The Relevance of *Marching with a Billion* Today

1. https://www.dailyo.in/politics/veer-savarkar-mahatma-gandhi-jawaharlal-nehru-narendra-modi-hindu-mahasabha-hindutva-sangh-parivar-rss/story/1/8698.html

Chapter 1

1. Milind Kamble, communication with the author, New Delhi, 6 September 2016.
2. Gaurav Vallabh, communication with the author, New Delhi, 21 September 2016.
3. Kishore Makwana, communication with the author, Ahmedabad, 11 September 2016.

Chapter 2

1. Saurabh Kumar, communication with the author, New Delhi, 25 March 2017.
2. Debjani Ghosh, communication with the author, New Delhi, 18 September 2016.
3. Sandeep Arora, communication with the author, New Delhi, 18 September 2016.
4. Dipak Kumar Dev, communication with the author, Indore, 7 October 2016.
5. Amit Paranjape, communication with the author, Pune, 29 September 2016.
6. Bhuvanesh Jha, communication with the author, New Delhi, October 2016.
7. Sunil Parekh, communication with the author, Ahmedabad, 4 October 2016.

Chapter 3

1. Rajeev Chandrasekhar, communication with the author, New Delhi, October 2016.
2. Manish Baradia, communication with the author, New Delhi, 14 April, 2017.
3. Richa Abhyankar, communication with the author, Pune, 12 February 2016.

4. Suchitra Raghavachari, communication with the author, Chennai, 12 February 2016.

5. Rana Bhaumik, communication with the author, New Delhi, 15 July 2016.

6. Akhilesh Mishra, communication with the author, New Delhi, 15 July 2016.

7. Gaurav Dwivedi, communication with the author, New Delhi, 15 July 2016.

8. Vidyut Thakar, communication with the author, New Delhi, 15 July 2016.

9. Prerita Chothaiwale, communication with the author, New Delhi, 14 July 2016.

10. Bhaskar Khulbe, communication with the author, New Delhi, 6 November 2015.

11. P.K. Sinha, communication with the author, New Delhi, 5 November 2015.

12. 'The End of Transfer–Posting Raj', *India Today*, 25 November 2015.

13. Investigation by the author, New Delhi, 11–12 April 2017.

14. P.K. Mishra, communication with the author, New Delhi, 12 April 2016.

15. Sarkar, Jadunath, *Shivaji and His Times*, London: Sangram Books, 1992.

16. Anurag Jain, communication with the author, New Delhi, 12 April 2016.

17. Anurag Jain, communication with the author, New Delhi, 12 April 2016.

18. Interview to *Swarajya*, 19 September 2016.

19. Surjit Bhalla, communication with the author, New Delhi, 30 September 2016.

20. Mahurkar, Uday, 'Unskilled Enterprise', *India Today*, 24 November 2016.

Chapter 4

1. Suresh Prabhu, communication with the author, New Delhi, 23 October 2016.
2. Keer, Dhahnanjay, *Veer Savarkar* and *His Times*, Popular Prakashan, 1950.
3. 'Chandrashekhar Rao Praises Modi', *Deccan Chronicle*, Hyderabad, 7 August 2016.
4. Vivek Katju, communication with the author, New Delhi, 30 October 2016.
5. Sudhir Mankad, communication with the author, Ahmedabad, 29 October 2016.
6. A.K. Sharma, communication with the author, 1 June 2016.
7. Gaurav Dwivedi, communication with the author, New Delhi, 15 July 2016.

Chapter 5

1. A.M. Naik, interviewed by the author, 2 March 2016.
2. Vikram Limaye, communication with the author, Mumbai, 1 March 2016.
3. Nitin Gadkari, in conversation with the author, 24 February 2016.
4. Nitin Gadkari, communication with the author, 24 February 2016.
5. Vaibhav Dange, communication with the author, 5 October 2016.
6. Arun Narendranath, communication with the author, 16 October 2016.
7. Arvind Kumar, communication with the author, Patna, 12 December 2016.
8. Hitesh Thakkar, communication with the author, Gandhidham, 15 December 2016.

9. Ravi Parmar, communication with the author, Gandhidham, 29 March 2016.

10. Rajgopal Sharma, communication with the author, New Delhi, 18 September 2016.

11. Mitesh Dharamshi, communication with the author, Gandhidham, 21 December 2016.

12. Arun Narendranath, communication with the author, 22 December 2016.

13. Prakash Goel, communication with the author, New Delhi, 12 August 2016.

14. Ranjit Kumar Chaudhary, communication with the author, 14 July 2016.

15. Aqueel Anjum, communication with the author, 14 July 2016.

16. Piyush Goyal, communication with the author, 12 August 2016.

17. Ashok Jhunjhunwala, communication with the author, Chennai, 12 March 2016.

18. Michael T. Eckhart, communication with the author, New Delhi, 28 February 2016.

19. Vinayak Chatterjee, at the launch of Energyinfrapost.com, New Delhi, 13 June 2016.

20. Piyush Goyal, at the launch of Energyinfrapost.com, New Delhi, 13 June 2016.

21. Keyur Shah, communication with the author, Vadodara, 15 February 2017.

22. Saurabh Kumar, communication with the author, New Delhi, 17 October 2016.

23. Santosh Vaidya, communication with the author, New Delhi, 29 October 2016.

24. Bhoovan Soral, communication with the author, New Delhi, February 2017.

25. Anant Swarup, communication with the author, New Delhi, 24 October 2016.

26. Suresh Prabhu, communication with the author, New Delhi, 29 October 2016.
27. Vipul Tuly, communication with the author, New Delhi, 15 March 2017.
28. Atanu Chakraborty, communication with the author, New Delhi, 18 December 2016.
29. Sashi Mukundan, communication with the author, New Delhi, 23 February 2017.
30. Piruz Khambatta, communication with the author, New Delhi, 25 February 2017.
31. Piruz Khambatta, communication with the author, New Delhi, 25 February 2017.
32. Hardeep Singh, communication with the author, 12 April 2017.

Chapter 6

1. Raj Chengappa of *India Today*, communication with the author, 2 March 2017.
2. Shalabh Kumar, speech at the India Today conclave, Mumbai, 19 March 2017.
3. Peter Lavoy, statement on CNN and other channels, Washington DC, 13 October 2016.
4. Strobe Talbott, interviewed by Nalin Mehta, *Times of India*, 23 December 2015.
5. Daniel Twining, communication with the author, Goa, 6 December 2016.
6. Walter Anderson, communication with the author, Goa, 6 December 2016.
7. R.S.N. Singh, interview to Doordarshan, New Delhi, 17 October 2016.
8. Sardesai, G.S., *History of Marathas*, Mumbai: Phoenix Publications, 1986.
9. Zaid Hamid, interview to Zen TV, Pakistan, 16 July 2016.

10. Syed Ata Hasnain, speech at the conference of the Forum for Integrated National Security, 22 November 2016.
11. Kanchan Banerjee, communication with the author, New Delhi, June 2016.
12. G. Parthasarathy, communication with the author, New Delhi, 20 October 2016.
13. *Hindustan Times*, 19 September 2016.

Chapter 7

1. Hasmukh Adhia, communication with the author, New Delhi, 17 September 2016.
2. Amitabh Kant, communication with the author, New Delhi, 17 October 2016.
3. Surjit Bhalla, communication with the author, New Delhi, 29 October 2016.
4. Interview to *Swarajya* magazine, 17 September 2016.
5. Nripendra Misra, communication with the author, new Delhi, 4 April 2017.
6. Vivek Dehejia, communication with the author, New Delhi, 21 January 2017.
7. Nirmala Sitharaman, communication with the author, 18 April 2017.
8. Abhishek Patel, communication with the author, Ahmedabad, 27 April 2017.
9. Ashok Zaveri, communication with the author, Rajkot, 30 October 2017.

Chapter 8

1. Kuldeep Ratnoo, interviewed by the author, New Delhi, 9 November 2016.
2. Surjit Bhalla, communication with the author, New Delhi, 20 January 2017.

3. Vivek Dehejia, communication with the author, New Delhi, 21 January 2017.
4. Interview to *Swarajya* magazine, 18 November 2016.
5. 'Demonetization, A Creative Disruption', *The Hindu Business Line*, 5 January 2017.
6. Amitabh Kant, interview to Doordarshan, 19 January 2017.
7. Jitendra Vakharia, communication with the author, Surat, 14 March 2017.
8. Viral Desai, communication with the author, Surat, 14 March 2017.

A Note on the Author

Uday Mahurkar is a senior journalist and deputy editor with *India Today*.